America's Backyard

The United States and Latin America from the Monroe Doctrine to the War on Terror

Grace Livingstone

Zed Books
London & New York

America's Backyard: The United States and Latin America from the Monroe Doctrine to the War on Terror
was first published in 2009 by Zed Books Ltd, 7 Cynthia Street, London N1 9JF, UK and Room 400,
175 Fifth Avenue, New York, NY 10010, USA, in association with
Latin America Bureau, 57b Tresco Road, London SE15 3PY, UK.

www.zedbooks.co.uk
www.latinamericabureau.org

Designed and typeset by Long House Publishing Services
Cover designed by Andrew Corbett
Printed and bound in the UK by MPG Books Group

Distributed in the USA exclusively by Palgrave Macmillan, a division of St Martin's Press, LLC,
175 Fifth Avenue, New York, NY 10010, USA.

A catalogue record for this book is available from the British Library
Library of Congress Cataloging in Publication Data available

ISBN 978 1 84813 213 9 hb
ISBN 978 1 84813 214 6 pb

Contents

Acknowledgements

I am very grateful to the following people who granted me interviews or sent me material: Adam Isacson; Victor Bulmer Thomas; Ronald H. Chilecote; Richard Gott; Jens Eric Gould; Peter Hakim; Pien Metaal; César Navarro MP; Oscar Olivera; Augusto Montiel Medina MP; Michael Reid; Daniel Samper Pizano; Michael Shifter; Peter H. Smith; Juan Gabriel Tokatlian; Carlos M. Vilas and Daisy Zamora. I would particularly like to thank Greg Wilpert for allowing me to read chapters of his book before publication: *Changing Venezuela by Taking Power: The History and Policies of the Chávez Government*, Verso Books, 2006.

I would like to give my grateful thanks to three US non-governmental organizations whose work I have found invaluable: the National Security Archive, the Center for International Policy and the Washington Office on Latin America. None of the above is responsible for the contents of this book.

I would like to thank Jean McNeil for her calm and assured editing; Ellen McKinlay for her well-informed advice; Pat Harper for her astute copy-editing; Kate Kirkwood for typesetting and design; Anne Rodford for proof-reading; Daniele Och for his production skills; and Sue Branford, who was a reassuring presence throughout the whole project. A big thank you also to Alex McHallam, Elizabeth Mistry and Kelly Walker for reading parts of the manuscript.

Lastly, I would like to give love and thanks to Dinah Livingstone, Francis McDonagh and Josh Cedar.

The research, writing and publication of *America's Backyard* have been supported by funds from Oxfam GB. The views and opinions expressed in this book are mine alone and not necessarily endorsed by Oxfam GB. Support for *America's Backyard* is undertaken as part of Oxfam GB's contribution to research and debate on issues in development and humanitarian relief.

This book was also written with support from the Authors' Foundation, for which I am very grateful.

The author and Zed Books gratefully acknowledge permission to reproduce the 1940 survey of US views of Latin Americans © Princeton University Press, A.H. Cantril, *Public Opinion 1935–1946*, Princeton, Princeton University Press, 1951.

The author and Zed Books gratefully acknowledge permission to reproduce an excerpt of the poem 'Asimilao' by Tato Laviera © T. Laviera, *AmeRícan*, Houston, Arte Público Press, 1985.

The author and Zed Books gratefully acknowledge permission to reproduce the poem 'The US Congress Approves Contra Aid' by Ernesto Cardenal © Katabasis, first published in E. Cardenal, *Nicaraguan New Time*, London, Journeyman, 1988

The author and Zed Books gratefully acknowledge permission of Sandra María Esteves to reproduce the poem 'Not Neither' first published in S.M. Esteves, *Tropical Rain: A Bilingual Downpour*, New York, African Caribbean Poetry Theater, 1984

The author and Zed Books gratefully acknowledge permission of Joan Jara and the Víctor Jara Foundation to reproduce the song 'Unfinished Song' by Víctor Jara, first published in J. Jara, *Victor: An Unfinished Song*, London, Jonathan Cape, 1983

The author and Zed Books gratefully acknowledge permission of the Fundación Pablo Neruda to reproduce a translation of the poem 'The United Fruit Co' by Pablo Neruda, first published in P. Neruda, *Canto General*, Mexico City, Talleres Gráficos de la Nación, 1950.

Latin America

1

Introduction

The United States' standing in the world was never so low as during the presidency of George Walker Bush (2001–9). The goodwill and sympathy extended to the US after the attacks of 11 September 2001 were squandered. More than at any time in history, the outlook of US leaders was at odds with global opinion. This disjuncture, this divergence of views, was acutely felt in the Americas. Latin America was pulsing with revolt against US-imposed neoliberal economics. The drumbeat of street protest sounded from Brazil to Guatemala – against privatization, spending cuts, job losses, free trade: the agenda of the International Monetary Fund (IMF), the World Bank and big corporations. At its apex, the swell of popular protest was so great that presidents were forced to flee ignominiously from Argentina, Bolivia and Ecuador. A 'pink tide' of progressive governments swept the Americas, promising to reverse decades of miserable poverty and entrenched privilege.[1]

While Latin America swung left, the US was governed by hardline right-wing ideologues. Even conservatives in Latin America felt alienated by an administration whose gaze was fixed on the Middle East and which, after 9/11, paid little attention to Latin America, except to paint it as a haven for criminals, drug smugglers and extremists ready to snake across the border at any time. US Secretary of Defense Donald Rumsfeld warned a Summit of the Americas in 2004 of the

> terrorists, drug traffickers, hostage takers and criminal gangs ... [who] find shelter in border regions or areas beyond the effective reach of government ... They watch, they probe looking for areas of vulnerability, for weakness and for seams in our collective security.[2]

Meanwhile General John Craddock, Commander of all US forces in South and Central America, spoke of 'under-governed sovereign territory and porous borders' creating an environment conducive to 'threats such as narco terrorism, illicit trafficking, urban gangs [and] organized crime'.[3]

1

The influential neoconservatives in the Bush administration were hardline right-wingers, but they professed democratic principles. They used the 'war on terror' as a new pretext for intervention in Latin America and tried to associate left-wing presidents with terrorism.[4] They also used the threat of terror to justify an ever growing military involvement in Colombia's counter-insurgency war. The Bush administration revived the scaremongering of the Cold War, but replaced the spectre of communism with 'radical populism', a term it adopted to describe the presidents of Venezuela, Bolivia, Nicaragua and Ecuador: 'Anti-globalization charlatans and the false prophets of populism [who] are trying – and, in some cases, succeeding – to undermine responsible policies and discredit responsible political leaders,' in the words of Assistant Secretary of State Roger Noriega.[5] It was not only the language that was reminiscent of the past: the Bush administration's support for an attempted coup against Venezuela's president Hugo Chávez in 2002 revived memories of one of the darkest days of the Cold War: General Pinochet's overthrow of elected president Salvador Allende in Chile in 1973. The tool of intervention most frequently used by Bush was the International Republican Institute (IRI), the international arm of the Republican Party (see Chapter 8). The IRI invited to Washington prominent Venezuelan opposition leaders who went on to play a key role in the short-lived coup against Chavez just weeks later; it also gave funds to organizations backing the coup. The IRI also worked with supporters of the old Haitian military regime who were plotting to unseat elected president Jean-Bertrand Aristide. The chairman of the IRI at that time was John McCain, the Republican Party's candidate for president in the 2008 presidential elections.

The United States has interfered in the affairs of Latin America for more than 180 years: dispatching marines, installing dictators, backing military coups, training repressive armed forces and destabilizing progressive governments. The US regards Latin America as its sphere of influence: a source of land, labour, raw materials and markets. It wants the strategic use of military bases, airstrips and ports throughout the Americas. To achieve its economic and geopolitical aims, the United States has sought pro-market, anti-communist governments. It has traditionally allied itself with Latin America's privileged elites, however reactionary or repressive they have been, and has regarded popular unrest or radical governments as a threat to its economic interests and hemispherical dominance. It has shaped Latin American history, intervening at key moments (Guatemala 1954; Chile 1973; Nicaragua 1979; El Salvador 1979–82), when reformers or revolutionaries were trying to uproot privilege and plant fairer societies. By protecting the rich and powerful, it has helped condemn Latin America to poverty and inequality.

Nowhere was this more evident than in Central America, home to the so-called 'banana republics', named for the disproportionate influence that US fruit companies wielded in these states, usually in collusion with corrupt dictators. When, in the 1980s, Nicaragua, El Salvador, Guatemala and to a lesser extent Honduras were convulsed by broad-based movements for change, US President Ronald Reagan (1981–89) declared, 'there must be no Soviet beachhead in Central America', and unleashed such terror – an illegal mercenary war, CIA airstrikes, the toleration of death squads and massacres, training and arming of repressive militaries – that the memory still haunts those countries now.[6] The depths to which Cold War governments sank to ward off communism or 'maintain stability' are chilling. The totalitarian dictatorships of the Southern Cone (Argentina, Chile, Paraguay and Uruguay), which became infamous for the 'disappearance' of thousands of their citizens, had the sympathy of Richard Nixon (1969–74), Gerald Ford (1974–77) and Secretary of State Henry Kissinger, the latter telling the Argentine junta soon after the 1976 coup, as details of barbaric torture filtered out, 'We would like you to succeed. I have an old-fashioned view that friends ought to be supported.'[7]

There has been a remarkable degree of continuity in US foreign policy despite the differing outlooks of presidents and their political affiliations. All administrations have had a bottom line: they have sought to defend strong, orderly, capitalist states; democracies if possible, dictatorships if necessary. The Good Neighbor Policy of President Franklin D. Roosevelt (1933–45) ended an era of repeated direct military intervention, but he relied on 'friendly dictators' in Central America to maintain order. The Alliance for Progress, launched by President John F. Kennedy (1961–63), was an ambitious plan to promote economic development and democracy in the region, but it also had a corresponding 'hard' side which entailed dispatching hundreds of US special forces to train Latin American militaries to combat 'subversives'. Kennedy, in fact, took a personal interest, reading guerrilla manuals to keep up to date with the latest counter-insurgency warfare techniques. Even the 'soft' side of the Alliance for Progress soon disintegrated because the intellectuals who designed it underestimated the resistance of the Latin American upper class to even moderate wealth redistribution, and were also alarmed at the raised expectations of the lower classes. When faced with peasant or labour unrest, which appeared to threaten stability or give the communists a foothold, the governments of Kennedy and Lyndon Johnson (1963–69) chose to tolerate or openly support the old elites. Within two years of the launch of the Alliance for Progress, six coups had taken place in Latin America.

The making of US foreign policy is a complex process and involves numerous actors: the White House, the Pentagon, the intelligence services, Congress and, indirectly, private companies. President Bill Clinton (1993–2001) was a popular figure in Latin America and impressed Latin American intellectuals such as Gabriel García Márquez with his cultured appreciation of Latin American literature. But he allowed the Pentagon and the corporations to shape his policy in Latin America. It was under Clinton's presidency that Plan Colombia, a heavily militarized counter-narcotics campaign, which raised the US military presence in Colombia and embroiled US forces in that country's counter-insurgency war, was launched. Clinton signed the North American Free Trade Agreement (NAFTA) and pushed for free trade throughout the Americas. Free trade suited the needs of large US corporations that were trying to compete with cheap imports, particularly from China, in the US domestic market. Corporations needed to use low-wage Latin American labour to manufacture goods which they could then send back to the US duty-free. They also wanted to tear down the barriers to investment as they aggressively sought out new markets for services, driving the privatization of basic amenities such as water and electricity in Latin America.

Clinton may have believed his own rhetoric that increased economic growth and trade would relieve poverty, but if so he underestimated the problems stemming from both the imbalance of power between rich and poor countries, and the deep structural problems within Latin America itself. It is not the poorest region in the world, but it is the most unequal. A minority own most of the wealth, while many more live in shacks on the outskirts of burgeoning cities, subsisting with no formal job, paying no tax and receiving no welfare. As Chapter 10 of this book shows, twenty years of free market economics (neoliberalism) has increased, and not diminished, the proportion of people living in poverty in Latin America.

The extent to which rich countries have shaped (or stunted) the development of poorer countries has been the subject of rich debate in Latin America. In the 1950s, modernization theorists had argued that all nations simply had to reach take-off point to become advanced capitalist economies. Nevertheless, after more than a decade of industrial growth following the Second World War, Latin Americans discovered that they were still reliant on the First World for financing and the most advanced technology. Academics began to investigate the structural barriers to growth and whether the rich countries themselves were responsible for inhibiting Third World development. The economic historian Andre Gunder Frank argued that the rich 'metropolis' devoured the resources of the 'periphery', enriching itself while keeping the poor impoverished.[8] Implicit in this argument is the idea that the metropolis's wealth stems from exploiting poor countries. Critics such as Nigel Harris pointed out that most global trade and investment took place *between* rich countries, so their wealth could not primarily come from the Third World.[9] He argued that a country's economic status was not static; poor countries were not destined to remain dependent and that many (for example, the Asian economies, Mexico and Brazil) were moving into the First World. Decades later, however, Mexico and Brazil might be industrial giants, home to a sizeable middle class, but the majority of the population still have not reached First World living standards. Much of Mexico's manufacturing industry is made up of maquiladoras (assembly plants), where all of the inputs are imported by foreign companies and simply assembled by the Mexican labour force. Even in powerful Brazil, the most dynamic, high-tech sectors of manufacturing industry are foreign-owned, with the exception of the country's world-class aerospace industry, Embraer.

A more nuanced version of dependency theory was put forward by Fernando Henrique Cardoso and Enzo Faletto in *Dependency and Development in Latin America*.[10] They argued that long-standing structural problems hindered Latin American economic development and that rich countries tend to reinforce these structural inequalities by allying with the reactionary elites. Poor countries are forever playing catch-up trying to acquire the latest technology, while rich countries use their dominant position to maintain their advantage. It was a sophisticated and dynamic argument that did not set out rigid precepts, but said that the interplay of classes within and between rich and poor countries should be studied.

Dependency theory was associated with the anti-imperialist movements of the 1960s and 1970s, the *fidelistas* (followers of Fidel Castro), the guerrilla movements, and the left-leaning reformist governments, both democratic (Chile) and military (Peru). Indeed some academics argued that only revolution could break the dependent structures. The popularity of dependency theory declined with the fortunes of the Left. Right-wing totalitarian dictatorships took over most countries, crushing the popular movement, and in the 1980s the debt crisis further drove down living standards, leading to drastically reduced political and economic aspirations. An updated version of modernization theory took hold: 'neoliberalism', the ethos of the free market, vigorously promoted by the United States and embraced as the only realistic solution by many Latin American leaders (including former dependency theorist Cardoso, who became President of Brazil).

Left-wing academic research splintered into a number of avenues; a minority continued to elaborate structural theories (world systems theory, modes of production theory), but the majority, particularly Latin Americanists in the United States, rejected grand narratives and moved the magnifying glass closer to the ground to look at individual social movements, indigenous communities, women's history, and gay issues, with a heavy emphasis on subjective viewpoints, influenced by the schools of postmodernism, cultural theory and post-colonial studies. While these studies have greatly enriched our knowledge of Latin America, there is a danger of losing the sight of the wood for the trees, and the need for an explanatory framework remains.

Dependency theory at its most crude was too rigid and reflected a specific moment in history; nevertheless the emphasis on the international context and the interplay of classes within and between countries was vital. It highlighted the barriers to equitable growth for countries shaped by colonialism and competing in a world where the rules are made by the powerful nations. One only needs to consider the power of US multinationals, the sway of the IMF and World Trade Organization (WTO) or the rich countries' double standards on agricultural subsidies to see that the argument still has relevance today.

In recent years, the neoconservative-led military campaigns in the Middle East, as well as the resurgence of the Left in Latin America in the late 1990s and the 2000s, have led to the re-emergence of the term 'imperialism' in academia, the media and on the political left.[11] But there remains a problem of definition. For some, 'imperialism' refers only to nineteenth-century colonial empire-building, while others simply use it as a loose term for a powerful nation seeking to dominate other countries. Some in the Marxist tradition still adhere to Lenin's thesis that imperialism is the highest stage of capitalism, while others have tried to differentiate between formal imperialism (colonies) and 'informal' imperialism (economic control).[12] In this book, the term 'imperialism' has only been used to describe the US's mid-nineteenth-century territorial expansion and early twentieth-century Rooseveltian policy of repeated military intervention and occupation. I have preferred to use the term 'hegemony', which implies that the US's military, economic and diplomatic power is vastly superior to that of its neighbours and can shape, but not necessarily control, their destinies.[13]

That early period of US imperial expansion brought with it a colonial mentality that the US establishment has never shaken off. Exaggerated fears of what lurks beyond the border have been stoked: from the nineteenth-century terror of 'Latin Indians' to today's panics about drugs gangs and migration. A hundred years ago, eugenicists wrote treatises on the superiority of Anglo-Saxon blood and the innate laziness of the 'Indian'; today Hollywood blockbusters treat us to unshaven corrupt Mexican policemen and gyrating *latinas*. US leaders chide Latin American politicians as if they were children, exhorting them to act 'responsibly' and 'maturely'. The term 'America's backyard' is an example of this colonial mindset. What is a backyard if not a place where you send the children to play; a wilderness that needs to be tamed; an extension of your property, that you can walk into and out of as freely as you please? The term is, of course, inaccurate: 'America' comprises both the United States and Latin America, as well as Canada and the Caribbean; 'American' describes all inhabitants of the Americas. The usurping of the title 'America' by the United States is symptomatic of an enduring imperial arrogance.

America's Backyard offers an overview of US foreign policy in Latin America, with a particular focus on the past three decades. It starts by charting the history of US–Latin American relations from the nineteenth century to the present day. It attempts to tell the story from the points of view of both the 'North' and the 'South' – of both the recipient and the manufacturer of foreign policy. The narrative is supported by many primary sources – congressional inquiries, declassified documents – which allow the reader to assess the evidence for themselves. These sources do not tell the whole story of US intervention in Latin America (not least because many documents remain classified) but they do provide a minimum of verifiable and reliable information. The second half of this book contains thematic chapters on drugs, money and culture. Chapter 9 explains why US counter-narcotics policy has failed to reduce the supply of cocaine but has caused widespread environmental damage. Chapter 10 demonstrates how two decades of free market economics have increased poverty and misery in Latin America. It explains how the IMF, the World Bank and the WTO have helped to keep the Third World poor and it examines the strategy of US corporations in Latin America today. Finally, Chapter 11 discusses how the people of the US and Latin America see each other and shows how cultural stereotyping has been used to justify intervention. It looks at the impact of US brands, media and music on Latin American culture and at how the increasingly politicized Latino community is changing the United States itself. In this book, the term 'Latin America' refers to the Spanish-, Portuguese- and French-speaking countries of the American mainland and the Caribbean.

In writing this book, I have relied not only on many Latin American sources, but also on the work of countless US academics, researchers and campaigners. Non-governmental organizations in the United States such as the Center for International Policy, the National Security Archive and the Washington Office on Latin America investigate, catalogue and report US actions in Latin America. The US public does not always agree with its own government's foreign policy, indeed it is often not told what is being done in its name. US activists and researchers have ferreted out information, brought it to public attention, and lobbied Congress to change course. Within Congress, some senators and representatives have laboured hard to change misguided policies and bring wrongdoings to light. From Irangate to the plots to make Fidel Castro's beard wilt, Senate reports have shone a light on the murkier corners of US foreign policy. Congress has at times reined back the excesses of the executive; it cut off aid to the Pinochet dictatorship; it prevented Reagan from colluding in the genocidal campaigns of Guatemala's Rios Montt, and it has tried, with limited success, to stop Colombian human rights abusers from receiving military aid. Perhaps it should go without saying that the US democratic system – the separation of powers, elected representatives and elected judges, backed up by a far-reaching freedom of information entitlement, has been admired throughout the world, not least in Latin America. What a pity, then, that the US has so often backed in the Third World, in the words of a once influential White House adviser, 'regimes whose origins and methods would not stand the test of American concepts of democratic procedure' and has so often 'conceded' that overseas 'harsh governmental measures of repression may be the only answer'.[14]

2

The Monroe Doctrine to the Second World War

Conquest and the Legacy of Colonialism

The history of the Americas is a history of conquest. Christopher Columbus's 'discovery' of the Americas in 1492 was a catastrophe for its original inhabitants. Thousands of indigenous people were massacred and millions more died through disease and overwork. The indigenous population in central Mexico alone fell from 25 million to just 1 million between 1519 and 1605, according to the most reliable studies.[1] The legacy of colonialism was equally devastating. The Spanish and Portuguese imported a feudal system; nobles lived on vast estates worked by indigenous indentured labour or imported African slaves. Latin America was left with a small white elite who felt they had little in common with the impoverished mass of the population.

Indigenous peoples in the fledgling United States of America were treated with equal brutality, hounded from their own lands and killed in their thousands during expansionist wars, but in contrast to Spanish America, feudalism was not introduced. Instead, homesteaders colonized the 'empty' land and set up farms of roughly similar size. As these families grew richer, some households experimented with technological innovations and found a ready market among their neighbours, thus creating the seeds of a dynamic capitalist economy, which ultimately helped the Northern states defeat the rich slave-owning Southern states in the civil war.

The nascent superpower's thirst for land, raw materials and labour fuelled an aggressive campaign of intervention in Central America and the Caribbean from the mid-nineteenth century onwards. After expanding to the west coast, US leaders went south, annexing half of Mexico's territory. By the 1930s, the US's economic grip on Central America was unassailable. The Good Neighbor Policy, associated with Franklin D. Roosevelt's presidency (1933–45) and heralded as the start of an era of harmonious peace and fraternity, was in part a recognition that direct military intervention was no longer necessary and that US objectives in Central America

Land Ownership in Latin America and North America, 1900s

Country, year	Proportion of household heads who owned land (%)
Mexico (rural areas), 1910	2.4
Argentina, 1895	
Chaco	27.8
La Pampa	9.7
Canada, 1901	87.1
United States, 1900	74.5

Source: D. Ferranti et al. *Inequality in Latin America: Breaking with History*, Washington, World Bank, 2004, p. 119.

could now usually be achieved by backing so-called friendly dictators. It also reflected the growing interest of US business in the more distant South America and its larger, richer countries which were less easy to dominate by plain brute force. The Second World War provided a crucial opportunity for the United States to extend its military influence in South America. By forming an alliance with right-wing elites, the US secured the use of ports and airbases across the hemisphere, and by supplying their armies with aid, training and hardware, a partnership was built with Latin American militaries that would endure throughout the Cold War and beyond.

The Latin American Independence Wars

The Latin American wars of independence of the early nineteenth century were led by the locally-born white elite (*criollo*), although many of their soldiers were *mestizos* (mixed-race indigenous and *criollo*). The independence leaders were inspired by the Enlightenment, but they found it impossible to build their idealized republics in countries that had virtually no middle class, and instead sported small, quarrelsome oligarchies who feared and loathed the poor and uneducated masses. Post-independence governance fluctuated between bouts of fragile constitutional rule and authoritarianism, and all governments faced regular budget crises because most inhabitants were too poor to tax. These countries were easy prey for a new generation of colonialists. European powers in particular sought markets, raw materials, investment opportunities, land and trade routes.

The Monroe Doctrine and Manifest Destiny

President James Monroe warned the European powers in 1823 that any incursions into the Western Hemisphere would be considered a threat to the peace and safety of the United States itself. Britain, France and Russia, as well as Spain, all were interested in Latin America's land, labour and raw materials. Britain, at the peak of its imperial might, sought new markets and strategic ports in the region. At the time, President Monroe's speech was essentially a defensive, isolationist statement, but the Monroe Doctrine, as it became known, was later used as a justification for US intervention in Latin America.

The Monroe Doctrine, 1823

'American continents, by the free and independent condition which they have assumed and maintain, are henceforth not to be considered as subjects for future colonization by any European powers ...

We owe it, therefore, to candor and to the amicable relations existing between the United States and those powers to declare that we should consider any attempt on their part to extend their system to any portion of this hemisphere as dangerous to our peace and safety. With the existing colonies or dependences of any European power we have not interfered and shall not interfere.'

President James Monroe (1817–25), Annual message to Congress, 2 December 1823

The United States began to expand westwards in the nineteenth century, consolidating and enlarging its territory at the expense of the Indian peoples and other colonial powers. In 1803 the US purchased Louisiana from France for US$15 million (the so-called 'Louisiana Purchase' also included fourteen other states and land which would eventually become two Canadian provinces) and in 1819 it acquired Florida from Spain. It ousted the British from Oregon in 1846 and in the same year provoked an aggressive war against Mexico in which Mexico lost half its land: Texas and the area now known as New Mexico and California. Within fifty years the United States had acquired 2.3 million square miles, increasing the size of its territory tenfold. The old defensive attitude was now replaced by the evangelical tones of Manifest Destiny:[2] a belief that the United States had a God-given mission to spread its way of life to new lands.

Challenging the British in the Caribbean and Central America

The United States began to vie with the British for control of the Caribbean and Central America. At the time, Britain was the largest naval power in the world. It dominated the Caribbean through its West Indian colonies and controlled parts of Central America's Caribbean coast. Both the US and Britain sought a trade route linking the Pacific and Atlantic oceans, and in 1850 they signed the Clayton Bulmer Treaty, which gave them joint access to a canal in Nicaragua. But by 1867 the US was powerful enough to defy the British and sign its own exclusive canal agreement with Nicaragua. As one US senator put it: 'If we want Central America, the cheapest, easiest, and quickest way to get it is to go and take it, and if France and England interfere, read the Monroe Doctrine to them.'[3]

In the 1880s US companies began to set up business in Cuba, Puerto Rico, Jamaica and Central America, producing sugar, fruit, tobacco and minerals. Within twenty years one company, United Fruit, controlled the export trade of the Central American isthmus and US fortune-seekers had invested US$30 million in Cuban plantations, mines and other businesses.

Filibusters and Manifest Destiny

Filibusters were private mercenaries who, inspired by the philosophy of Manifest Destiny, raided lands in Mexico, Central America and the Caribbean in the mid-nineteenth century. The best-known of these was William Walker who invaded Nicaragua in 1855 with a force of 58 men. He declared himself president and reintroduced slavery. He was forced out by British-backed Nicaraguan conservatives in 1857. The US government did not support Walker, but he received backing from US entrepreneurs and politicians from the slave-owning Southern states.

[The term *filibuster* derives from the Dutch *vrijbuiter* — 'freebooter' which evolved into the Spanish *filibustero*.]

'That which you ignorantly call "Filibusterism" is not the offspring of hasty passion or ill-regulated desire; it is the fruit of the sure, unerring instincts which act in accordance with law as old as the creation. They are but drivellers who speak of establishing fixed relations between the pure white American race, as it exists in the United States, and the mixed Hispano-Indian race, as it exists in Mexico and Central America, without the employment of force. The history of the world presents no such Utopian vision as that of an inferior race yielding meekly and peacefully to the controlling influence of a superior people. Whenever barbarism and civilization, or two distinct forms of civilization, meet face to face, the result must be war. Therefore, the struggle between the old and the new elements in Nicaraguan society was not passing or accidental, but natural and inevitable. The war in Nicaragua was the first clear and distinct issue between the races inhabiting the northern and central portions of the continent. But while this contest sprang from natural laws ... the stronger race kept throughout on the side of right and justice.'

William Walker, *The War in Nicaragua*, New York and Mobile,1860, pp. 429–30

Cuba and the Platt Amendment

Nationalists in Cuba, inspired by the writings of the exiled patriot José Martí, in the late nineteenth century began to press for independence from Spain. US marines were dispatched to the island in 1898, ostensibly to support the Cuban independence movement, and within a few months they had defeated Spain. But freedom from Spain did not mean independence for Cuba. The island remained under US military occupation until a constitutional convention agreed to limit the new nation's sovereignty. The Platt Amendment, appended to the Cuban constitution in 1901, effectively made Cuba a protectorate of the US. The Platt Amendment gave the US the right to intervene militarily and it forbade Cuba from entering into treaties with foreign powers or seeking loans without US approval. It also required Cuba to provide the US armed forces with naval and coaling stations on the island to 'enable the

United States to maintain the independence of Cuba'. The peace terms of the Spanish American war also gave the United States direct control of Puerto Rico, Guam and the Philippines (for a payment of US$20m), indicating that the war was not fought to secure the liberty of a small nation but to further US imperial ambitions.

Roosevelt and the Big Stick

By 1900 the United States was an industrial superpower. More than half its population lived in cities, its national income was three times that of England and it produced more iron, steel and coal than any European country. This powerful economic engine had a voracious appetite for raw materials and new markets. US business and government alike began to look further south, to Latin America. The territorial expansionism of the nineteenth century was over. Racism prevented US presidents from trying to subsume the rest of the Americas into the United States. Politicians, scholars and journalists agreed that lazy, inferior 'Latin Indians' would drain the vigour of the thrusting new nation and dilute the purity of Anglo-Saxon blood. On the other hand, European-style colonies were expensive and unnecessary. Instead the United States found it could dominate its 'sphere of influence' through economic weight and a judicious use of military intervention. Between 1898 and 1934 the United States intervened militarily in Central America and the Caribbean

---

The Roosevelt Corollary to the Monroe Doctrine, 1904

'All that this country desires is to see the neighboring countries stable, orderly, and prosperous. Any country whose people conduct themselves well can count upon our hearty friendship. If a nation shows that it knows how to act with reasonable efficiency and decency in social and political matters, if it keeps order and pays its obligations, it need fear no interference from the United States. Chronic wrong-doing, or an impotence which results in a general loosening of the ties of civilized society, may in America, as elsewhere, ultimately require intervention by some civilized nation, and in the Western Hemisphere the adherence of the United States to the Monroe Doctrine may force the United States, however reluctantly, in flagrant cases of such wrongdoing or impotence, to the exercise of an international police power ...

We would interfere with them only in the last resort, and then only if it became evident that their inability or unwillingness to do justice at home and abroad had violated the rights of the United States or had invited foreign aggression to the detriment of the entire body of American nations. It is a mere truism to say that every nation, whether in America or anywhere else, which desires to maintain its freedom, its independence, must ultimately realize that the right of such independence can not be separated from the responsibility of making good use of it ...'

President Theodore Roosevelt (1901–09), Annual message to Congress, 6 December 1904

more than thirty times. This mood of belligerent interventionism was epitomized by President Theodore Roosevelt (1901–09), an unabashed imperialist, whose maxim was 'speak softly but carry a big stick'. Roosevelt updated the Monroe Doctrine to include an explicit defence of US intervention in other countries, a corollary which reflected the confidence and conceit of the rulers of an emerging world power.

The Panama Canal

The US need for a canal connecting the Atlantic and Pacific oceans grew more pressing as its imperial ambitions widened. The acquisition of the Philippines was seen as a stepping stone to penetration of the vast markets of China. Most US ports and bases were on its eastern seaboard, but to protect its Asian interests the US needed easy access to the Pacific. A transoceanic canal would also cut the cost of trade with Latin America, and the cost of trade between the eastern and western coasts of the United States. Strategically, by straddling the Central American isthmus, a waterway would allow the US to dominate the Western Hemisphere and see off any rival powers. Having wooed Nicaragua for decades, Theodore Roosevelt finally decided Panama would be the ideal location for such a canal. Panama, however, was a province of Colombia. In August 1903, Colombian senators unanimously rejected the terms of a US offer to lease the Panamanian territory for 100 years. Damning the Colombians as 'jackrabbits', Roosevelt fomented a secessionist rising in the province of Panama, sent troops to support the rising and recognized it as an independent state in November 1903. Fifteen days later a treaty was signed with the new Panamanian government. It gave the United States the exclusive rights, in perpetuity, to a ten-mile-wide strip of land across Panama on which to construct a canal. The US was also granted the rights to all of the islands within the Canal Zone and 'the use, occupation and control of any other lands and waters outside of the zone … which may be necessary and convenient for the construction, maintenance, operation, sanitation and protection' of the canal. The Canal Zone remained under the control of the United States until 1999, an ever-present reminder of US military might and a source of nationalist indignation in Panama for nearly a century.

US Military Interventions in Central America and the Caribbean, 1898–1934

Costa Rica	1921*
Cuba	1898–02, 1906–09, 1912, 1917–22
Dominican Republic	1903, 1904, 1914, 1916–24
Guatemala	1920
Haiti	1915–34
Honduras	1903, 1907, 1911, 1912, 1919, 1924, 1925
Mexico	1913, 1914, 1916–17, 1918–19
Nicaragua	1898, 1899, 1909–10, 1912–25, 1926–33
Panama	1903–14, 1921, 1925

*A US naval warship stood by during a boundary dispute with Panama; troops did not land

To Roosevelt

Mighty Hunter, the way to reach you would be
with voice of the Bible or a Walt Whitman poem.
Primitive and modern, simple and complex,
one part Washington, to four of Nimrod.

You are the United States,
you are the future invader
of America the innocent, with her indigenous blood,
who still speaks in Spanish and prays to Christ.

You are a proud, strong specimen of your kind,
you are cultured and clever, you go against Tolstoy.
Taming horses or killing tigers,
you are an Alexander–Nebuchadnezzar.
(You are a professor of energy,
as the fashionable madmen cry.)

You think life is fire,
progress an eruption,
the future wherever
your bullet strikes.
   No.

The United States is big and powerful.
When it shivers, a deep shudder runs
down the Andes' giant spine.
If it shouts, it sounds like a roaring lion.

As Hugo told Grant: 'The stars are yours.'
(Argentina's sun is just up and shining,
Chile's star is rising...) You are rich.
As well as Hercules, you worship Mammon;
and, lighting the pathway to easy conquest,
Liberty lifts its torch in New York.

But our America has had her poets
since the far-off times of Nezahualcoyotl,
great Bacchus' footprints are still preserved there
and Pan's alphabet she learned long ago;
she consulted the stars and knew Atlantis,
whose name echoes down to us from Plato.

➔

➜ From her life's earliest origins
she's lived with light, fire, fragrance and love.
America of great Moctezuma and the Inca,
perfumed America of Christopher Columbus,
Catholic America, Spanish America,
America where noble Cuauhtémoc declared:
'I am not on a bed of roses,' America,
hurricane-shaken, alive with love.
Yes, you with Saxon eyes and barbarous souls, she's alive.
And dreams. And loves, and quivers; she is the sun's daughter.
Take care! Long live Spanish America!
A thousands cubs have sprung from the Spanish Lion.
Roosevelt, God himself would have to make you
the terrible Gunman, the mighty Hunter,
for you to grasp us in your iron claws.

And though you've got it all: one thing you lack: God!

Rubén Darío (1867–1916)
Translated by Dinah Livingstone

Interventions and Dollar Diplomacy

The United States intervened to ensure that neighbouring countries were ruled by pliant and friendly governments – or, as Theodore Roosevelt put it, to 'show those Dagos that they will have to behave decently'.[4] All the military interventions took place in Central America and the Caribbean; warships were dispatched to the coasts of Venezuela and Chile in South America to exert pressure during disputes, but did not land. (US troops never invaded a South American country in the twentieth century, although troops had been sent to Argentina, Colombia, Paraguay, Peru and Uruguay in the nineteenth century.)

The Roosevelt administration dispatched marines to Cuba in 1906 because it was unhappy with the results of elections on the island. The elections were annulled and William H. Taft, later to become the 27th US President, was named as provisional governor. US officials also 'oversaw' elections in Panama in 1906, 1908 and 1912. The US elite was particularly unnerved by the Mexican revolution in 1911; although the Taft administration had allowed Francisco Madero to arm and organize his revolt against the Mexican president, Porfirio Díaz, in Texas, US officials feared the radical nature of the revolution once the dictator had fallen. On orders from Washington, the US ambassador Henry Lane Wilson manoeuvered against Francisco Madero's new progressive government; the evidence suggests that he conspired with Madero's enemy, Victoriano Huerta, to assassinate him. US military forces were sent to Mexico four times between 1913 and 1919.

Increasingly, marines were sent to protect US property and investments. In the late nineteenth century, European gunboats had often been dispatched to Latin America and the Caribbean to collect unpaid debts. Washington was determined to keep rival imperialist powers out of its sphere of influence, and encouraged US banks to assume the debts of European creditors. It then took over the debtor country's customs houses to ensure payment – dollar diplomacy. Economic intervention invariably led to military action. It became clear that dollar diplomacy was not so much about 'replacing bullets with dollars', the suggestion of one of President William H. Taft's officials, as about using bullets to protect US investors' dollars.[5]

The Dominican Republic experienced a classic case of dollar diplomacy. The Dominican government agreed to let the US take over customs collection in 1907 after it had defaulted on debts. When, in 1916, a new government refused to sign a treaty granting the US control of its customs, treasury and armed forces, US Marine Captain H. S. Knapp declared martial law, closed the parliament and named himself 'supreme legislator'. US troops occupied the country until 1924. Another example of dollar diplomacy was Haiti, which had assumed strategic importance to the US after the completion of the Panama Canal, because it lay between the US's eastern coast and the Canal. In 1914 marines occupied the country, took over the customs houses and established martial law; they remained until 1934.

Nicaragua also suffered a prolonged military occupation. The United States backed a rising against the nationalist president José Santos Zelaya in 1910. Once he was deposed, the new Conservative government agreed to let the US supervise customs houses in return for a loan. This deal caused a national outcry and eventually led to a revolt by the Liberals. Marines arrived to crush the rising in 1912 and occupied Nicaragua until 1925. They returned in 1926 after the results of a US-supervised election provoked civil war. US Under-Secretary of State Robert Olds wrote thus in a State Department memorandum in 1927:

> We do control the destinies of Central America and we do so for the simple reason that the national interest absolutely dictates such a course ... Until now Central America has always understood that governments which we recognize and support stay in power, while those we do not recognize and support fail.[6]

However, one Nicaraguan general, Augusto C Sandino, refused to accept the US-brokered peace terms following the 1926-27 civil war and continued to demand that US marines leave Nicaraguan territory. Four thousand troops were sent to defeat Sandino's guerrilla army, which demanded national sovereignty, land redistribution and justice for the poor. Sandino was still undefeated in 1933 when the marines left, but he was assassinated a year later by the US-trained Nicaraguan National Guard.

With Sandino in Nicaragua

Journalist Carleton Beals interviewed Augusto Sandino for The Nation *in 1928. His weekly reports embarrassed the US government and won international support for Sandino's cause.*

'Several days ago I rode out of the camp of General Augusto C. Sandino, the terrible "bandit" of Nicaragua who is holding the marines at bay. Not a single hair of my blond, Anglo-Saxon head had been injured. On the contrary, I had been shown every possible kindness. I went, free to take any route I might choose, with permission to relate to anybody I encountered any and every thing I had seen and heard. Perhaps my case is unique. I am the first and only American since Sandino began fighting the marines who has been granted an official interview and I am the first bona fide correspondent of any nationality to talk to him face to face.

"Do you still think us bandits?" was his last query as I bade him goodbye.

"You are as much a bandit as Mr Coolidge is a Bolshevik" was my reply.

"Tell your people" he returned, "there may be bandits in Nicaragua, but they are not necessarily Nicaraguans" ...'

Cited in R. Holden and E. Zolov (eds), *Latin America and the United States: A Documentary History*, New York, Oxford University Press, 2000, p. 132

Banana Republics

Central America and the Caribbean consisted of small agricultural economies. They exported one or two products and were dependent on the vagaries of the world market. Their development had been stunted by colonialism and upon independence they were easily dominated by the US. For example, US companies quickly gained control of sugar production in Cuba, Puerto Rico, Haiti and the Dominican Republic, although the industry on the English-speaking islands remained largely British-owned. In Central America, meanwhile, coffee farms tended not to be foreign-owned, but remained in the hands of local oligarchies (with the exception of large German holdings in Guatemala). However, foreign companies made the biggest profits by processing, transporting and marketing the coffee. Banana production was entirely in the hands of US companies, primarily United Fruit and the smaller Standard Fruit. United Fruit initially gained control of the banana trade by building the railways and ports to export the fruit. It later bought the plantations, and by the 1930s it owned 3.5 million acres of land across Central America and the Caribbean; its vast network of plantations earned it the nickname *el pulpo* – 'the octopus'. In Guatemala, United Fruit was the largest landowner, the largest employer, the largest exporter and the owner of almost all the country's railways. The company was so powerful, it could veto presidents and dictate

The United Fruit Co.

When the trumpet sounded,
everything on Earth was ready
and Jehovah shared out the world
between Coca-Cola Inc., Anaconda,
Ford Motors and other corporations:
the United Fruit Company Inc.
got the juiciest bit,
my land's middle coast,
America's sweet waist.
It rechristened its territories
Banana Republics,
and over the sleeping dead,
over the unquiet heroes,
who had won greatness,
freedom and flags,
it set up a comic opera:
it disposed of free will,
granted imperial crowns,
unsheathed envy, attracted
the dictatorship of flies,
Trujillo flies, Tacho flies,
Carías flies, Martínez flies,
Ubico flies, flies sticky with
blood of the poor, with jam,
drunken flies buzzing
over the people's graves,
circus flies, clever flies
who knew about tyranny.
Among the bloodthirsty flies
United Fruit disembarked,
sweeping the coffee and fruits
into its ships that stole away
laden with treasure
from our overrun lands.

Meanwhile Indians fall
into the harbours' sugary depths,
to be buried in morning mist:
a body rolls, a nameless
thing, just a number,
a bunch of bad fruit
dumped to rot.

Pablo Neruda. Translated by Dinah Livingstone.
Spanish orginal first published in P. Neruda, *Canto General*, Mexico City, Talleres Gráficos de la Nación, 1950. © Fundación Pablo Neruda.

government policy, and for this reason the small nations of Central America became known as banana republics.

The United States and South America

In the first half of the twentieth century, the influence of the United States in the larger and more distant republics of South America was far weaker than its influence in Central America and the Caribbean. Here the railways and ports were financed by European investors, particularly the British. South American countries bought manufactured goods such as clothing and household goods from the British empire and exported raw materials to Europe. The debts of their governments were mainly owed to British banks. Gradually, US capital began to move south. In 1914, 78 per cent of US investment in Latin America went to Central America and the Caribbean, while only 22 per cent went to South America. By 1929, the proportion invested in South America had risen to 56 per cent.[7] Nevertheless, in 1929, British investment in Latin America was still greater than that of the United States; it was not until the Second World War that the US overtook Britain.[8] Nor did the United States dominate trade with South America as it did with Central America. In 1918, 83 per cent of Central America's exports were sold to the US and 78 per cent of its imports came from there, whereas in the same year the proportions for South American trade with the United States were just 35 per cent (exports) and 26 per cent (imports). The US did not become the Southern Cone's number one trading partner until the Second World War. Even then, it never came to monopolize trade in South America as it did in Central America.

The Good Neighbor Policy and Friendly Dictators, 1933–39

The Good Neighbor Policy introduced by President Franklin D. Roosevelt aroused hopes that an era of continental fraternity and mutual respect had begun. At inter-American conferences in Montevideo in 1933 and in Buenos Aires in 1936, the US recognized the principle of legal equality between nations and signed joint declarations condemning intervention. In the 1930s, it abrogated Cuba's hated Platt Amendment (but kept possession of Guantánamo Bay) and agreed to limit its freedom of action in Panama (but kept control of the Canal Zone).

The Good Neighbor Policy was, at root, a recognition that intervention was no longer the most effective way of maintaining hegemony. Interventions had become increasingly costly, in terms both of money and of lives. In Nicaragua alone more than 100 marines had died fighting Sandino's irregular army. The threat of European meddling in the region had subsided and the US found it could often maintain political influence and protect its markets through economic leverage.

In Central America and the Caribbean, which had borne the brunt of military intervention, the US protected its interests by grooming friendly dictators. Before the US marines withdrew from Nicaragua in 1933, the US created, trained and equipped a local police force, the National Guard, and appointed Anastasio Somoza

---

The Good Neighbor Policy and Mexican Oil Nationalization

Mexico has always had a prickly relationship with the US, one neatly encapsulated by the Mexican lament 'Poor Mexico! So far from God and so close to the United States.' Between 1836 and 1920, the US sent troops to Mexico fifteen times to protect its interests. Since the Mexican revolution (1910–17) the US has been more circumspect, but has tried a variety of indirect methods to maintain its influence across the border.

In 1938 Mexico nationalized the oil industry and expropriated the property of sixteen US oil companies. Roosevelt, who was keen to have Mexico as an ally in the impending world war, ignored the oil companies' calls for intervention, and negotiated. Mexico agreed to pay US$40 million in compensation and in return Roosevelt promised loans and military aid and agreed to buy Mexican silver at world market prices. This pragmatic deal paved the way for good relations during the Second World War and the early stages of the Cold War.

Source: David Dent, *The Legacy of the Monroe Doctrine: A Reference Guide to US Involvement in Latin America and the Caribbean*, Connecticut, Greenwood Press, 1999. The phrase quoted belongs to Porfirio Díaz, President of Mexico 1896–80 and 1884–1911

---

its commander. Somoza seized power in 1936 and his violent regime was supported by the US until his assassination in 1956. The same tactic was used in the Dominican Republic, where Rafael Trujillo was appointed head of a US-trained National Guard. Trujillo led a coup in 1930 and established a tyranny that lasted until 1961. By the mid-1930s, dictatorships had been established across Central America: Jorge Ubico in Guatemala (1931–44), Tiburcio Carías Andino in Honduras (1931–48) and Maximiliano Hernández Martínez in El Salvador (1931–44). In Cuba, the US refused to recognize the left-wing government established after the fall of the dictator Gerardo Machado in 1933. State Department officials built up a relationship with the corrupt and sadistic sergeant Fulgencio Batista, helping him to dominate the Cuban political scene until his election as president in 1940. Batista was invited to Washington to meet Roosevelt in 1938; Roosevelt personally met Somoza at the station when he visited Washington in 1939, and Trujillo was invited for tea with the president and his wife at the White House in 1940. President Roosevelt had become, as Peruvian politician Víctor Raúl Haya de la Torre said, 'the good neighbour of tyrants'.[9]

The Second World War

During the Second World War, an alliance was forged between the militaries of the United States and Latin America. Pentagon planners wanted to be able to use Latin American ports and airbases and sought to strengthen Latin American military forces so that they could defend the Western Hemisphere from potential Nazi aggression. Latin American governments received US$450 million in military aid, and by 1941 US military missions had been assigned to almost all Latin American countries.[10] US advisers helped to modernize local police forces and armies by introducing new training methods and military hardware. Many junior officers were sent to train in US military academies, establishing a relationship that would endure throughout the Cold War and beyond. At the behest of the United States, all Latin American governments declared war on the Axis powers, although Argentina, which had sympathies with Nazi Germany, left it as late as March 1945 (see below).

The war was fought in the name of democracy, but many of the beneficiaries of US military assistance in Latin America were dictatorships, including that of the US's most important ally: Brazil's Getúlio Vargas. Latin America was crucial to the United States during the war as a supplier of vital raw materials, including oil, tin, manganese and copper. Its strategic importance increased after the Japanese occupation blocked off rubber supplies from Southeast Asia.

The war also stimulated the development of Latin America's economies because, in addition to the sharp rise in demand for its exports, isolation from Europe and the subsequent lack of imported manufactured goods gave its fledgling domestic industries a chance to grow.

Post-war Dominance

The United States emerged from the Second World War as a truly international power. The war had decimated Europe's economies and brought the British empire to its knees. In contrast, the US army had grown into an enormous military machine with troops stationed all over the world. Economically, it was the undisputed global leader, producing a third of the world's exports and half of the world's industrial output. The United States sought to build a stable international system that would allow it unrestricted access to the world's markets and raw materials. The World Bank and International Monetary Fund (IMF) were established in 1944 to regulate international banking, stabilize currencies and encourage overseas investment. US corporations were now expanding in Europe and the Far East, but the US interest in Latin America remained significant. In 1946–47 Latin America bought a quarter of US exports and in 1950 it received a third of its overseas investment.

Juan Perón

Argentina, having long-standing links with both Britain and Germany, had enraged the United States by remaining neutral for most of the war. In 1943 a group of nationalist officers staged a coup. They closed the Argentinian congress and banned political parties, and, like the democratic government before them, refused to declare war on Germany (until 1945 when Allied victory was assured). Unsurprisingly, the State Department feared that the junta had pro-Nazi sympathies. Colonel Juan Perón was labour minister in this administration. By encouraging the creation of trade unions and granting large wage rises, Perón built up a powerful and loyal labour movement and in 1945 he stood for President. Suspicious about his sympathies and uneasy at the appearance of thousands of militantly nationalist workers on the streets, the United States sought to prevent his election. Ambassador Spruille Braden openly campaigned against Perón and two weeks before the election published the 'Blue Book', a State Department document outlining Perón's alleged links with the Nazis during the war. But this blatant meddling in Argentina's domestic affairs backfired, stoking anti-US sentiment, and, with the slogan 'Braden or Perón', Perón won a resounding 54 per cent majority.

Although Perón was undoubtedly authoritarian, he was not a Nazi. He is better described as a populist – a common figure in Latin American politics – whose power rested on a cross-class alliance of workers, industrialists and junior military officers. Despite its initial hostility, the US made peace with the increasingly authoritarian Perón in the 1950s, as its security planners turned their attention from the Nazis to the Communists.

3

The Cold War
The Guatemalan Coup and the Cuban Revolution

Our problem then is to create where such do not already exist incentives which will impel the governments and societies of the Latin American countries to resist communist pressures ... Where the concepts and traditions of popular government are too weak to absorb successfully the intensity of the communist attack, then we must concede that harsh governmental measures of repression may be the only answer; that these measures may have to proceed from regimes whose origins and methods would not stand the test of American concepts of democratic procedure; and that such regimes and such methods may be preferable alternatives, and indeed the only alternatives, to further communist success.

Secret report by George F. Kennan submitted to Secretary of State Dean Acheson in 1950. Kennan was the State Department's leading expert on the Soviet Union.[1]

Diplomatic 'finesse and patience' are all right under the Marquis of Queensberry rules, but they may bring defeat if applied in a bar-room brawl, such as we are engaged in with the Kremlin ... Frequently it is necessary to fight fire with fire. No one is more opposed than I to interfere in the internal affairs of other nations. But... we may be compelled to intervene ... Communism is so blatantly an international and not internal affair, its suppression, even by force, in an American country, by one or more of the republics, would not constitute an intervention in the internal affairs of the former ...

Spruille Braden, Assistant Secretary of State under Truman, calling for intervention in Guatemala in 1953.[2]

The Cold War was one of the most disturbing periods in the history of US foreign policy towards Latin America. In the name of 'containing Communism', the United States supported dictators, undermined legitimately elected governments and colluded with authoritarian governments to repress dissent. It distorted Latin American political life to such an extent that it changed the course of history for several sovereign nations in the region. The Guatemalan coup is perhaps the best example of this, at least during the Cold War period: by the overthrow of the moderately left-wing president Jacobo Arbenz in 1954, Guatemala lost a chance of peaceful reform and the country was thrown into a 36-year-long civil war. As the Guatemalan case shows, the US regarded all reformers, not just communists, as a threat to its economic and military hegemony in the region.

Fidel Castro, the leader of the Cuban revolution of 1959, was not originally a Communist, but was pushed towards the Soviet Union by the intransigence of Cold War US administrations. Neither Eisenhower nor Kennedy would tolerate a left-wing, avowedly nationalist government on an island ninety miles off the coast of Florida, particularly one which had been until then the playground of wealthy Americans, and a source of lucrative income from illicit industries such as gambling. But such obduracy has backfired. Although Fidel's Cuba was not the socialist paradise painted by its supporters, the example of a small nation withstanding the enmity of the world's greatest power, so close to its shores, inspired radicals and anti-imperialists worldwide and has been a source of profound irritation to the White House for fifty years.

Containing alleged Soviet aggression became the top priority of US foreign policy in the late 1940s. In a speech to Congress in 1947, President Harry Truman declared: 'I believe it must be the policy of the United States to support free peoples who are resisting attempted subjugation by armed minorities or by outside pressures.'

The Truman Doctrine, as it became known, summed up the new theory of 'containment' and indicated that the US was willing to take action anywhere in the world to prevent the spread of Soviet communism. In Latin America, the Cold War was initially used as a pretext to shore up US military and geopolitical dominance. All the American nations signed a military pact, the Rio Treaty, in 1947. The signatories agreed to defend each other from attack and to confer before taking action when faced by a 'fact or situation that might endanger the peace of America'. In practice US military superiority allowed it to determine what constituted a danger and, more important, Latin American nations had limited their own room for manoeuvre by agreeing to confer with the US before taking any security issue to the United Nations.

The Organization of American States (OAS) was formed in 1948 and established a framework for resolving regional problems. Although the OAS charter, which included a non-intervention clause, was celebrated by Latin Americans, the imbalance of power between the member states meant that the OAS became little more than a tool of US foreign policy. US priorities were evident when, at its founding conference, the OAS issued a resolution calling for 'urgent measures' to stop the spread of communism in the hemisphere: '[We] declare: That, by its anti-democratic nature and its interventionist tendency, the political activity of international communism or any other totalitarian doctrine is incompatible with the concept of American freedom.'

The threat of communism was greatly exaggerated in Latin America. As in Europe, communist parties had grown during the war years, partly because the Soviet

Union was an ally in the fight against fascism. Communists could boast prestigious supporters in the region, such as the Chilean poet Pablo Neruda and Mexican artists Diego Rivera and Frida Kahlo, but the number of communist party members in Latin America never rose above half a million at a generous estimate. The growth of the Left was part of a much wider movement towards democracy, as the middle class and urban working class demanded greater participation in national affairs. Dictatorships fell across Latin American in 1945– 46; free (or freer) elections were held and opposition parties took power. Although wartime Allied propaganda had encouraged these democratic movements, the US now was uneasy about the upheavals, fearing a threat to stability.

This democratic flowering did not last long, as the traditional landowning classes resorted to their old methods of control. In the late 1940s and early 1950s the military took power in Venezuela, Peru, Ecuador, Cuba, Paraguay and Colombia, while the Central American dictatorships that had survived now abandoned promises of liberalization. By 1954, only four democracies remained: Uruguay, Costa Rica, Chile and Brazil. Cold War ideologues viewed the dictatorships as a bulwark against communism. George Kennan, the State Department's most influential adviser and the author of containment policy, wrote, 'It is better to have a strong regime in power than a liberal one if it is indulgent and relaxed and penetrated by Communists.'[3] The US gave diplomatic recognition and military assistance to the military governments and even awarded the Legion of Merit to two of the most hated dictators in the region at the time, Manuel Odría of Peru and Marcos Pérez Jiménez of Venezuela.

The CIA and Covert Action

The National Security Act of 1947 created the National Security Council and the Central Intelligence Agency (CIA) and merged the Departments of War and Navy into the Department of Defense. The CIA's mandate was much broader than simple intelligence gathering. This National Security Council memorandum of 1948 outlines some of its other tasks:

'Any covert activities related to propaganda, economic warfare; preventative direct action, including sabotage, anti-sabotage, demolition and evacuation measures, subversion against hostile states, including assistance to underground resistance groups, and support of indigenous anti-communist elements in threatened countries of the free world.'

Cited in M. McClintock, *Instruments of Statecraft: US Guerilla Warfare, Counter-Insurgency and Counter-Terrorism, 1940-1990*, New York, Pantheon Books, 1992, p. 29.

For their part, the authoritarian regimes in the region began an onslaught against communists, left-wing activists and the trade unions – an onslaught that the US applauded while urging democratic governments to follow suit. Communist parties were banned in nine countries and in democratic Chile and Brazil elected communists were removed from congress and local government. Communist party membership in Latin America fell to below 200,000 by 1952. Labour attachés from the US were appointed to its embassies in Latin America in order to lobby governments to confront the militant independent trade unions that had erupted onto the scene during the Second World War. Trade unions were disbanded or taken over by the state, activists were arrested and anti-strike legislation was introduced. Crackdowns on labour movements were not restricted to those countries ruled by the military, but also occurred in Chile, Brazil, Costa Rica and Mexico. Meanwhile, the US-led American Federation of Labor (AFL) was given thousands of dollars to wage a campaign against so-called communist trade unions and to set up alternative pro-US unions.

The Coup in Guatemala, 1954

The Guatemalan dictator Jorge Ubico, feared and despised by the bulk of Guatemala's population but approved of by the United States, was overthrown in 1944 by a movement led by teachers and reformist military officers. José Arévalo, a professor and political moderate, was elected President in 1945. For the first time Guatemalans enjoyed freedom of speech, freedom of the press and freedom to organize.

At the time, Guatemala was an overwhelmingly agricultural country: 90 per cent of the labour force worked in the countryside. A tiny oligarchy accounting for just 2.2 per cent of all landowners owned 70 per cent of the country's arable land, while the vast majority of the population lived in poverty. Arévalo was a cautious reformer, but even the modest Labour Code introduced in 1947 attracted the ire of United Fruit, the country's largest employer. The Labour Code gave urban workers and rural workers on large plantations (although not on medium-sized farms) the right to join unions. United Fruit, which owned half a million hectares, making it the largest landowner in Guatemala, threatened to leave the country when the Labour Code was promulgated, and when labourers on banana plantations started strikes for higher wages the company began to lobby US politicians in earnest, warning of a communist threat in Guatemala.

Defence minister Jacobo Arbenz was elected President in 1950, promising to raise living standards by tackling the inequality and backwardness of the economy. Arbenz may have been a radical nationalist, but he was not a communist. His 1952 agrarian reform law allowed only for the expropriation of uncultivated parts of large plantations; medium-sized farms and cultivated plantations would not be touched. Compensation would be paid on the basis of tax returns, a clause that angered United Fruit, which for years had deliberately undervalued its land in order to pay less tax.

On assuming power in 1953, President Eisenhower complained that his pre-decessor had been 'soft on communism', and it was he who in August 1953 authorized the CIA to remove Arbenz. Eisenhower's administration was particularly susceptible to United Fruit's lobbying because many of its officials had links with the fruit company (see box). In September 1953 the CIA drew up a 'General Plan of

---

United Fruit and the Eisenhower Government

United Fruit had a tight web of connections to the government of President Dwight D. Eisenhower (1953–61).

- The family of John Moors Cabot, Assistant Secretary of State for Inter-American Affairs, owned stock in United Fruit. His brother was president of the company in 1948.
- US ambassador to the UN Henry Cabot Lodge was a stockholder in United Fruit.
- The wife of Edmund Whitman, United Fruit's public relations director, was President Eisenhower's personal secretary.
- Undersecretary of State Bedell Smith was seeking an executive job with United Fruit while helping to plan the 1954 coup. He later sat on the board of directors.
- Robert Hill, US ambassador to Costa Rica, was close to United Fruit, having worked for Grace Shipping Lines, which had interests in Guatemala.
- Secretary of State John Foster Dulles had been a senior partner in a law firm that did legal work for Schroder Banking Corp, which was an adviser to International Railways of Central America (IRCA). United Fruit took over IRCA and Dulles handled the negotiations.
- Allen Dulles, director of the CIA, was on the board of directors of Schroder Bank. Schroder Bank was a depository of secret CIA funds for covert operations.

Source: S. Schlesinger and S. Kinzer, *Bitter Fruit: The Story of the American Coup in Guatemala*, London, Sinclair Browne, 1982, p. 106.

Action' which has recently been declassified.[4] It outlined its preparations under headings including 'Paramilitary action'; 'Economic pressure'; 'Official discrediting of Guatemala' and 'Psychological warfare'; under the latter it stated: 'A complete psychological warfare campaign for Guatemala is in the planning stage.' Two months later the CIA had drawn up a detailed six-stage plan to destabilize and overthrow Arbenz. This document, which has also been declassified, starts by succinctly stating the CIA's objectives:

1. To remove covertly, and without bloodshed if possible, the menace of the present Communist-controlled government of Guatemala.
2. To install and sustain, covertly, a pro-US government in Guatemala.[5]

The document then goes on to outline the tasks ahead:

3. Stage Three – Build Up
   a. Create maximum antagonism to target regime
   b. Fan passive will to resist
   c. Apply internal and external economic pressure to create serious difficulties …
   d. … apply diplomatic pressures

    e. Demonstrate urgency by speeding military build-up of neighboring countries (not including Mexico)

    f. Accentuate para-military preparation

    g. Initiate passive sabotage program …

4. Stage Four – Critical Period

    a. Apply maximum economic pressure

    b. Accentuate divisionist activity within the target

    c. Intensive rumor campaign stimulating fear of war …

    d. Constitutional revolutionary forces claim support of the people

    e. Para-military force in readiness

    f. Passive sabotage evident …

The Coup

For the coup the CIA recruited, armed and trained a force of Guatemalan exiles and foreign mercenaries. Carlos Castillo Armas, a Guatemalan officer who had led an abortive coup in 1950, was chosen to lead the 'liberating forces'. Anti-communist propaganda including newspaper articles, radio broadcasts and 25,000 cartoons and posters was distributed throughout Guatemala and Latin America. Three days before the invasion, Eisenhower told a White House meeting, 'I want all of you to be damn good and sure you succeed … I'm prepared to take any steps that are necessary to see that it succeeds, for if it succeeds, it's the people of Guatemala throwing off the yoke of Communism. If it fails, the flag of the United States has failed.'[6]

'I have made a sad and cruel judgement'

President Jacobo Arbenz made a final address to the people of Guatemala on the evening of Sunday 27 June 1954. [Many Guatemalans did not hear his words as the radio transmission was jammed by the CIA.]

'Workers, peasants, patriots, my friends – people of Guatemala: Guatemala is enduring a most difficult trial. For fifteen days a cruel war against Guatemala has been underway. The United Fruit Company, in collaboration with the governing circles of the United States, is responsible for what is happening to us …

In whose name have they carried out these barbaric acts? What is their banner? We know very well. They have used the pretext of anti-communism. The truth is very different. The truth is to be found in the financial interests of the fruit company and the other US monopolies which have invested great amounts of money in Latin America and fear that the example of Guatemala would be followed by other Latin countries …

I have made a sad and cruel judgement. After reflecting with a clear revolutionary conscience, I have made a decision that is of great importance for our country in the hope of containing this aggression and bringing peace to Guatemala. I have decided to step down …'

Source: S. Schlesinger and S. Kinzer, *Bitter Fruit: the Story of the American Coup in Guatemala*, London, Sinclair Browne, p. 199.

The CIA transported the few hundred mercenaries to the Guatemalan border, where they launched the 'invasion' on 18 June 1954. CIA planes bombed Guatemala City and strategic sites, a campaign that was particularly effective because the US had refused to sell the Guatemalan government anti-aircraft equipment. A CIA radio station broadcast misinformation which unsettled the population and wore down the resolve of Guatemala's military leaders, who, on 27 June, persuaded Arbenz to resign.

The Legacy of Guatemala

The destabilization of Arbenz's government had devastating consequences for Guatemala. The country missed a chance of peaceful reform. Big landowners retained their power, leaving most people in poverty. As a consequence, the country soon descended into a 36-year-long civil war in which more than 200,000 Guatemalans lost their lives. Arbenz's overthrow also had a profound impact on Latin America, which went beyond the angry crowds that jostled and spat at a

---

The Bolivian Revolution

The US reaction to the Bolivian revolution of 1952 contrasted with its unmitigated hostility to the Guatemalan reformist government. The Movimiento Nacional Revolucionario (MNR), a nationalist progressive movement backed by militant tin miners' unions, led a popular insurrection and its leaders immediately assured the United States that it would respect private property and international agreements. The revolutionary government had no links with the official communist party, which had labelled the MNR 'pro-fascist' during the Second World War.

Unlike in Guatemala, US investors had no large landholdings in Bolivia, so were not affected by the government's land reforms. US investors owned a 20 per cent stake in one of the three large tin mining companies that were nationalized, but the Bolivian government paid generous compensation to the former owners. Tin was of strategic value to the US, but there was no danger of supplies being cut off; on the contrary, the Bolivian government was desperate for foreign exchange and urged the US government to sign long-term sales agreements.

In 1956, when the Bolivian economy faced crisis, the US offered an aid package on the condition that the government agreed to implement severe austerity measures. President Hernán Siles Suazo implemented the cuts despite mass protests, a battle that left the defeated mining unions too weak and dispirited to pose a revolutionary threat. A few years later the government laid off thousands of tin miners. Economic collaboration with the US government continued, and Bolivia became the largest recipient of US aid in Latin America throughout the 1950s.

shaken Vice-President Nixon when he attempted a goodwill tour of the Americas in 1958. A generation of young Latin Americans now began to question whether change could come through peaceful democratic means.

The Cuban Revolution

Fidel Castro, described by *New York Times* reporter Herbert Matthews as 'a powerful six-footer, olive-skinned with a straggly beard', toured the island of Cuba in an open-top jeep greeting cheering crowds before making his triumphant entrance to Havana aboard a tank on 8 January 1959. His guerrilla army had defeated the hated dictator Fulgencio Batista. Matthews had met Castro in his guerrilla encampment in the mountains two years earlier:

> The personality of the man is overpowering. It was easy to see that his men adored him and also to see why he has caught the imagination of the youth of Cuba all over the island. Here was an educated, dedicated fanatic, a man of ideals of courage and of remarkable qualities of leadership.[7]

Batista's fall was not due simply to the efforts of Castro and his fighters. Cuba was a relatively advanced economy and the standard of living, in the cities at least, was higher than in most Latin American countries. The country had a well-educated middle class and active student and trade union movements. Batista had seized power in 1952, and as his regime became more corrupt and repressive, the opposition grew to include not only students and workers, but most of the middle class as well. Even the US government could see that its former protégé was losing his grip on power and in late 1958 it withdrew its support. Castro, the heroic guerrilla in the mountains, had become a symbol of resistance who had also managed to unite the disparate forces of his country.

For five decades, an agonized debate has taken place in the US about what went wrong in Cuba. Could the US have stopped Cuba from becoming communist? If the US had been friendly to Castro, would he still have turned to the Soviet Union? If the US had not imposed a trade embargo, would capitalism have gradually flourished in Cuba? Or, more prosaically, if the Bay of Pigs invasion had not been such a fiasco, could the revolution have been stopped in its tracks?

Surely it was bungling of historic proportions to turn a movement that simply wanted to overthrow a dictator and improve the lot of the poor into a hardline Soviet ally? But this argument is not so straightforward: Cuban revolutionaries possessed a blazing desire for sovereignty. Indignation and resentment against the US had smouldered since 1898, when Cuba won freedom from Spain with US help, but instead of gaining true independence became a *de facto* US protectorate. The anti-dictatorial struggle necessarily had a anti-US tinge, because the dictator Batista had been groomed by the US. Anti-imperialism in this context could not help but be anti-Yankee; a yearning for sovereignty meant a yearning for independence from the US.

Castro was above all a nationalist who saw himself completing the task started by

Cuba's independence leader, José Martí. In his first speech, Castro pledged that the revolution would not repeat the mistakes of 1898 when 'the North Americans came and made themselves masters of our country'.[8] The manifesto of Fidel's 26th of July Movement called for an end to 'the colonial mentality'; 'foreign economic domination'; 'political corruption' and 'military intemperance'. Castro's brother Raúl had been a young communist and his comrade-in-arms Che Guevara was a socialist, but Castro's aims were vague. Having seen poverty first-hand in the Cuban countryside, however, he was determined to end the servitude of the peasantry and to improve the lot of the urban poor. The first acts of his government included slashing rents, forbidding landlords from evicting tenants, decreeing a minimum wage for sugar cane cutters, and cutting the price of medicines and phone calls. Reforms like these could not help but cause friction with the US, which had an octopus-like hold on the economy: US businesses owned 90 per cent of Cuba's telephone and electricity services, 50 per cent of the railways and 40 per cent of the sugar industry.

The US gave official recognition to the new government, reassured by the appointment of two traditional politicians as prime minister and president. It was not long, however, before the US State Department was discomforted by the public trial and execution of several hundred of Batista's officers and cohorts, and by Cuba's management takeover of the US-owned giant International Telephone & Telegraph (ITT). When Castro came, unannounced, to Washington in April 1959, President Eisenhower did not meet him, choosing instead to play golf. Vice-President Nixon concluded after a two-hour-long discussion with Castro that he was 'either incredibly naïve about Communism or under Communist discipline – my guess is the former'.[9] From that point on, Nixon advocated the removal of Castro. But it was the land reform bill of June 1959 that really marked the breakdown of relations. It was a moderate reform – landowners could keep up to 1,000 acres of land, the excess being liable to expropriation – but Americans, who owned vast estates in Cuba, regarded it as communistic. This view was shared by the moderate politicians in Castro's cabinet, who had been disturbed by the growing influence of the Cuban Communist Party. The head of the Cuban air force left the country and, a month later, the president resigned. Castro, whose own base of power was small, increasingly turned to the communists, the best-organized and most disciplined left-wing party in the country, to carry through his reforms.

In June 1959, just six months after Fidel's triumphant arrival in Havana, the US National Security Council began discussing how to get rid of Castro. Four months later, in October 1959, President Eisenhower approved support for Cuban dissidents trying to topple Castro.[10] In December, the head of the CIA's Western Hemisphere division, J.C. King, fleshed out a programme of covert and propaganda operations against the regime. Within weeks, the CIA began sabotaging sugar refineries and other targets. King also proposed the 'elimination' of Castro, setting in motion a series of bizarre assassination plans, from poison pens to drugged cigars – some of which, in the words of a US Senate committee, 'strain the imagination' (see box, overleaf).

CIA Plots to Assassinate Fidel Castro

A US Senate committee investigated numerous CIA attempts to assassinate Fidel Castro. Below is an extract of the committee's 1975 report:

' [We have found] concrete evidence of at least eight plots involving the CIA to assassinate Fidel Castro from 1960 to 1965. Although some of the assassination plots did not advance beyond the stage of planning and preparation, one plot, involving the use of underworld figures, reportedly twice progressed to the point of sending poison pills to Cuba and dispatching weapons to commit the deed. Another plot involved furnishing weapons and other assassination devices to a Cuban dissident. The proposed assassination devices ran the gamut from high-powered rifles to poison pills, poison pens, deadly bacterial powders and other devices which strain the imagination ...

... From March through August 1960, during the last year of the Eisenhower Administration, the CIA considered plans to undermine Castro's charismatic appeal by sabotaging his speeches ... an official in the [CIA'S] Technical Services Division (TSD) recalled discussing a scheme to spray Castro's broadcasting studio with a chemical which produced effects similar to LSD, but the scheme was rejected because the chemical was unreliable. During this period TSD impregnated a box of cigars with a chemical which produced temporary disorientation hoping to induce Castro to smoke one of the cigars before delivering a speech. The [CIA] Inspector General also reported a plan to destroy Castro's image as 'The Beard' by dusting his shower with thallium salts, a strong depilatory that would cause his beard to fall out ...

... An [CIA] official was given a box of Castro's favorite cigars with instructions to treat them with lethal poison. The cigars were contaminated with a botulinum toxin so potent that a person would die after putting one in his mouth. The official reported that the cigars were ready on October 7 1960 ... they were delivered to an identified person on February 13, 1961. The record does not disclose whether an attempt was made to pass the cigars to Castro.'

Source: *US Senate Select Committee on Governmental Operations Alleged Assassination Plots Involving Foreign Leaders*, 1975.

Pushed into the Arms of the Soviet Union

Even *before* Castro formed an alliance with the Soviet Union, the United States had already decided to get rid of him. But this strategy backfired; by pursuing the Cuban leader and seeking to topple his regime, the US made it impossible for Castro to take any other course if he and his revolution were to survive.

An initial contact with the Soviet Union was made in July 1959 when, as part of a tour to drum up trade with the Third World, Che Guevara – then minister of the economy – signed a preliminary deal with Russia to buy half a million tonnes of sugar. The Cubans were keen to reduce their dependency on US trade, as the United States bought two thirds of Cuban exports and supplied 70 per cent of its imports. In February 1960 the Russian deal was expanded into a five-year commitment to buy a million tonnes of sugar per year. The US responded with fury. The CIA bombed a ship in Havana harbour, killing one hundred people, in March 1960 and in the same month Eisenhower approved a CIA policy paper entitled 'Program of Covert Action against the Castro Regime', authorizing the CIA to mount an operation to overthrow Castro. This order led to the bungled Bay of Pigs invasion a year later.

In the meantime a series of tit-for-tat actions drove Cuba ever eastward towards the Soviet empire. In April 1960, the first consignment of Soviet oil arrived, but the refineries owned by Shell, Texaco and Standard Oil, under pressure from the US government, refused to refine it. The Cuban government confiscated the oil companies' assets. In July, the US, which had for years bought Cuban sugar at a preferential price, reduced Cuba's sugar quota by 700,000 tonnes. In retaliation Castro announced the nationalization of large US properties, including thirty-six sugar mills and their plantations, as well as oil, telephone and electricity companies. US banks were seized in September and over the next three months US-owned railways, ports, hotels and cinemas were taken over. In October 1960, the US imposed an economic embargo, banning US companies from selling anything to Cuba except food and medicine. This embargo, which endures fifty years later, made Cuba economically dependent on the Soviet Union until the early 1990s.

Bay of Pigs

Fourteen hundred fighters landed on Girón beach on the Bay of Pigs, on the southern coast of Cuba, in the early hours of 17 April 1961. The CIA had trained Cuban exiles in Guatemala and supplied them with arms, munitions and transport, but the invading force was defeated within seventy-two hours after heavy fighting with government-armed militias and Cuba's small air force. The invasion was an embarrassing disaster for the US. It had underestimated the strength of popular support for the Cuban government and had made crucial military and intelligence blunders – Castro had been alerted to the imminent attack by a CIA air strike on Cuba two days earlier, and the US did not back up the invasion with air power, leaving the rebels isolated on the beach. The Bay of Pigs invasion provoked years of bitter recriminations not only among Cuban exiles in the US, but between the CIA and President Kennedy's administration, which the CIA blamed for the disaster. The US never again attempted to invade Cuba, but it did continue trying to destabilize the Castro government. Just seven months after the failed invasion, Kennedy approved Operation Mongoose, another programme of covert action and dirty tricks aimed at ousting Castro. But for Cuba, the Bay of Pigs was a turning point. In a speech after the CIA air attacks Castro for the first time defined the revolution as 'socialist', and in December 1961 he described himself as a 'Marxist Leninist' and joined the Cuban Communist Party.

Bay of Pigs Declassified

This CIA policy paper, approved by President Eisenhower in March 1960, set in motion the Bay of Pigs invasion of Cuba. The document was declassified in 1996.

' PROGRAM OF COVERT ACTION AGAINST THE CASTRO REGIME
16 MARCH 1960

1 Objective: The purpose of the program outlined herein is to bring about the replacement of the Castro regime with one more devoted to the true interests of the Cuban people and more acceptable to the US in such a manner as to avoid any appearance of US intervention ...

2 a. The first requirement is the creation of a responsible, appending and unified Cuban opposition to the Castro regime, publicly declared as such and therefore necessarily located outside of Cuba ...

   b. So that this opposition may be heard and Castro's base of popular support undermined, it is necessary to develop the means for mass communication to the Cuban people so that a powerful propaganda offensive can be initiated in the name of the declared opposition. The major tool proposed to be used for this purpose is a long and short wave gray broadcasting facility probably to be located on Swan Island ... This will be supplemented by broadcasting from US commercial facilities paid for by private Cuban groups and by the clandestine distribution of written material inside the country.

   c. Work is already in progress in the creation of a covert intelligence action organization within Cuba which will be responsive to the orders and directions of the 'exile' opposition ...

   d. Preparations have already been made for the development of an adequate paramilitary force outside of Cuba, together with mechanisms for the necessary logistic support of covert military operations on the Island. Initially a cadre of leaders will be recruited after careful screening; and trained as paramilitary instructors ...

4 Cover: All actions undertaken by the CIA in support and on behalf of the opposition council will, of course, be explained as activities of that entity (insofar as the actions become publicly known at all). The CIA will, however, have to have direct contacts with a certain number of Cubans and, to protect these, will make use of a carefully screened group of US businessmen with a stated interest in Cuban affairs and a desire to support the opposition ....'

Source: Peter Kornbluh (ed.), *Bay of Pigs Declassified*, New York, New Press, 1998, p. 103.

The Cuban Missile Crisis

Secretary of the Treasury Douglas Dillon was one of a core group of advisers selected by President Kennedy following the discovery of Soviet nuclear bases in Cuba. In this memo to the President he advocates air strikes on Cuba if it fails to agree within 24 hours to remove the bases.

'MEMORANDUM FOR THE PRESIDENT
OCTOBER 17 1962

It is my view that the Soviet Union has now deliberately initiated a public test of our intentions that can determine the course of world events for many years to come.

If we allow the offensive capabilities presently in Cuba to remain there, I am convinced that sooner or later and probably sooner we will lose all Latin America to Communism because all credibility of our willingness to effectively resist Soviet military power will have been removed in the eyes of the Latins. We can also expect similar reactions elsewhere, for instance in Iran, Thailand and Pakistan.

I therefore believe that the survival of our nation demands the prompt elimination of the offensive weapons now in Cuba ....'

Source: L. Chang and P. Kornbluh (eds), *The Cuban Missile Crisis, 1962: A National Security Archive Document Reader*, New York, New Press, 1992, p. 18.

The Cuban Missile Crisis

> Within the past week, unmistakable evidence has established the fact that a series of offensive missile sites is now in preparation. The purpose of these bases can be none other than to provide a nuclear strike capability against the Western Hemisphere.

President Kennedy's words, broadcast in a televised address on the evening of 22 October 1962, stunned the world audience. Over the following six days the superpowers came closer to nuclear war than they have ever been, before or since. As Robert McNamara, Kennedy's Defense Secretary, said some years later: 'No one should believe that had US troops been attacked with tactical nuclear warheads, the United States would have refrained from responding with nuclear warheads. And where would it have ended? In utter disaster.'[11]

Locating nuclear missiles on Cuba had not been a Cuban idea. As the historian Richard Gott has shown, the Cuban government sought a conventional military alliance with the Soviet Union in the wake of the Bay of Pigs.[12] The Soviets responded by offering to send 42,000 troops to secretly construct nuclear missile bases, comprising 16 intermediate-range ballistic missile launchers and 24 medium-range launchers, each equipped with two missiles and a nuclear warhead. The Cubans, who believed that another US invasion was imminent, accepted the offer, but with some reluctance because they were aware that the move could damage the image of the revolution in Latin America and the Third World.[13] CIA reconnaissance planes photographed the sites on 16 October. President Kennedy spent a week discussing with his closest advisers what to do and came close to launching air strikes on Cuba. However, it was decided that the best option was to impose a naval blockade and attempt to negotiate. In the days following Kennedy's televised address it was not clear how the Soviet Union would respond, and US conventional and nuclear forces were put on full alert worldwide. But to the relief of millions, the Soviet leader, Nikita Khrushchev, did not attempt to break the US blockade and on 28 October agreed to withdraw the bases from Cuban soil. In return Kennedy agreed to remove US nuclear warheads in Turkey, and gave an informal assurance that it would not invade Cuba. The Cuban government played no part in the negotiations and was dismayed that the Soviet Union prioritized the removal of missiles in Turkey rather than the dismantling of the US naval base in Guantánamo.[14] Cuba had discovered the cost of allying itself with one strategically minded superpower in order to keep another at bay.

Exporting Revolution in Latin America and Che Guevara

The Cuban revolution was an inspiration to intellectuals, reformers and revolutionaries not only in Latin America, but throughout the world. Poets, artists and writers including Gabriel García Márquez, Carlos Fuentes, Jean-Paul Sartre, Roberto Matta, Pablo Neruda and Simone de Beauvoir flocked to the island to witness the revolution. Cuba's literacy campaign of 1961 won worldwide acclaim. In its early years, the Cuban revolutionary government still permitted vigorous debate, and the possibility of spreading the revolution in Latin America seemed real. Che Guevara assured readers of his handbook Guerrilla Warfare (1960) that the Cuban example could be repeated; a dedicated group of guerrillas could defeat a conventional army, he argued. Giving hope to dozens of would-be revolutionaries he added: 'It is not always necessary to wait until all the conditions for revolution exist; the insurrectional guerrilla foco [unit] can create them.' When the Organization of American States (OAS) expelled Cuba in 1962, Fidel Castro responded with the Second Declaration of Havana in which he called for continent-wide revolution: 'It is the duty of the revolutionary to make the revolution.' Small guerrilla groups duly sprang up across Latin America in the 1960s, but nearly all were wiped out by the end of the decade. The reasons for their failure varied from country to country, but many were formed by middle-class idealists who failed to win support from the peasantry, and became easy prey for the military. The main exception was Colombia, where the guerrillas had deep roots in peasant communities. A second wave of guerrilla warfare took place in the 1970s, often in the cities, but again most failed to win broad support and were annihilated, with the notable exception of the insurgencies in Central America.

'Create two, three ... many Vietnams, that is the watchword'

Che Guevara left Cuba in 1965 to lead revolutionary struggles across the world, from the Congo to Bolivia. In April 1967 he gave this message to a meeting in Havana of the Organization of Solidarity with the Peoples of Asia, Africa and Latin America (the Tricontinental):

'... The Yankee agents of repression will increase in number. Today there are advisers in all countries where armed struggle is going on. It seems that the Peruvian army, also advised and trained by the Yankees, carried out a successful attack on the revolutionaries of that country. But if the guerrilla *focos* are led with sufficient political and military skill, they will become practically unbeatable and will make new Yankee reinforcements necessary ... Little by little the obsolete weapons that suffice to repress the small armed bands will turn into modern weapons and the groups of advisers into US combatants ... This is the road of Vietnam ... It is the road that Latin America will follow, with the special feature that the armed groups might establish something such as coordinating committees to make the repressive tasks of Yankee imperialism more difficult and to help their own cause.

Latin America, a continent forgotten in the recent political struggles for liberation, is beginning to make itself heard through the Tricontinental in the voice of the vanguard of its people: the Cuban revolution. Latin America will have a much more important task: the creation of the world's second or third Vietnam, or second *and* third Vietnam ... How close and bright would the future appear if two, three, many Vietnams flowered on the face of the globe, with their quota of death and immense tragedies, with the daily heroism, with their repeated blows against imperialism, forcing it to disperse its forces under the lash of the growing hatred of the peoples of the world! ...

Our every action is a battle cry against imperialism and a call for the unity of the peoples against the great enemy of the human race: the United States of North America.'

Source: D. Deutschmann (ed.), *The Che Guevara Reader*, Melbourne, Ocean Press, 2003, p. 350

Guevara left Cuba in 1965 to fight a guerrilla war in the Congo and, a year later, Bolivia. Cuba's dreams of exporting revolution ended in 1967 when Guevara was killed by the Bolivian military. The staid, cautious Soviet bureaucracy had frowned upon Cuba's attempts to foment revolution, which it feared could upset the international balance of power. The end of the dream for many of Cuba's admirers came in 1968, when Castro succumbed to such 'realism' and backed the Soviet invasion of Czechoslovakia.

The Cuban revolution coloured US policy towards Latin America for the next half-century. The US intelligence services maintained their campaign of sabotage and dirty tricks, in collusion with Cuban exiles, and since the revolution over 3,500 people have been killed in US-sponsored terrorist attacks, according to one pro-Cuban source.[15] The embargo endured – indeed was strengthened – giving Cuba little choice but to rely on the USSR for oil and other essentials. US intransigence simply strengthened hardliners in Cuba who used the external threat to justify restrictions on civil liberties. Avoiding 'another Cuba' became an obsession for the Pentagon, the State Department and the CIA and gave US presidents another excuse for backing authoritarian regimes and abusive militaries in Latin America.

4

The Alliance for Progress

The US answer to the Cuban revolution was the Alliance for Progress, an ambitious plan to promote economic and social development in Latin America. It aimed to prevent more Cuban-style revolutions in Latin America by promoting moderate reform from above. 'Those who make peaceful reform impossible will make violent revolution inevitable,' declared President Kennedy at the launch of the Alliance in August 1961. Venezuela's president, Rómulo Betancourt, put it more succinctly: 'We must help the poor … to save the rich.' The Alliance would plough loans of US$20 billion into Latin America over a decade, half of which would come from private investors. Latin American governments were encouraged to draw up national development plans, with the help of US advisers, to stimulate economic growth and promote redistribution. As the credit began to flow, the IMF and the World Bank began to play an increasingly prominent role in shaping governments' policies.

The most radical element of the Alliance for Progress was land reform. Its architects, recognizing just how crucial the land question was for Latin American development, declared that 'unjust structures and systems of land tenure' should be replaced by 'an equitable system of property', so that the 'land will become for the man who works it the basis of his economic stability, the foundation of his increasing welfare and the guarantee of his freedom and dignity'. But land reform was a failure. Fewer than one million families across the region were given land, while 10 to 14 million families received nothing. The number of landless families actually increased due to population growth. US planners had not counted on the intransigence of Latin American oligarchs who were not prepared to give up their land, no matter who was behind the land reform schemes. Nor was US agribusiness in favour of dividing up large estates, and a growing paranoia that communists would penetrate peasant unions meant Washington did little to promote agrarian reform. Instead the emphasis was increasingly put on modernization, technical improvements and cheaper credit for large farmers. In some countries the position of rural workers actually deteriorated because their jobs were taken by machines. Whilst most Latin American economies achieved moderate growth in the 1960s, there was very little wealth redistribution.

Counter-insurgency

From the beginning, the Alliance for Progress was a two-pronged strategy: it sought to undercut support for the Left through economic development, while using military methods to suppress guerrillas and other 'subversives'. The reforms petered out, but the military side of the Alliance endured. Military aid and training programmes rose dramatically in the 1960s; annual US military assistance in the first five years of the decade was double what it had been in the 1950s. Between 1964 and 1968 alone, 22,059 Latin American military officials were trained at the School of the Americas in the Panama Canal Zone and at other US military training schools. Thousands more were instructed in the field in Latin America by the US special forces. The special forces or 'Green Berets' were elite US army units trained in jungle warfare, psychological operations and covert action, and equipped with the latest lightweight field radios, helicopters and high-powered rifles. Some 1,100 special forces were stationed at Fort Gulick in the Panama Canal Zone, and between 1962 and 1968 four hundred special forces mobile training teams were sent on missions in Latin America. Latin American police forces were also trained and equipped.

The US military, which had honed its unconventional warfare techniques in Greece, Korea and Laos, developed counter-insurgency doctrine to confront the guerrilla challenge in Vietnam. President Kennedy, who visited Vietnam, took a personal interest in this type of warfare. He read treatises on guerrilla warfare by Mao Zedong and by Che Guevara and urged Pentagon officials to do the same. He spelt out the threat in a 1962 speech:

> Subversive insurgency is another type of war, new in its intensity, ancient in its origins – war by guerrillas, subversives, insurgents, assassins, war by ambush instead of by combat, by infiltration instead of aggression. It requires … a whole new kind of strategy, a wholly different kind of force and therefore a new and wholly different kind of training.[1]

Project X, a secret Pentagon campaign which has only recently come to light as a result of declassifying material, aimed to teach Latin American militaries the lessons that had been learnt in Vietnam. US army instructors in Latin America were provided with manuals and teaching materials containing the latest counter-insurgency techniques. Students at the School of the Americas studied psychological warfare, clandestine operations, defoliation, the use of informants, the interrogation of prisoners, handling mass rallies and meetings, intelligence photography and polygraphs.[2] Counter-insurgency doctrine argued that unconventional tactics were needed to combat irregular forces. Particularly ominous was a shift of focus onto civilians, based on the premise that guerrillas needed the support of the local population in order to survive. Counter-insurgency doctrine stated that the civilian population should be dissuaded from supporting insurgents, by means of either 'hearts-and-minds' civic programmes or coercion. An example of this type of thinking is given in the 1962 army field manual *Psychological Operations*:

> Civilians in the operation area may be supporting their own government or collaborating with an enemy occupation force. An isolation program designed to instill doubt and fear may be carried out, and a positive political action program designed to elicit active support ... also may be effected. If these programs fail, it may become necessary to take more aggressive action in the form of harsh treatment or even abductions. The abduction and harsh treatment of key enemy civilians can weaken the collaborators' belief in the strength and power of their military forces.[3]

In many of the US training manuals, no distinction is made between guerrilla fighters and their civilian supporters; both are viewed as 'subversives'. This doctrine provided the justification for some of the worst atrocities of Latin America's military governments and left a lasting legacy in the form of right-wing death squads which regard trade unionists and human rights lawyers, among others, as legitimate targets.

The School of the Americas and Torture Training Manuals

The United States established a training school for Latin American soldiers in the Panama Canal Zone in 1949. Originally called the Army Caribbean School, it was renamed the School of the Americas in 1963, when a new curriculum was introduced offering courses in counter-insurgency, military intelligence and psychological warfare. In 1984, the school was moved to Fort Benning, Georgia, USA, and in 2001, in an attempt to improve its image, its name was changed again to the Western Hemisphere Institute for Security Cooperation.

More than 60,000 Latin American soldiers have been trained at the school, among them some of the region's most notorious dictators and human rights abusers.

In 1996, the Pentagon declassified seven training manuals used at the School of the Americas. The manuals advocated the use of 'fear, payment of bounties for enemy dead, beatings, false imprisonment, executions and use of truth serum', according to the Department of Defense's own summary.* The manuals also included detailed interrogation techniques and use the term 'neutralization', which the Department of Defense admits is a euphemism for illegal execution.

More than a thousand copies of the manuals were distributed to the armed forces in Latin America between 1987 and 1991. They quoted verbatim from military training materials written in the 1960s, as part of Project X, and from a notorious CIA manual *KUBARK: Counterintelligence Interrogation*, written in 1963 (see box below).

* Memorandum for the Secretary of Defense, from Werner E. Michel, Assistant to Secretary of Defense, 'Improper Material in Spanish-Language Intelligence Training Manuals', 10 March 1992.

CIA's Handbook for Torturers

The 1963 manual *KUBARK: Counterintelligence Interrogation* (KUBARK is the CIA's codename for itself) deals at length with the psychological aspects of interrogation. Citing numerous academics, the section on 'non-coercive' interrogation gives step-by-step instructions on how to disorientate a suspect and weaken his will in order to obtain information. The manual then examines 'coercive techniques' which are extracted below.

In 1983 the CIA published the *Human Resource Exploitation Training Manual*, which is strikingly similar to the 1963 manual, and was used in CIA and special forces training in Latin America from 1983 to 1987.

ꞌINDEX: IX THE COERCIVE COUNTERINTELLIGENCE INTERROGATION OF RESISTANT SOURCES.

Restrictions
The Theory of Coercion
Arrest
Detention
Deprivation of Sensory Stimuli
Threats and Fear
Debility
Pain
Heightened Suggestibility and Hypnosis
Narcosis
The Detection of Malingering
Conclusion

The theory of coercion

Coercive Procedures are designed not only to exploit the resistant source's internal conflicts and induce him to wrestle with himself but also to bring a superior outside force to bear upon the subject's resistance ... All coercive techniques are designed to induce regression. As Hinkle notes in 'The Physiological State of the Interrogation Subject as it Affects Brain Function' the result of external pressures of sufficient intensity is the loss of those defenses most recently acquired by civilized man: ... 'the capacity to carry out the highest creative activities, to meet new, challenging, and complex situations, to deal with trying interpersonal relations and to cope with repeated frustration. Relatively small degrees of homeostatic derangement, fatigue, pain, sleep loss, or anxiety, may impair these functions.' As a result 'most people who are exposed to coercive procedures will talk and usually reveal some information that they might not have revealed otherwise.' ...

→

Detention

... Control of the source's environment permits the interrogator to determine his diet, sleep pattern, and other fundamentals. Manipulating these into irregularities, so that the subject becomes disorientated, is very likely to create feelings of fear and helplessness ... In short the prisoner should not be provided a routine to which he can adapt and from which he can draw some comfort – or at least a sense of his own identity ...

Deprivation of sensory stimuli

The chief effect of arrest and detention and particularly of solitary confinement is to deprive the subject of many or most of the sights, sounds, tastes, smells and tactile sensations to which he has grown accustomed ...

The more completely the place of confinement eliminates sensory stimuli, the more rapidly and deeply will the interrogatee be affected. Results produced only after weeks or months of imprisonment in an ordinary cell can be duplicated in hours or days in a cell which has no light (or weak artificial light which never varies), which is sound-proofed, in which odors are eliminated, etc. An environment still more subject to control, such as a water-tank or iron lung, is even more effective ...

Threats and fear

The threat of coercion usually weakens or destroys resistance more effectively than coercion itself. The threat to inflict pain, for example, can trigger fears more damaging than the immediate sensation of pain. In fact, most people underestimate their capacity to withstand pain ... Threats delivered coldly are more effective than those shouted in rage ...

Pain

It has been plausibly suggested that, whereas pain inflicted on a person from outside himself may actually focus or intensify his will to resist, his resistance is likelier to be sapped by pain which he seems to inflict upon himself. [Hinkle observes] 'In the simple torture situation the contest is one between the individual and his tormentor (... and he can frequently endure). When the individual is told to stand at attention for long periods, an intervening factor is introduced. The immediate source of pain is not the interrogator but the victim himself. The motivational strength of the individual is likely to exhaust itself in this internal encounter ...'

Source: *KUBARK: Counterintelligence Interrogation*, 1963, National Security Archive

Military Governments

The starkest failure of the Alliance for Progress was its promise to promote democracy in the region. Within two years of its launch, six military coups had taken place: Argentina (March 1962); Peru (July 1962); Guatemala (March 1963); Ecuador (July 1963); the Dominican Republic (September 1963) and Honduras (October 1963). Further coups took place in Brazil (1964), Bolivia (1964) and Argentina (1966). By the end of the decade most Latin American countries were once again ruled by dictators. The Kennedy administration had envisaged that enlightened but anti-communist governments would carry out its reforms, taking the Christian Democrats in Chile and Acción Democrática in Venezuela as ideal examples. But there was a distinct lack of this type of middle-class party in Latin America, and where such parties did exist they did not have the political strength or the inclination to challenge the privileges of the oligarchy. At the same time, Washington felt threatened when the peasantry and trade unions agitated for reforms. President João Goulart in Brazil, for example, was constantly harried by the Kennedy administration for allowing 'communist' penetration of the unions.

Kennedy initially took a hard line on military takeovers: he responded to the coup in Peru by cutting off aid and recalling his ambassador; his administration also tried to dissuade the Honduran military from overthrowing President Raúl Villeda. But his position later softened, and coups in Guatemala and Ecuador were tolerated. Just as efficiency replaced equity as the goal of the Alliance, so 'stability' became more important than promoting democracy. With the accession of Lyndon Johnson to the presidency in late 1963 after Kennedy's assassination, this trend was even more pronounced. Johnson's administration played an active part in the overthrow of the Brazilian reformist president Goulart. A year later it invaded the Dominican Republic to prevent the elected president, Juan Bosch, from regaining power after he was ousted in a coup. Nixon's administration, which took office in 1969, gave up any pretence of promoting democracy and openly supported the dictatorships of the late 1960s and 1970s.

The Invasion of the Dominican Republic, 1965

The dictator Rafael Trujillo ruled the Dominican Republic with the blessing of the United States for three decades after coming to power in 1930. After 1959, however, the State Department began to fear that his brutality could provoke another revolution in the Caribbean. US businesses also resented Trujillo's stranglehold on the economy; his family owned an estimated 75 per cent of Dominican land and businesses. Trujillo was assassinated in 1961 by men who received CIA aid.[4] His death prompted Kennedy's famous remark: 'There are three possibilities … a decent democratic regime, a continuation of the Trujillo regime, or a Castro regime. We ought to aim at the first but we really can't renounce the second until we are sure we can avoid the third.'[5]

The Dominican Republic's first ever free elections were held in 1962. Juan Bosch, a poet, journalist and lifelong opponent of Trujillo, was elected president. Bosch was a moderate reformer who greatly admired Kennedy. He initially had the support of the Kennedy administration but US officials began to worry when he sought to restrict foreign capital, spoke up for the rights of the peasantry, tolerated left-wing groups and refused to sell off the assets of Trujillo, which now belonged to the state.

Seven months after he took office, Bosch was ousted in a military coup. The US role in the coup was ambiguous. The historical record shows that staff in the US embassy in Santo Domingo knew the coup was coming, and that the military and labour attachés regarded Bosch as a communist sympathizer and approved of the coup. The US ambassador, however, asked the State Department to send an aircraft carrier to warn off the coup plotters, but was told that there would be no show of force unless there was a threat of a communist takeover. Kennedy condemned the coup and cut off aid, but a decision was made early on not to reinstate Bosch, who was considered unreliable.[6]

A conservative junta replaced Bosch, but progressive army officers rose up in April 1965 and tried to reinstate him as the constitutionally elected president. As the Bosch forces gained ground, President Lyndon B. Johnson sent 500 marines to the Dominican Republic. Within a month, more than 20,000 US troops were sent to the island, a strategy of using overwhelming force that was soon to be tried in Vietnam. In a televised broadcast on 2 May 1965 Johnson spelt out what became

---

'The invasion by North American capitalist companies'

The deposed president of the Dominican Republic, Juan Bosch, wrote his own account of US motives:

'Intervention is carried out for fear of communism, but is consolidated through the installation of industrial, banking and commercial companies that grow thanks to the patronage of the military power that replaces the weakened political power of the now occupied country. This is what happened in the Dominican Republic, which was occupied by the United States armed forces for fear that communism would be established in the country, and in the end was turned into a neocolony supplying cheap labour and opportunities for setting up businesses, both industrial like Gulf and Western or Falconbridge and financial like Bank of America, Citibank or Chase Manhattan Bank.

In the phase that might be called the invasion by North American capitalist companies ... the United States government becomes the agent that makes the contacts for the companies, and in some cases that government is represented by its highest officials. At least, that's what happened in the Dominican Republic, where Gulf and Western Incorporated ... was brought in by a direct recommendation of President Johnson to President Joaquín Balaguer.'

J. Bosch, *La República Dominicana: Causas de la Intervención Militar Norteamericana de 1965*, Santo Domingo, Editora Alfa & Omega, 1985

known as the Johnson Doctrine: 'The American nations cannot, must not, and will not permit the establishment of another Communist government in the Western Hemisphere.' The Bosch forces were defeated. In the subsequent elections, the US poured US$13 million into the campaign of its preferred candidate, Joaquín Balaguer. An ally of former dictator Trujillo, Balaguer was to rule the Dominican Republic for twenty-two of the next thirty years.

Within a few years of the invasion, foreign companies had bought up the rights to the Dominican Republic's natural resources. Rosario Resources gained control of the country's gold deposits; Alcoa dominated its bauxite industry and Falconbridge its nickel.[7] But the biggest beneficiary was Gulf & Western, which bought a third of the country's sugar plantations, as well as interests in ranching, tobacco, beef, citrus fruits, tourism and luxury hotels.

The Quiet Intervention: Brazil, 1964

João Goulart, a left-wing populist, became President of Brazil in 1961, at a time when the economy was on the brink of crisis and popular organizations were growing in strength. Goulart was indecisive and vacillated on certain key decisions, but passed laws that upset the elite; for example, a law giving rural workers the right to join trade unions incensed landowners and sparked a wave of land occupations. Goulart also expropriated privately owned Brazilian (although not foreign) oil refineries and promised to control rents. He spoke directly to crowds of low-ranking soldiers, which angered the military. The US was concerned by the drift to the left, the oil refinery expropriations, which they viewed as an attack on private property, and a law limiting the amount of profits foreign companies could transfer abroad. Goulart was overthrown by the Brazilian military in 1964.

The US ambassador to Brazil, Lincoln Gordon, and Defense Attaché Vernon A. Walters were in close touch with the conspirators while they were planning the coup. Walters had been a liaison officer with the Brazilian Expeditionary Force in Italy during the Second World War and knew the officers well. Gordon and Walters offered arms and munitions as well as fuel because it was believed the government and its supporters might resist for a number of days or even weeks and keep control of the oil refineries. In the event, the military met little resistance and the US supplies were not needed. In her book *Brazil and the Quiet Intervention*, Phyllis Parker raked through declassified US official communications to uncover the extent of US involvement in the coup.[8] The following account is based on those declassified cables and memos.

- 27 March 1964: Ambassador Gordon sends a lengthy top-secret message to the White House, the Secretary of State, the Defense Secretary, the CIA director and the Joint Chiefs of Staff requesting that fuel and military back-up be sent to Brazil to support the military conspirators.
- 30 March: a Brazilian general issues a manifesto denouncing the Goulart government. On the morning of 31 March he orders his tanks to start rolling towards Rio. Other Brazilian generals join the coup that evening.

Destabilization in Guyana

Cheddi Jagan, a US-educated dentist, was a leading figure in Guyana's struggle for independence in the years after the Second World War. In 1950 he founded the People's Progressive Party which demanded independence and radical social reforms. Jagan was elected chief minister of Guyana in 1953. But the British government, claiming he was a communist, declared a state of emergency and sent troops to depose him.

Jagan remained popular, and months after Kennedy was inaugurated as president, Jagan's party won the Guyanese parliamentary elections. The CIA began a destabilization campaign, working with the American Federation of Labor (AFL) to provoke strikes, damage the economy and stir up racial tensions. With US backing, a more moderate politician, Forbes Burnham, was elected prime minister in 1964. Guyana became independent from Britain two years later. Burnham remained in power until his death in 1986, rigging elections and spying on political opponents.

Cheddi Jagan was elected President of Guyana in 1992, but by this time he had abandoned his radical nationalism and was no longer viewed as a threat by the US.

Source: D. Dent, *The Legacy of the Monroe Doctrine: A Reference Guide to US involvement in Latin America and the Caribbean*, Connecticut, Greenwood Press, 1999

- 31 March: US Secretary of State Dean Rusk, Defense Secretary Robert McNamara, Chairman of the Joint Chiefs of Staff General Maxwell Taylor, the US Commander in Chief of the Southern Forces Lt. Gen. Andrew O'Meara and CIA director John McCone hold a meeting in which they approve sending arms, munitions, fuel and a carrier fleet to Brazil as contingency support for the conspirators. The plan is codenamed 'Brother Sam' and is activated in the afternoon.
- A heavy attack aircraft carrier and supporting destroyers are ordered to set sail to Brazil. Additional support for the ships include oil, ammunitions and provisions.
- The US Joint Chiefs of Staff issue instructions for 250 twelve-gauge shotguns and 110 tons of small arms and ammunition to be airlifted to Brazil. Planes for the airlift include seven transport aircraft, eight fighter aircraft, up to eight tanker aircraft, one communications aircraft and one airborne command post.
- The US Joint Chiefs of Staff issue instructions that four tankers be loaded with 36,000 barrels of motor gas, 272 barrels of jet fuel, 87,000 barrels of aviation gas, 33 barrels of diesel and 20,000 barrels of kerosene to be sent to Brazil.
- 1 April: in the early hours the leader of the Brazilian senate illegally declares the Brazilian presidency vacant and an interim president is sworn in. Goulart flies to the southern state of Rio Grande do Sul that evening.

- 2 April: President Johnson gives formal recognition to the new regime.
- Ambassador Gordon says in a teleconference to Washington: 'Just received confirmation from Castelo Branco [the general leading the coup] that all resistance has ceased in Porto Alegre and the democratic forces [sic] now in full control of Rio Grande do Sul. This eliminates last pocket of military resistance.'
- Gordon cables Washington stating that Goulart's 'de facto ouster' is a 'great victory for [the] free world'. Failure would have risked a 'total loss to [the] West of all South American Republics'.
- 3 April: the US Joint Chiefs of Staff postpone the airlift of arms. The material is stored pending transit to Brazil until 7 April when the airlift is finally cancelled. The fuel *en route* to Brazil is diverted elsewhere.
- 4 April: Goulart takes refuge in Uruguay. Fearing that the Uruguayans might receive Goulart as the legitimate Brazilian president, US Secretary of State Dean Rusk cables the US embassy in Montevideo stating: 'It would be useful if you could quietly bring to the attention [of] appropriate officials the fact that despite his allegations to [the] contrary Goulart has abandoned his office.'

The military remained in power in Brazil for the next twenty-five years, until 1989.

Historical Roots of Latin American Dictatorships

The United States may have smiled upon the dictators of Latin America, but historical and economic factors also help to explain the region's susceptibility to military rule.

The military has always played a predominant role in Latin American politics. Deriving its strength from the independence wars of the nineteenth century, it traditionally defended the oligarchy, but regarded itself as the arbiter of class conflict and guardian of the national interest. Latin American economies were reaching a crisis point in the 1960s. Their main income continued to come from exporting raw materials, but since the 1930s the larger countries had been following a policy of import substitution industrialization (ISI), manufacturing products such as clothes, processed food, electrical goods, which had previously been imported. Nevertheless, they still had to import the necessary machinery (capital goods) from the rich countries. The cost of importing capital goods was greater than the amount Latin America made from its exports (typically commodities and foodstuffs such as coffee, sugar, beef, copper and bananas) so governments continually faced foreign exchange crises which led to budget deficits, inflation and indebtedness. A further problem with the ISI strategy was Latin America's small market. Most of the population was too poor to buy many manufactured goods, so industries found it hard to expand. Land reform would have helped raise living standards and expand the market, but Latin America's landed oligarchy, still the dominant class, opposed any such move. Furthermore the imported capital-intensive technology provided relatively few jobs, so landless people moving to the cities found it hard to find work.

This model of development gave Latin America a peculiar social structure. Latin

America's small professional class (lawyers, accountants, exporters) differed from the traditional European model because, as Skidmore and Smith note, despite living in the cities, many of its interests were tied to the agrarian sector.[9] Far from seeking to break the power of landed aristocrats, they were often allies of the oligarchy. The industrial working class was small but powerful, particularly in high-tech industries and the export sector; a strike affecting the railways, docks or mines, for example, could cut off a Latin American country's export earnings very quickly. There was also a growing number of unemployed or semi-employed people, a group sociologists describe as 'the informal sector', who lived a precarious existence in the cities.

A small industrial bourgeoisie emerged from the 1930s onwards. During the 1940s and 1950s, industrialists formed temporary 'populist' alliances with the working class to promote national development, but these alliances prospered only in times of economic growth. The growth of the state also created a large number of public sector workers. These poorly paid but educated employees, schoolteachers and lecturers among them, often joined trade unions and radical parties.

As the ISI model ran out of steam, the choices for Latin America's radicals and dictators alike appeared to be stark: either break the power of the landed elite and redistribute wealth, or use escalating repression to silence the clamour for higher living standards. Repression won. As we have seen, military governments took power in most countries in the 1960s and 1970s, as economic crises led to political polarization. These military governments, often described as 'bureaucratic authoritarians', with Brazil (1964) and Argentina (1966) being the archetypal examples, sought to take Latin America to the next stage of economic development by raising investment and suppressing wages. They did this by repressing trade unionists, peasant activists and dissenters, while at the same time forming an alliance with multinational corporations. Foreign companies cornered the market in high-tech industries such as cars, while military governments ran up huge debts building mega projects and investing in 'strategic' nationalized industries. Brazil, notably, built a significant capital goods sector, and a small number of industries emerged (such as aircraft manufacturing) that could compete on a global scale. But, on the whole, Latin America remained – and remains today – dependent on the First World and multinational corporations for the latest technology. Latin America was left with huge debts, many of them squandered on white-elephant projects and siphoned away by corrupt officials. And when interest rates rose in 1979 the debt bubble burst, to spectacular effect.

5

The Military Governments of the 1970s

Soon after he took office, President Nixon (1969–74) asked Nelson Rockefeller to travel to Latin America, meet its leaders and report back with policy ideas. Rockefeller, a Republican state governor and philanthropist, made four trips to Latin America, where he was often met by angry demonstrators. He submitted a controversial report in which he warned of a growing communist threat and argued that, in the interests of national security, the United States should be more tolerant of military governments:

> Rising frustrations ... over poverty and political instability have led increasing numbers of people to pick the United States as a scapegoat and to seek out Marxist solutions to their socio-economic problems. At the moment there is only one Castro among the twenty-six nations of the hemisphere, there can well be more in the future. And a Castro on the mainland, supported militarily and economically by the communist world, would present the gravest kind of threat to the security of the Western Hemisphere and pose an extremely difficult problem for the United States ... Military leaders throughout the hemisphere are frequently criticized here in the United States. However, we will have to give increasing recognition to the fact many new military leaders are deeply motivated by the need for social and economic progress ... In many cases, it will be more useful for the United States to try to work with them in these efforts, rather than to abandon or insult them because we are conditioned by arbitrary ideological stereotypes.[1]

Nixon needed little persuading. He was a firm supporter of the Latin American military, once telling a White House meeting: 'I will never agree with the policy of downgrading the military in Latin America. They are power centers subject to our influence. The others [the intellectuals] are not subject to our influence. We want to give them some help.'[2]

Rockefeller's recommendations also chimed with new thinking in Washington. After setbacks in Vietnam, the United States was reluctant to commit US forces

50

abroad, so looked to the Latin American military to keep communism in check.

This Cold War mentality led Nixon and his successor, Gerald Ford, to support the most brutal and frightening totalitarian governments the continent has ever seen. All but four Latin American countries were ruled by the military by the mid-1970s. The Southern Cone dictatorships of Argentina, Chile and Uruguay were particularly chilling. Inspired by anti-communist national security doctrine, these military governments methodically tortured and killed thousands of their citizens and gave a new word to the Spanish American lexicon: *los desaparecidos* (the disappeared).

Allende and the Coup in Chile

The overthrow of Salvador Allende in Chile in 1973 shocked the world and raised questions that are still pertinent in Latin America today. Would the United States ever allow a socialist to remain in power in its backyard? Would it allow an elected leader to make radical reforms which challenged private property rights? Allende's Chile raised such passions because, to supporters, it appeared to be on the brink of creating a new society, not through violence but through the ballot box – 'the elected road to socialism' – a road that perhaps other Latin Americans could travel. As in Guatemala in 1954, there seemed to be a chance to break the old structures of entrenched privilege; the Allende years represented a key moment when the trajectory of Latin American history could have changed. Perhaps the Allende government would have collapsed in economic disarray and internal division; perhaps the Chilean military would have been able to overthrow him without the help of a US-abetted destabilization campaign. But the US ensured that the Allende government never had a chance. The extraordinary story of US covert action in Chile, which begins a decade before Allende was elected President, is documented in a US Senate report (1975) and thousands of official US documents declassified in the 1990s.[3] The following account is based on those official sources.

The 1964 Election

Chile had the strongest tradition of democracy in Latin America, and since 1932 had enjoyed uninterrupted democratic rule. In the years after the Second World War, the electorate had split fairly evenly between three political currents: the Right (various parties merging to form the National Party), the centre (the Christian Democratic Party) and the Left (the Socialist Party). Salvador Allende, a socialist, was the Left's candidate in the elections of 1952, 1958, 1964 and 1970. Advocating a 'peaceful transition to socialism', his manifesto called for the nationalization of Chile's copper mines, redistribution of wealth and agrarian reform.

The US was determined to prevent Salvador Allende from winning the 1964 elections (Allende had come a close second in 1958). The CIA alone spent US$3 million trying to influence the results of the vote. More than half the campaign of the Christian Democrat candidate, Eduardo Frei, was funded by the CIA, although he was not aware of it. The CIA also gave funds to a more right-wing candidate, Julio

Durán of the Radical Party, 'in order to enhance the Christian Democrats' image as a moderate progressive party being attacked from the right as well as the left'.[4] The CIA also tried to win influence in student organizations, a prominent women's group, trade unions and a private citizens' group. It spent tens of thousands of dollars on an anti-communist propaganda campaign. According to the Senate report:

> Extensive use was made of the press, radio, films, pamphlets, posters, leaflets, direct mailings, paper streamers and wall painting. It was a 'scare campaign' which relied heavily on images of Soviet tanks and Cuban firing squads and was directed especially towards women ... Disinformation and black propaganda material which purported to originate from another source, such as the Chilean Communist Party, were used as well.[5]

By the end of the campaign, the CIA was distributing 3,000 posters a day, producing 24 daily radio news bulletins and 26 weekly 'commentary' shows. Frei won the election in September with 57 per cent of the vote.

Allende's Election Victory

The Frei administration launched a 'revolution in liberty', undertaking modest agrarian reform and stepping up Chilean control of the copper mines. But the reforms alienated the Chilean Right while failing to meet the expectations they raised among the poor. Land occupations, unofficial strikes, and trade union membership increased in number. As the 1970 election approached, the CIA ploughed US$1 million into anti-Allende propaganda, once again using the press and radio and infiltrating civic organizations. During the campaign, US businesses in Chile contacted US officials to express their concern about Allende. Three months before the election, the head of the CIA's Western Hemisphere Division met the chairman of the board of the US-owned telephone company ITT, which had extensive interests in Chile. The meeting was set up by former CIA director John McCone, who sat on ITT's board of directors.[6] It was the first of many meetings between the CIA and ITT in Chile. The CIA channelled US$350,000 of ITT funds to Allende's opponents and a similar amount was provided by other US companies. However, the Chilean Right made a tactical blunder, fielding their own candidate, Jorge Alessandri, instead of backing Radomiro Tomic, the Christian Democrat. The split vote enabled Allende, heading Unidad Popular (Popular Unity) a coalition of socialists, communists and other left-wing groups, to win the election in September 1970 with 36.3 per cent of the vote. His supporters were ecstatic; at last they had elected a government that would challenge Chile's age-old inequities.

Planning a Coup

Under Chile's electoral system, if a candidate does not win an outright majority then congress decides who should be president. After the election but before the Chilean congress appointed a president on 24 October 1970, the United States launched a campaign to prevent Allende from taking office. This campaign ran on two tracks: a

US Companies in Chile

After the 1970 election, US companies with investments in Chile wasted no time in expressing their concerns about Allende to the Nixon administration. Within two weeks of the poll, Nixon's Security Adviser, Henry Kissinger, held meetings with David Rockefeller of Chase Manhattan Bank and Donald Kendall, president of Pepsi-Cola, to discuss the Chilean situation.

Meanwhile, ITT hoped that Allende's ascension to power might be blocked through a coup or economic sabotage, hopes revealed in a series of memos leaked to the press in 1972. The documents included memos sent by ITT officials between 14 September and 18 November 1970 and a report submitted to Kissinger. One of the memos is excerpted below.

Confidential Memo   New York – September 29, 1970

To: Hal Hendrix [public relations director for ITT in Latin America]
From: Robert Berrellez [head of ITT's public relations organization for Latin America, based in Buenos Aires]
Dictated today by telephone from Buenos Aires to New York

1. A congressional defeat for Allende seems unlikely at this point ...
2. Despite the pessimism, efforts are continuing to move Frei and/or the military to act to stop Allende. Efforts are also continuing to provoke the extreme left into a violent reaction that would produce the climate requiring military intervention.
3. Although its chances of success are slender, a roadblock to Allende's assumption of power through an economic collapse should not be dismissed.

cc: E.J. Gerrity [Senior Vice President of ITT, in charge of public relations]
    E.R. Wallace [ITT Vice-President with responsibilities for public relations]
    K.M. Perkins [Director of Public Relations]

Source: *Subversion in Chile: a Case Study in US Corporate Intrigue in the Third World,* Nottingham, Spokesman Books/Bertrand Russell Peace Foundation, 1972, p. 42

committee headed by Henry Kissinger, the President's National Security Adviser, ordered the CIA to use propaganda, political and economic pressure to persuade the Chilean congress to approve Allende's opponent. This tactic was known among its instigators as Track One. Track Two was more ominous. On 15 September, Nixon held a meeting with Kissinger, CIA director Richard Helms and Attorney General John Mitchell. In the words of the US Senate report:

> President Nixon informed ... Helms that an Allende regime in Chile would not be acceptable to the United States and instructed the CIA to play a direct role in organizing a military coup d'etat in Chile to prevent Allende's accession to the Presidency.[7]

Urgent Directive sent from CIA Director Richard Helms to the CIA Station in Santiago, 7 October 1970 (Declassified July 2000)

' Secret

October 7 1970
Immediate Santiago

1. [censored word] instructs you to contact the military and let them know USG [US Government] wants a military solution, and that we will support them now and later.

2. [censored paragraph]

3. [censored word] requires that you use all available assets and strategems including the rumor-mill to create at least some sort of coup climate. If major reaction by the left cannot be provoked, this effort to be topped [deleted word] which can be used by military as pretext.

4. [censored word] are your instructions for action between now and 24 October. All other considerations are secondary, and you should not let any other activity by you and your [censored word] officers vitiate this three-pronged task. Every hour counts. Do not concern yourself with PDC [Christian Democrat Party], Frei, Vital Centre and PN [National Party].

5. Your efforts to prepare for future while necessary should be considered second priority [we are approving your sponsorship of divisive tactics in UP [Allende's Unidad Popular] by [censored word] in separate message].

6. In sum, we want you to sponsor a military move which can take place, to the extent possible, in a climate of economic and political uncertainty. Work to that end with references as your charter.

End of message '

Source: Peter Kornbluh, *The Pinochet File: A Declassified Dossier on Atrocity and Accountability*, New York, New Press, 2003, p. 58.

Notes scrawled on a scrap of paper by Helms during the meeting with Nixon have recently been declassified:

- 1 in 10 chance perhaps, but save Chile!
- worth spending
- not concerned risks involved
- no involvement of embassy
- US$10,000,00 [sic] available, more if necessary
- full-time job – best men we have
- game plan

- make economy scream
- 48 hours plan of action.[8]

CIA operatives made contact with several groups conspiring within the Chilean military. At this stage, the plotters were rather peripheral figures, because there was uncertainty about whether the Chilean top brass would support a coup. All the conspiracies centred on the removal of the Chilean chief of staff, General Rene Schneider, who was committed to uphold the constitution. The plan was to kidnap Schneider and make the kidnap look like the work of left-wing extremists. This, the CIA calculated, would prompt the military to carry out a coup to prevent the congress from ratifying Allende as president, a vote that was scheduled for 24 October. After looking around for possible candidates to lead the coup, the CIA began to focus its efforts on a right-wing extremist general, Roberto Viaux, but became concerned that Viaux did not have broad enough support within the military and that precipitate action could ruin any hope of a successful coup. On 16 October, CIA headquarters sent the following memo to the CIA station in Santiago:

… It is firm and continuing policy that Allende be overthrown by a coup. It would be preferable to have this transpire prior to 24 October, but efforts in this regard will continue vigorously beyond this date…

… After most careful consideration it was determined that a Viaux coup attempt carried out by him alone with the forces at his disposal would fail. Thus, it would be counterproductive to our [word censored] objectives. It was decided that [word censored] get a message to Viaux warning him against precipitate action. In essence our message is to state '… We have come to the conclusion that your plans for a coup at this time cannot succeed. Failing, they may reduce your capabilities for the future. Preserve your assets. We will stay in touch. The time will come. When together with all your other friends you can do something. You will continue to have our support.'

… Our objectives [are] as follows
(a) to advise him of our opinion and discourage him from acting alone
(b) continue to encourage him to amplify his planning
(c) encourage him to join forces with other coup planners so that they may act in concert either before or after 24 October
(NB. Six Gas Masks and Six CS Canisters are being carried to Santiago by special [word deleted] courier ETD Washington 1100 Hours 16 October) …[9]

A Senate investigation concluded that the Nixon administration called off the Viaux plot at the last minute, but this declassified memo shows that he was ordered to continue working towards a coup. Other newly declassified documents show that the CIA went on to deliver materiel to Viaux and other conspirators.[10] On 19 October Viaux's men, armed with the gas grenades delivered by the CIA, made an abortive attempt to grab Schneider. On 20 October six machine guns and ammunition were sent in a diplomatic pouch to the US embassy in Santiago and at 2am on 22 October they were given to another group of conspirators led by General Camilo

Valenzuela. At 8am on that day Schneider's car was surrounded by five men. He resisted and was shot three times at close range. He died three days later. After his death, the Viaux group was given US$35,000 by the CIA, according to the CIA's own report.[11] This piece of state-sponsored terrorism did not, however, have the effect that the CIA had hoped for. The guilty men were arrested. Viaux was convicted of kidnapping, and both he and Valenzuela were convicted of conspiracy to cause a coup. The Chilean congress approved Allende on 24 October 1970 and on 3 November he was inaugurated as Chile's first Socialist president.

The US Role in the 1973 Coup

Three days after Allende took office, President Nixon told a meeting of the National Security Council:

> Our main concern in Chile is the prospect that he can consolidate himself and the picture projected to the world will be his success ... No impression should be permitted in Latin America that they can get away with this, that it's safe to go this way. All over the world it's too much the fashion to kick us around.[12]

The meeting decided to adopt a 'cool and correct' public position towards Allende, but continued to work on various tracks to undermine his government. The first overt method was to give Allende, in Nixon's words, 'cold turkey' on the economic front. The US cut economic aid and credit and encouraged private companies and international financial institutions to do the same. On a country that had been a showpiece of the Alliance for Progress and which was used to receiving generous US assistance, the impact was enormous. Bilateral aid to Chile dropped from US$45 million in 1969 to US$1.5 million in 1971, while US export-import bank credits dropped from US$234 million in 1967 to zero in 1971. Credit from the Inter-American Development Bank (IDB) fell from US$46 million in 1970 to US$2 million in 1972 and the World Bank provided no new loans during the Allende government's lifetime. The US economic boycott seriously affected the Allende government's ability to buy replacement parts and machinery for the most critical sectors of the economy: copper, steel, electricity, petrol and transport. By late 1972, one third of the trucks at Chuquicamata copper mine, one third of privately owned and state-run city buses and 21 per cent of taxis could not operate because of the lack of spare parts or tyres.[13] President Nixon also ordered his officials to sell copper from the US stockpile in order to reduce the world copper price and slash Chile's export earnings.

Providing covert assistance to the opposition and sowing division within the government was the second track of the campaign to destabilize Allende. In the three years of Allende's government, US$7 million was spent on CIA propaganda and on funding opposition groups. The money was approved by Kissinger's 40 committee, a grouping of government officials whose job was to oversee US covert action. Kissinger famously remarked to this committee: 'I don't see why we have to let a country go Marxist just because its people are irresponsible.' Funds were given to the right-wing National Party of Chile, the Radical Party, the Christian Democrat Party and several splinter groups, enabling the larger parties to buy their own radio stations and newspapers. The CIA produced several magazines with national circulations and large numbers of books. It planted stories in Chilean daily newspapers, two weekly broadsheets, radio stations and several television shows on three channels. The right-wing daily *El Mercurio*, which had a circulation of 300,000 but severe financial problems, was given US$1.5m to stay afloat. *El Mercurio* went on to 'play a significant role in setting the stage for the military coup', according to the US senators' report.[14] The CIA also funded 75 per cent of a research body that drafted congressional bills for opposition politicians in Chile. The CIA gave only a small amount of money directly to the striking truck drivers, but provided generous indirect support; US$100,000 was given to three pro-strike groups – a businessmen's organization, an association of small businesses and an umbrella opposition alliance – as part of an overall package of US$1.5 million for Chilean opposition groups. The CIA not only tried to sow divisions in Allende's Unidad Popular alliance but also sought to infiltrate the Christian Democrats to ensure that left-wing members of that party would not back the government.

The final element of the US destabilization plan was its relationship with the military. While all other US aid was cut, military aid rose during the Allende years, as the United States tried to improve the capabilities of the Chilean armed forces. After the debacle of the aborted Viaux coup, the CIA sought to improve and extend its relationship with Chilean military leaders and let it be known that it would be sympathetic to an overthrow of Allende. The CIA actually passed on fabricated material to the Chilean high command to encourage it to make a move against Allende. (The material purported to prove that the Cubans were helping Allende to gather intelligence on the Chilean army.)[15] The CIA also subsidized a small anti-government newsletter directed at the armed forces. Most ominously, it collected operational intelligence that would be necessary in the event of a coup – arrest lists, lists of key civilian installations and personnel that would need protection, lists of government installations that would need to be taken over, and details of government contingency plans that would be used in case of a military uprising. The CIA claims it did not pass this information on to the Chilean military. The CIA received detailed reports of the coup plans as they developed over the three months leading to 11 September 1973. The US government kept in touch with high-level military contacts until the day of the coup, and upon its success it immediately sent a message of support to the junta.

According to the documentary evidence so far released, the United States helped to create a climate favourable to a coup, and let the plotters know they would have any assistance they required, but did not directly organize the 1973 coup. The 1975 Senate report concluded:

> Was the United States DIRECTLY involved, covertly, in the 1973 coup in Chile? The Committee has found no evidence that it was. However, the United States sought in 1970 to foment a military coup in Chile; after 1970, it adopted a policy, both overt and covert, of opposition to Allende, and it remained in intelligence contact with the

---

The Chile Declassification Project

Human rights campaigners have for many years called for the release of all the records relating to US activities in Chile. Only a small number of the documents reviewed by the Senate Intelligence Committee in 1975 were released to the public. The Clinton administration came under renewed pressure to release the files in 1998 when General Pinochet was arrested in London on charges of torture and conspiracy to murder.

Clinton's government launched the Chile Declassification Project in 1999 which led to the release of 2,200 CIA records, 18,000 State Department records and 3,800 records from the White House, the National Security Council, the Pentagon and the FBI covering the period 1970–1990. In all, 24,000 documents were declassified, making it the biggest discretionary presidential release of records in US history. Many of these documents were collected by Peter Kornbluh, director of the National Security Archive's Chile Documentation project, and published in his book *The Pinochet File: A Declassified Dossier on Atrocity and Accountability*, New York, New Press, 2003.

Chilean military, including officers who were participating in coup plotting ... [The] CIA's information-gathering efforts with regard to the Chilean military included activity which went beyond the mere collection of information ... They put the United States government in contact with those Chileans who sought a military alternative to the Allende presidency.

Yet the full story of US covert action in Chile during the Allende years still cannot be told. Many US documents are still classified, and those that have been released are heavily censored. Large chunks of the text have been blacked out, particularly in parts relating to covert action and the military, leaving the historian to wonder what the US security services still have to hide.

The Pinochet Coup

Before entering politics, Salvador Allende had been a doctor. He was a witty, educated man, who promised to be Chile's first '*compañero presidente*', a comrade and friend of the workers. At a victory speech in Chile's national stadium he spelt out his aims:

> We shall abolish the monopolies which grant control of the economy to a few dozen families. We shall abolish a tax system which favours profiteering and which has always put a greater burden on the poor than the rich. We are going to nationalize credit. We shall abolish the large estates which condemn thousands of peasants to serfdom. We shall put an end to the foreign ownership of our industry and our sources of unemployment. The road to socialism lies through democracy, pluralism and freedom.[16]

The first acts of the government were to raise the minimum wage by 67 per cent and provide a daily free glass of milk to every schoolchild. A year later, Chile's copper mines were nationalized, a law that was backed by the opposition Christian Democrats. Copper was Chile's most important export, accounting for 80 per cent of the country's export earnings; US companies controlled 79 per cent of the industry. The government calculated that 'excessive profits' made over the past fifteen years were greater than the amount of compensation due so the companies were given nothing, a decision that caused consternation in Washington. The economy grew rapidly during Allende's first year of office as higher wages stimulated demand, but the boom did not last. Falling world copper prices, high government spending, sabotage by the economic elite and a US-orchestrated international credit squeeze all led to hyperinflation and indebtedness.

Chile was a highly polarized society. Allende's victory had provoked enormous expectations among the poor and apprehension among the upper and middle classes. In October 1972, lorry drivers began a strike which soon won the support of shopkeepers, factory owners and banks and escalated into a nationwide business lock-out which aimed to bring down the government. Allende survived by calling a partial state of emergency, but the strike crippled the economy and created an atmosphere of chaos. A second truckers' strike launched in mid-1973 lasted until Allende fell. While the Right sought to undermine the government, Allende's supporters were impatient for change. Peasants began to occupy farms, and workers took over factories that had been shut down by their owners. To allay right-wing fears, Allende invited three generals to join the cabinet in 1972, but dissident generals and colonels had already begun plotting a coup. On 22 August 1973 Allende appointed Augusto Pinochet as Commander-in-Chief of the army, believing he was a constitutionalist. The night before, Pinochet had told Allende, 'President, be aware that I am ready to lay down my life in the defence of the constitutional government that you represent.'[17] Yet less than three weeks later, when Pinochet was told of the coup plot by the conspirators, he agreed to lead it. On 11 September 1973, Pinochet ordered warplanes to bomb the presidential palace. Allende remained in the palace; even as rockets tore through the roof, he managed to broadcast a message to the nation on live radio (see box, p. 60). Allende died in the palace that day. The darkest era in Chile's history had begun.

There was no precedent in Chilean history for the barbarous acts committed by the armed forces after the coup. Soldiers were given orders to shoot 'extremists' on sight. Army convoys were sent to housing estates and working-class areas to kill or arrest militants. Tanks were sent to universities where hundreds of students and teachers were taken prisoner. Thousands of people, including children, were taken to makeshift torture centres all over the country. Santiago's national stadium was turned into a nightmarish torture camp. The types of torture inflicted were detailed in the charges brought, years later, by the Spanish authorities when they sought the extradition of General Pinochet. In the case of one victim these included:

- giving him electric shocks by passing electric current through his chest, his penis and his toes;
- placing him on board a helicopter, then pushing him out with ropes tied to his trousers, and dragging him through thorns;

'I shall sacrifice my life in loyalty to my people'

'This is certainly the last time I shall speak to you. The air force has bombed all our radio stations. My words flow more from disappointment than from bitterness – let them serve as a moral condemnation of those who betrayed their oath, these Chilean soldiers ...

Faced with all these events, there is only one thing I can say to the workers: I shall not surrender.

History has given me a choice. I shall sacrifice my life in loyalty to my people, in the knowledge that the seeds we have planted in the noble consciousness of thousands of Chileans can never be prevented from bearing fruit.

Our enemies are strong; they can enslave the people. But neither criminal acts nor force of arms can hold back this social process. History belongs to us; it is the people that make history ...

Workers of my country: I want to thank you for the loyalty you have always shown, for the trust you have always placed in a man who has been no more than the interpreter of your great desire for justice, a man who undertook publicly to respect the constitution and the law and who did not betray that undertaking. This is the last chance I shall have to speak to you, to explain to you what has happened. Foreign capital and imperialism have allied with the forces of reaction to produce a climate in which the armed forces have broken with tradition ...

I have faith in Chile and in its destiny. Other Chileans will come forward. In these dark and bitter days, when treachery seeks to impose its own order, you may be assured that much sooner than later, the great avenues towards a new society will open again, and the march along that road will continue.

Long live Chile!

Long live the people!

Long live the workers!

These are my last words. I know my sacrifice has not been in vain. May it be a lesson for all those who hate disloyalty, cowardice and treachery.'

Salvador Allende
9.30am, 11 September 1973

- tying him to a rope and lowering him into a well, until he was nearly drowned;
- forcing him to take all his clothes off in the presence of the captive Rodríguez family who had been arrested with their sons, forcing him to witness torture of that family as the father was made to bugger his son, as simultaneously that son was made to bugger his younger brother;
- forcing him to bugger one of those sons himself.[18]

Many of those arrested were never seen again and their families were not told what had happened to them. The Chilean Truth and Reconciliation Commission found that at least 2,025 people were killed or 'disappeared' during the military regime – although the actual number is thought to be higher.

The military junta closed the Chilean congress, censored the press, banned left-wing parties and restricted the activity of other parties. In 1974 Pinochet assumed the title of Supreme Chief of the Nation. He remained in power until 1990.

Victor Jara: An Unfinished Song

Victor Jara was a popular folk singer who supported Salvador Allende and who sang at Unidad Popular rallies and festivals. Born to a peasant family, he was one of the founders of the 'New Song' movement which revived traditional Chilean folksongs.

On 12 September he was taken to Santiago's national stadium, where he was held with five thousand other prisoners. He was tortured and his hands and wrists were broken so he could not play the guitar. He was machine-gunned to death; his body was found on 16 September.

While he was in the national stadium he wrote a final song:

There are five thousand of us here
in this small part of the city.
We are five thousand.
I wonder how many we are in all
in the cities and in the whole country ...

How much humanity
exposed to hunger, cold, panic, pain,
moral pressure, terror and insanity? ...

How hard it is to sing
when I must sing of horror.
Horror which I am living
horror which I am dying.
To see myself among so much
and so many movements of infinity
in which silence and screams
are the end of my song.
What I see, I have never seen
What I have felt and what I feel
will give birth to the moment ...

Source: Joan Jara, *Victor: An Unfinished Song*, London, Jonathan Cape, 1983. © Joan Jara and the Victor Jara Foundation

The US and the Pinochet Regime

Two days after the US coup the State Department sent a secret cable to its embassy in Santiago:

1. We welcome General Pinochet's expression of junta. Desire for strengthened ties between Chile and the US. You are requested to convey at the earliest possible opportunity informal response to General Pinochet along the following lines and by whatever private means you deem appropriate.

2. The USG [US government] wishes make clear its desire to cooperate with the military junta and to assist in any appropriate way. We agree that it is best initially to avoid too much public identification between us. In meantime we will be pleased to maintain private unofficial contacts as the junta may desire ...[19]

Publicly the Nixon administration kept its distance and did not give formal recognition to the junta until two weeks after the coup; secretly it gave help to the regime during that time. On 15 September the Chilean air force requested 1,000 steel helmets and 1,000 flares 'for illumination purposes in military operations against extremist groups'. The US ambassador in Chile told his superiors: 'I believe it is advisable to accommodate this request – discreetly if possible.' A fortnight later the Chileans asked for a 'detention center advisor' as well as tents and portable housing for prisoners. The ambassador again recommended complying with the request.

Three days after the coup the Nixon administration established a task force, the Washington Special Action Group, to consider 'anticipated short, medium and long term Chilean assistance requirements.' On 20 September, Kissinger chaired a meeting of the Action Group which instructed the ambassador

... to talk to the Junta ... to inform them of our goodwill ... of our intention to recognize and when; when the emergency food supplies will be delivered and authorizing the Ambassador to discuss with Junta, Chile's middle and long-term economic needs.

Economic aid to the junta poured in. The Nixon and Ford administrations approved US$186 million in economic assistance for Chile between 1974 and 1976, compared with a total US$19.8 million during the Allende years. International financial institutions also turned the credit taps back on. The Inter-American Development Bank (IDB) approved US$237 million of credit and the World Bank US$66 million during the first three years of the military government. The United States also helped to design and implement the junta's economic policies. The US Senate later reported that 'CIA collaborators were involved in preparing an initial overall economic plan which has served as the basis for the Junta's most important economic decisions.'[20]

The US also helped to 'assist the Junta [to] gain a more positive image, both at home and abroad'. According to the 1975 US Senate report:

Access to certain Chilean media outlets was retained in order to enable the CIA Station in Santiago to help build Chilean public support for the new government as well as to influence the direction of the government, through pressures exerted by the mass media. These media outlets attempted to present the Junta in the most positive light for the Chilean public and to assist foreign journalists in Chile to obtain facts about the local situation. Further, two CIA collaborators assisted the Junta in preparing a White Book, of the Change of Government in Chile. The White Book, published by the Junta shortly after the coup, was written to justify the overthrow of Allende. It was distributed widely both in Washington and in other foreign capitals.[21]

The CIA worked closely with the Chilean security and intelligence services after the coup. According to the CIA's own report: 'The CIA actively supported the military junta after the overthrow of Allende.'[22] The document goes on to state: 'The CIA offered the [Chilean security] services assistance in internal organization and training to combat subversion and terrorism from abroad,' but claims it did not collaborate in internal repression. However, the CIA has admitted that many officers responsible for human rights abuses were in fact agents or contacts of the CIA. The head of the notorious Chilean secret service, the DINA, General Manual Contreras, was himself a paid CIA informant. The full extent of the CIA's involvement in human rights abuses still remains to be revealed. The CIA has fought hard to keep its activities in Pinochet's Chile secret. The report cited above was written only after the US Congress passed legislation in 2000 forcing it to do so. It tells the bare minimum, mainly confirming information already in the public arena.

Missing

Two US citizens, Charles Horman and Frank Teruggi, were taken from their houses, tortured and killed by the Chilean security forces in the days following the coup. Horman's family issued a lawsuit alleging US involvement in their son's killing. They have been met with years of official obfuscation and denials. Their struggle for justice was dramatized in the film *Missing*.

In 1980, the US government gave the Horman family solicitors a file of heavily censored official documents. One of these documents, a State Department memo written in 1976, appeared to provide no new information.

In 1999, this same memo was declassified and some of the formerly blacked-out passages were revealed. It was now possible to see that the memo said there was evidence to suggest that 'US intelligence may have played an unfortunate part in Horman's death.' The author of the memo goes on to lament that their investigations involving the CIA have suffered from a 'lack of candor' which only 'heightens our suspicions'.

Source: 'US Department of State Memorandum, Subject Charles Horman Case, August 25 1976, from ARA/BC Fimbres', www.foia.state.gov. To view the previous version see National Security Archive.

Operation Condor

The military governments of Chile, Argentina, Paraguay, Brazil and Bolivia joined forces in the 1970s to track down and kill 'subversives' anywhere in the world. They called this collaboration Operation Condor, after the majestic but menacing bird of prey of the Andes. Under Operation Condor, assassination units were sent abroad to 'eliminate Marxist terrorist activities'. Among the victims was the former commander of the Chilean army, General Carlos Prats, a constitutionalist and friend of Allende. He and his wife were killed in a car bomb in Buenos Aires in 1974. Orlando Letelier, Allende's former foreign minister and ambassador to the United States, was killed along with US citizen Ronni Moffit by a car bomb in Washington DC in 1976 – a shocking and audacious attack in the heart of the US capital. These were the most high-profile of the assassinations; many other dissidents were hunted, tortured and murdered in Latin America. The US intelligence services helped the Southern Cone militaries to track down subversives; a recently declassified document shows that a US communications installation in the Panama Canal Zone was used 'to coordinate intelligence information among Southern Cone countries'.[23] The CIA also provided computers and Telex encoding machines for Condor operations.[24] US police and intelligence officers even carried out surveillance and interrogation of suspects in the US.[25] The architect of Operation Condor was

---

Investors' Paradise

Chile became a testing ground for the radical free market policies advocated by a new breed of US economists trained at the University of Chicago known as the 'Chicago Boys'. State industries were privatized, labour laws abolished, unions outlawed and private investment encouraged. US investors could not contain their enthusiasm for the new Chile.

'While the winds of nationalism continue to buffet much of Latin America, Chile claims to be a safe refuge for all foreign investors. Unlike many developing countries where foreign investment is considered a necessary evil at best, Chile's new governors have widely publicized their position that foreign investment is "indispensable".

The pro-foreign investment sentiment is widely espoused in Chilean government circles today. From the governing military junta, its key civilian economic ministers and advisors, down to the officers that deal routinely with foreign investors, the favorable attitude prevails. This uniformity assures investors that what they have been promised at the highest levels will be acted upon at lower echelons.'

Source: *Chile After Allende: Prospects for Business in a Changing Market*, New York, Business International Corporation, 1975, p. 63

General Contreras, the paid CIA informer. The CIA continued working with Contreras even after the murder of Letelier and Moffit in Washington.

Nixon, Kissinger and Congress

News of the atrocious human rights abuses in Chile caused an outcry among politicians and the public in the United States. Press leaks suggesting that the United States was complicit in the coup led to the Senate intelligence committee inquiry of 1975. The report revealed the US's role in destabilizing Allende's government and its efforts to prop up the Pinochet junta. A year later Congress voted to ban arms sales and reduce economic aid to Pinochet's regime and to limit economic aid to US$27.5 million. Nixon and Kissinger regarded Congress's actions with great irritation. When Kissinger had become Secretary of State in 1973, he had told his staff: 'I think we should understand our policy: that however unpleasant they act, the government is better for us than Allende was.'[26] As the human rights lobby gathered strength in 1976, Kissinger told his Assistant Secretary of State, 'I am not on the same wavelength with you guys on this [human rights] business. I am just not eager to overthrow these guys... I think we are systematically undermining them.'[27] Days later, on 8 June 1976, Kissinger met Pinochet at a conference of the Organization of American States (OAS) in Santiago. Under pressure from the US Congress to be tough on human rights, Kissinger privately assured the dictator that he had US approval:

> **Pinochet:** This is a country of warm-hearted people who love liberty. This is the reason they did not accept Communism when the Communists attempted to take over the country ... I have always been against Communism. During the Viet-Nam War, I met with some of your military and made clear to them my anti-Communism, and told them I hoped they could bring about its defeat.
> **The Secretary:** In Viet-Nam, we defeated ourselves through our internal divisions. There is a world-wide propaganda campaign by the Communists.
> **Pinochet:** Chile is suffering from that propaganda effort. Unfortunately, we do not have the millions needed for counter propaganda.
> **The Secretary:** I must say your spokesman (Sergio Diez) was very effective in this morning's General Assembly session in explaining your position. In the United States, as you know, we are sympathetic with what you are trying to do here. I think that the previous government was headed toward Communism. We wish your government well. At the same time, we face massive domestic problems, in all branches of the government, especially Congress, but also in the Executive, over the issue of human rights. As you know Congress is now debating further restraints on aid to Chile. We are opposed. But basically we don't want to intervene in your domestic affairs. We can't be precise in our proposals about what you should do. But this is a problem which complicates our relationship and the efforts of those who are friends of Chile.
>
> I am going to speak about human rights this afternoon in the General Assembly. I delayed my statement until I could talk to you. I wanted you to understand my position. We want to deal in moral persuasion, not by legal sanctions.

In my statement, I will treat human rights in general terms, and human rights in a world context. I will refer in two paragraphs to the report on Chile of the OAS Human Rights Commission. I will say that the human rights issue has impaired relations between the US and Chile … It would really help if you would let us know the measures you are taking in the human rights field. None of this is said with the hope of undermining your government. I want you to succeed and I want to retain the possibility of aid.

… I want to see our relations and friendship improve. I encouraged the OAS to have its General Assembly here. I knew it would add prestige to Chile. I came for that reason. We have suggestions. We want to help, not undermine you. You did a great service to the West in overthrowing Allende. Otherwise Chile would have followed Cuba. Then there would have been no human rights or a Human Rights Commission.[28]

A Friend in Paraguay

Alfredo Stroessner was dictator of Paraguay for 35 years (1954–89). Stroessner used the army and secret police to retain his grip on power; political opponents were imprisoned and tortured. Stroessner won over 80% of the vote in every election, even after 1963, when he allowed some opposition parties to take part.

Cold War US governments saw Stroessner as a valuable anti-communist ally and gave Paraguay generous economic and military aid. Stroessner met President Eisenhower in 1953 and 1956 and assured him that Paraguay was '100% anti-Communist'. During a visit to Paraguay in 1958, Vice-President Nixon said: 'In the field of international affairs, I do not know of any other nation which has risen more strongly than yours against the threat of communism and this is one reason why I feel especially happy to be here'.

Stroessner reacted with indignation to Jimmy Carter's human rights policy, condemning 'Carter-Communism' at the Congress of the World anti-Communist League in 1977, but he nevertheless felt compelled to release almost 1,000 political prisoners. Carter cut military aid, but continued to send economic assistance to Paraguay. To Stroessner's surprise, the Reagan administration was also critical of Paraguay's human rights record (in part to offset criticism of Reagan's war against left-wing Nicaragua). But the Reagan administration also ensured that Paraguay was granted full certification enabling it to receive US aid on 'national security grounds'.

Stroessner was overthrown in a palace coup in 1989 and spent his final years in exile in Brazil.

Source: D. Dent, *The Legacy of the Monroe Doctrine*, Connecticut, Greenwood Press, 1999, p. 318. Additional sources: J. Painter, *Paraguay in the 1970s: Continuity and Change in the Political Process*, London, Institute of Latin American Studies, 1983 and C. Miranda, *The Stroessner Era: Authoritarian Rule in Paraguay*, USA, Boulder Press, 1990

Argentina's Dirty War

Military coups were common in Argentina during the twentieth century; the armed forces habitually took control during periods of economic crisis or political strife. But, as in Chile, nothing had prepared Argentina for the savagery of the regime that took power in March 1976. Generals ousted Isabel Perón, the widow of Juan Perón, to end a period of economic chaos, rising labour unrest and attacks by left-wing guerrillas. Argentina's totalitarian new leaders, imbued with anti-communist and anti-Semitic ideology, launched a National Reorganization Process to restructure every facet of Argentine life. Congress was shut down, all the Supreme Court judges were sacked, political parties and trade unions were banned, and television and radio stations were taken over. Argentinians now had to face the 'overwhelming monotony of living with fear', as one Argentinian historian has put it. The junta launched a 'dirty war' to eliminate 'subversion' but their targets were not just guerrilla fighters. General Videla, the leader of the junta, told the press: 'A terrorist is not just someone with a gun or a bomb, but someone who spreads ideas that are contrary to Western and Christian civilization.'[29] Thousands of people were abducted from their homes and tortured. Secret torture centres were set up all over the country. The Navy Mechanical School was a notorious torture centre in residential Buenos Aires: guards played loud music to cover the screams of victims. The national football stadium was just a few blocks away and prisoners could hear the cheers as Argentina hosted and won the 1978 World Cup.

Many of the prisoners disappeared. Their families were not told of their whereabouts or what had happened to them. They simply never heard from them again. Argentina's official report lists the names of 8,960 people who 'disappeared', but human rights groups and the secret services estimate that the real number is higher than 20,000.[30] Some of the 'disappeared' were drugged, and taken on the so-called 'Death Flights': put into a helicopter and thrown out into the Atlantic Ocean or the River Plate. Bodies washed up on shore, and in recent years it has been possible to identify these victims by exhuming the bodies and using DNA forensic techniques. Examinations of the cadavers have shown they had been thrown from a height. One of the most chilling acts of the military regime was the treatment of pregnant women prisoners. After they had given birth in prison, their babies were taken from them and given to childless military couples to adopt. The mothers were then killed. Argentinian families today are now facing the emotional and legal consequences of these secret adoptions.

Kissinger Welcomes the Junta

Washington initially welcomed the coup, but as the scale of the abuse became apparent, the Ford administration came under pressure from Congress to break its ties with Argentina. Secretary of State Henry Kissinger met Argentina's foreign minister, Admiral César Augusto Guzzetti, in Santiago in June 1971. According to a

---

US Congress Stands Up for Human Rights

The Nixon and Ford governments may have been sympathetic to Latin American dictators, but Congress became increasingly disturbed by the human rights violations being reported. Senators and Representatives introduced several pieces of legislation cutting aid to dictatorships. When President Carter took office in 1977, military aid to the remaining dictatorships was cut.

1975   The Harkin Amendment gave Congress the right to reduce economic aid to human rights violators.

1976   Legislation was passed which allowed Congress to reduce military aid to human rights violators.
        Economic and military aid was cut off to Uruguay, a Southern Cone dictatorship (1973–85) responsible for two hundred disappearances and seven thousand political prisoners. Representative Edward Koch led the campaign for the ban.

1977   Economic and military aid to Chile was suspended. Following President Carter's inauguration, military and economic aid to Argentina was suspended.

1978   Military aid for Guatemala, El Salvador, Paraguay and Brazil was suspended.

---

recently declassified State Department memorandum of conversation, Kissinger told Guzzetti:

> We have followed events in Argentina closely. We wish the new government well. We wish it will succeed [sic]. We will do what we can to help it succeed. We are aware you are in a difficult period. It's a curious time, when political, criminal and terrorist activities tend to merge without any clear separation. We understand you must establish your authority.[31]

The memorandum shows that the tone of the meeting was friendly even though the US embassy in Buenos Aires had raised concerns that three US women had been kidnapped and tortured by the Argentinian authorities.[32] Kissinger tells Guzzetti that he will see what he can do on the economic front. He promises to 'use our influence in the private sector'; to phone the banker David Rockefeller; and to meet Argentina's finance minister 'as a symbolic gesture'. When Guzzetti complains about the foreign press 'interpreting events in a very peculiar manner,' Kissinger sympathizes: 'The worst crime as far as the press is concerned is to have replaced a government of the left.'

Kissinger met Guzzetti again in October 1976, this time at the Secretary of State's suite in the Waldorf Astoria Hotel in New York. Kissinger told the Argentinian foreign minister:

Look, our basic attitude is that we would like you to succeed. I have an old-fashioned view that friends ought to be supported. What is not understood in the United States is that you have a civil war. We read about human rights problems but not the context. The quicker you succeed the better ... We want a stable situation. We won't cause you unnecessary difficulties. If you can finish before Congress gets back, the better. Whatever freedoms you could restore would help.[33]

The Argentinian foreign minister was 'euphoric' about this reaction from the United States, according to Robert Hill, the US ambassador in Buenos Aires at the time. Hill had been sympathetic to the coup at first, but had become disturbed by the extent of the human rights violations. (Hill was no soft liberal; he had helped to plan the overthrow of Arbenz in Guatemala in 1954.) After the Kissinger–Guzzetti meeting, Hill sent a telegram to Washington complaining that the Argentinian foreign minister had been given the impression that the US was unconcerned about abuses in Argentina:

[Guzzetti] considered his meeting with Secretary of State Kissinger a success ... Guzzetti went to US fully expecting to hear some strong, firm, direct warnings on his government's human rights practices, rather than that, he has returned in a state of jubilation, convinced there is no real problem with the USG over that issue.[34]

Carter, Reagan and Dictatorships

Democratic President Jimmy Carter took office in 1977. Military aid to Argentina was immediately banned and he launched a vocal international campaign criticizing human rights violations by the junta. A year later Carter cut off military aid to the dictators of Brazil, Guatemala, El Salvador and Paraguay. It is true that the US government continued to provide commercial credit to dictatorships through the Export-Import Bank during the Carter years, mainly as a result of lobbying by US businesses and the apolitical pragmatism of the Treasury.[35]

There were also ways round the restrictions on military aid: the channelling of aid to the military police through the anti-narcotics budget, for example. However, Carter's principled attempt to penalize human rights violators in Latin America was in stark contrast to the actions of both his predecessor and his successor.

In 1981 the new Republican president, Ronald Reagan, signalled a clear change of policy when he received the leader of the Argentinian junta General Roberto Viola as his first official guest from Latin America. Reagan immediately sought to lift the ban on arms sales, military aid and loans to Argentina and Chile, but Congress resisted. A compromise was agreed which allowed the sale of arms and the resumption of military aid to the Southern Cone dictators if the US government verified that human rights had improved. The Reagan administration soon began supplying loans to the Argentinian junta and inviting the navy to take part in joint exercises. Reagan went on to enlist Argentina's military help in Central America, a collaboration that led to more atrocious violations, reprising the darkest days of the Cold War.

6

Reagan and the Central American Tragedy

Central America's problems do directly affect the security and well being of our own people. And Central America is much closer to the US than many of the world trouble spots that concern us ... El Salvador is nearer to Texas than Texas is to Massachusetts. Nicaragua is just as close to Miami, San Antonio, San Diego and Tucson as those cities are to Washington ... But nearness on the map does not even begin to tell the strategic importance of Central America, bordering as it does on the Caribbean – our lifeline to the outside world ...

President Ronald Reagan: Address to Joint Session of Congress, 27 April 1983[1]

We deplore the Marxist Sandinista takeover of Nicaragua and the Marxist attempts to destabilize El Salvador, Guatemala and Honduras ... [We] pledge a strong new United States policy in the Americas. We will stand firm with countries seeking to develop their societies while combating the subversion and violence exported by Cuba and Moscow.

The Republican Party platform, 1980

Central America is the most important place in the world for the United States today.

Jeane Kirkpatrick, US Ambassador to the UN, 1981

Ronald Reagan and the New Right

The New Right, which formed the backbone of Ronald Reagan's presidential campaign, sought to reassert US global supremacy. The establishment had been traumatized and divided by defeat in Vietnam. Liberals in the Democratic Party believed that the war had been a mistake and that it had been a mistake to view Vietnam as an extension of the conflict with Moscow and Beijing. From now on, they argued, Third World politics should no longer be viewed through the lens of the

Cold War.[2] But an alternative view began to gain support: that the United States had lost Vietnam because it did not use sufficient force early on in the conflict. According to this view, the Soviet Union was, in fact, the greatest threat facing the United States, and sponsorship by the USSR of Third World liberation movements could leave the US isolated in a hostile world. Mozambique, Angola, Ethiopia, Iran, Grenada and Nicaragua were all seen by the New Right as examples of Soviet aggression. Intellectuals such as Paul Nitze, Richard Pipes and Eugene Rostow set up the Committee on the Present Danger to campaign for a new arms programme to confront the alleged Soviet threat. For the New Right the global economic crises of the late 1970s compounded the uneasy sense that the standing of the US in the world was fragile and in jeopardy.

The New Right rounded on President Jimmy Carter for the 'loss' of Nicaragua and Iran, two countries in which dictators had been overthrown by revolution in 1979. One of Ronald Reagan's closest advisers, Jeane Kirkpatrick, argued in an influential essay that Carter's human rights policy had allowed anti-American forces to come to power:

> Universal in its rhetoric ... but almost invariably anti-Western in its application, the Carter human rights policy alienated nondemocratic but friendly nations, enabled anti-Western opposition groups to come to power in Iran and Nicaragua and reduced American influence throughout the world.[3]

The Reaganites made a distinction between totalitarian regimes (the Soviet bloc) and pro-Western authoritarian regimes. Dictatorships in Latin America were no longer viewed as international pariahs but instead were seen as valuable allies in the new Cold War. Kirkpatrick explained:

> If we are confronted with the choice between offering assistance to a moderately repressive autocratic government which is also friendly to the United States and permitting it to be overrun by a Cuban-trained, Cuban-armed, Cuban-sponsored insurgency, we would assist the moderate autocracy.[4]

But the Reaganites' biggest preoccupation was preventing the spread of the Nicaraguan revolution to other Central American countries – the so-called Domino Theory. 'I think it's time the people of the United States realize', said Ronald Reagan in 1980, 'that we're the last domino.'[5]

Carter and the Nicaraguan Revolution

President Jimmy Carter may have been the target for the wrath of the Reaganites over his Nicaragua policy, but he was in fact following in a long-held tradition of US policy: dropping dictators once they served their purpose and/or became an embarrassment. The regime of Anastasio Somoza was brutal, autocratic and corrupt, characteristics which were laid bare when an earthquake devastated the capital Managua in 1972. Somoza and his officials stole more than half the international funds donated for the relief effort, while his undisciplined National Guard looted the

The Somoza Dynasty: Loyal Allies of the USA

The Somoza dynasty ruled Nicaragua for forty-three years (1936–79) and all three Somoza presidents were firm allies of the United States, receiving economic aid, arms and military training over four decades.

US marines occupied Nicaragua during 1912–25 and 1926–33. When the marines left in 1933, they appointed Anastasio Somoza García ('Tacho I') as head of the new US-trained National Guard. Somoza had studied bookkeeping and advertising at the Pierce Business School in Philadelphia and was fluent in English. He was so close to the Americans during the occupation that he was known among his compatriots as 'El Yanki'. He seized power in 1936 and became president a year later. Somoza used the state to amass a US$60 million fortune within eight years. Somoza and his wife were received with full state honours by President Roosevelt in Washington in 1939. After the Second World War, Somoza ruled through a series of puppet presidents. Always a loyal anti-communist ally, Somoza allowed the CIA to use Nicaragua as a base for the overthrow of President Arbenz of Guatemala in 1954. Tacho I was assassinated in the Nicaraguan city of León in 1956 by the poet Rigoberto López Pérez.

Somoza had two sons, Luis and Anastasio Somoza Debayle ('Tacho II', or 'Tachito'). Both sons studied at La Salle Military Academy on Long Island, New York. When he was sixteen, Tacho II went to study at the United States Military Academy at West Point, while his brother Luis studied agronomy at Louisiana State Academy. Tacho II lived in the US from the age of eleven until he was twenty-one, and Spanish became his second language. In 1956, he was made head of the National Guard.

On his father's death, Luis declared himself acting president, while Tacho II used the National Guard to crack down on the opposition. Again a puppet president was installed while the Somoza brothers remained in control. Tacho II attended John F. Kennedy's inauguration, where he met Alan Foster Dulles and offered to help destabilize Castro's new government. The US-backed exiles launched their failed Bay of Pigs attacks from Nicaragua's Atlantic Coast, with the Somozas' blessing. The Somoza dynasty's assets were enormous, including vast estates, a merchant shipping line and the national airline.

Tacho II became president in 1967 in a fraudulent election. His brother Luis died later that year, leaving Tacho II as president, head of the National Guard and owner of a personal fortune. Tacho II's dictatorship was particularly brutal. Among the torture methods used by his National Guard were electric shocks, mutilation and rape. The National Guard dreamed up new methods of torture such as tying a button to the end of a string, forcing a victim to swallow it, then tugging it back up again.

Nixon admired Somoza's anti-communist credentials. Somoza was a 'special honored guest' at a White House dinner hosted by Nixon for West Point graduates in 1971. Somoza repaid the favour by contributing US$1 million to Nixon's presidential campaign in 1972. US ambassadors became close friends of Somoza; Thomas E. Whelan enjoyed a round of poker with the dictator, while the obsequious Turner B. Shelton became Somoza's closest confidant.

Tacho II was a great fan of the US and despised his own people. He loved to chat to foreign news correspondents. In June 1979, as the FSLN guerrillas launched their final offensive against his regime, a drunken Somoza told reporters: 'I'm enjoying the hell out of getting together with you guys, because you know something? You are just human beings like I am – you're a bunch of shits. You know we ought to clear the air. Forget about me being president. Let's just be men and then we should get together and say, all right, what the fuck is good for this goddamn undeveloped country and what is good for these bastards who are trying to make hay in situations that are not realistic.'

Source: B. Diederich, *Somoza and the Legacy of US Involvement in Central America*, New York, E. P. Dutton, 1981, pp. 2, 89.

disaster areas. Somoza alienated the Nicaraguan business class by awarding all the reconstruction contracts to his cronies. All classes were now tired of the dictatorship; the nationalist left-wing guerrilla group *Frente Sandinista de Liberación Nacional* (FSLN), which had been formed a decade earlier, began to win widespread support.

Carter's policy was confused and inconsistent. He suspended aid in early 1977 only to send the regime US$2.5 million worth of arms and munitions later that year. US aid flowed throughout 1978 and was only finally cut in 1979, just months before Somoza was ousted. This contradiction stemmed from a split within the Carter administration. His National Security Adviser, Zbigniew Brzezinski, was steeped in Cold War politics and primarily concerned about Soviet ambitions in the region, whereas Carter's Secretary of State, Cyrus Vance, suggested – more plausibly – that the roots of the conflict could be found in Central America. Congress was also divided. Whilst eighty-six congressmen tried to cut aid to Nicaragua on human rights grounds, Somoza could count on over seventy senators and representatives to vote in his favour. The dictator boasted that he had more friends in Congress than Carter, who he dismissed as 'that Baptist'. The most vocal of Somoza's friends was Representative John Murphy who had studied with him in La Salle Academy.

As it became clear that the dictatorship was unravelling, Washington tried desperately to preserve 'Somocismo without Somoza'. A US mission headed by William Bowdler was sent to Nicaragua in October 1978 and spent months trying to split the moderates from the FSLN and trying to persuade them to preserve the dictator's hated National Guard. As the FSLN launched a final offensive in June 1979, US officials began casting around desperately for a way to prevent the guerrillas from taking power. Carter asked the OAS to send a 'peacekeeping' force to Nicaragua, but the proposal was voted down by other Latin American countries. Popular uprisings broke out in the provinces and the US began round-the-clock negotiations with the Sandinistas' five-person junta, trying, unsuccessfully, to persuade them to keep the National Guard and include Somoza's liberal party in the junta. Somoza fled to Paraguay on 17 July 1979. A US attempt to oversee an orderly transition collapsed when the head of the caretaker government refused to step down and the National Guard began to desert its posts. The Sandinistas pressed on to all-out military victory and took the capital on 19 July.

For the Pentagon it was 'the worst-case scenario' and officials were 'stunned' by the disintegration of the National Guard.[6] The CIA immediately began to reorganize Somoza's officers. The Chairman of the US Joint Chiefs of Staff summed up the dominant mood among US military and intelligence services: 'Now we have a Cuba on the continent proper and the Soviets are going to use it as a launching pad to support Central American movements. This is a target of opportunity for Havana and Moscow.'[7]

However, the President's Office and the State Department took a more pragmatic view. They sought to strengthen moderate elements within the government to ensure that private property and US investments would be protected.[8] The US approved US$35 million of aid in 1979 and even offered the Sandinistas military training (an offer that was declined). The following year, the Carter administration drew up a US$80 million aid package, but in line with its aim of strengthening the moderates it stipulated that 60 per cent of the funds must go to the private sector. Right-wingers within Congress held up the aid for eight months and added many more conditions.

The Sandinistas were a broad-based movement. Their aims had been to end the dictatorship, to improve the living standards of the people and to assert national sovereignty in a country which, they believed, had been a vassal of the United States for too long. The liberation war had a terrible cost; 50,000 people had died and 40,000 children were orphaned. Somoza had made off with the country's reserves, leaving a US$1.5 billion debt. The new government made reconstruction the top priority, as well as the improvement of health and education. All of Somoza's properties were nationalized as well as the banks (which were on the point of collapse), but the only foreign companies affected were two small mining concerns which had joint ventures with Somoza. Standard Fruit and United Brands continued operating.

The Sandinistas were desperate for foreign aid to rebuild their devastated economy. In 1980 while the US Congress was laboriously debating its aid package Nicaraguans sought help from Europe and the Soviet bloc. The Soviet Union provided U$100 million of credit. This only accounted for 19 per cent of Nicaragua's foreign loans, but the offer aroused great suspicion in Washington. The Sandinistas sought the help of the Cubans, experts in public health and education provision, to design literacy and immunization campaigns, a move that also alienated Washington. The FSLN's decision to postpone general elections, the resignation of two prominent moderates from the governing junta, and the appointment of Sandinista Humberto Ortega as defence minister brought a further decline in relations with the US. In late 1980, Carter ordered the CIA to launch a covert action campaign, starting with the funding of opposition political parties, trade unions and the anti-Sandinista press.

Whilst Carter had spent some time exploring the possibility of accommodation with the Sandinistas, he took immediate military action after the revolution to ensure it did not spread. In October 1979 he announced the formation of a permanent Caribbean contingency task force and within weeks the US navy began carrying out manoeuvres in Caribbean waters.[9] Overriding human rights concerns, in late 1979 a military aid package worth US$10–20 million was approved for the eastern Caribbean and the military governments of Central America. Much of the aid went to El Salvador, where the Pentagon was concerned by the growing guerrilla movement. The military regime of Honduras, which along with El Salvador bordered Nicaragua, was another large recipient. A further US$9 million of military aid was given to El Salvador and Honduras in 1980, paving the way for the all-out Central American offensive launched by Carter's successor, the Republican Ronald Reagan, when he took power in 1981.

Reagan's War on Nicaragua

The Reagan administration unleashed unparalleled military and economic aggression against a tiny country with a population of only three million. The Contra War, so named for the counter-revolutionaries (*contrarevolucionarios*) who fought against the Sandinista revolution, left 30,864 people dead and 20,064 wounded. In a case brought against the United States at the International Court of Justice, the Nicaraguan government estimated the total cost of the war and the accompanying economic embargo at US$17.8 billion. The court ruled that the United States had broken international law and violated Nicaragua's sovereignty. It ordered the US to stop 'arming and training' the Contra rebels, a judgement the Reagan administration ignored.

Exhausted by war and hardship, the Nicaraguan people would vote the Sandinistas out of office in 1990. The Sandinistas, 'a cruel clique of committed Communists at war with God and man', according to Reagan, accepted the result and stepped down, the first transfer of power in fair elections in Nicaraguan history. The outgoing president, Daniel Ortega, handed power to the victorious US-backed candidate, Violeta Chamorro, in a sorrowful yet dignified embrace. It was a sad moment for the Sandinistas and a turning point for Nicaragua; after ten years of aggression, another sovereign country's attempt to steer its own course through history had been wrecked.

The Contras
Determined to overthrow the Sandinistas but convinced the US public would not accept a conventional invasion in the aftermath of Vietnam, the Reagan administration seized upon a new military strategy: Low Intensity Warfare. Like the counter-insurgency doctrines of the 1960s, Low Intensity Warfare was a combination of paramilitary, psychological and economic warfare. Crucially, it did not require large numbers of US troops, but relied on special forces and intelligence operatives

to train foreign paramilitary forces. The covert paramilitary war against Nicaragua began in spring 1981. The CIA offered military training and equipment to exiled opponents of the Sandinistas. Many of the Contras were former members of Somoza's National Guard. Most were trained in Honduras, but paramilitary training camps were also set up in Florida, California and Texas even though this violated the 1794 Neutrality Act.[10] To keep the operation secret, the CIA paid Argentinian military intelligence to train the Contras. Using tactics honed in the Dirty War the Argentinian secret services were in charge of training the Contras until the 1982 Falklands War, when the Argentinian junta fell out with Reagan over his support for Britain.

The number of Contras escalated rapidly, from 500 in 1981 to 15,000 in 1984. Supplied by the CIA with trucks, planes, automatic weapons and artillery, the Contras launched a campaign of terror in the Nicaraguan countryside, targeting peasant farms, agricultural collectives, schools and health clinics in order to disrupt the economy and the Sandinistas' social programmes. By the end of 1985 the Contras had killed 3,652 civilians and kidnapped 5,232. Reagan described the Contras as 'the moral equivalent of our founding fathers'. However, the former director of the CIA, Stansfield Turner, was closer to the truth when he testified to Congress that the Contras' actions 'have to be characterized as terrorism, as State-supported Terrorism'.[11]

Psychological Operations in Guerrilla Warfare

The CIA manual *Psychological Operations in Guerrilla Warfare* was written in 1983. Two thousand copies were printed and at least 200 were distributed to Contras. When a copy was leaked to the US press, it became known as the 'Murder Manual' because one section advocates the illegal assassination of Nicaraguan officials.

'SELECTIVE USE OF VIOLENCE FOR PROPAGANDISTIC EFFECTS:
It is possible to neutralize carefully selected and planned targets, such as court judges, mesta [local] judges, police and State Security officials, CDS chiefs, etc. For psychological purposes it is necessary to gather together the population affected so that they will be present, take part in the act, and formulate accusations against the oppressor ...
An armed guerrilla force can occupy an entire town or small city that is neutral or relatively passive in the conflict ...
• Destroy the military or police installations and remove the survivors to a 'public place' ...
• Kidnap all officials or agents of the Sandinista government and replace them in 'public places' with military or civilian persons of trust to our movement: in addition carry out the following...
• Shame, ridicule and humiliate the 'personal symbols' of the government of repression in the presence of the people and foster popular participation through guerrillas [contras] within the multitude, shouting slogans and jeers ...'

The Freedom Fighter's Manual

The Freedom Fighter's Manual, published by the CIA in 1983, was a bilingual Spanish and English picture book, which illustrated ways to sabotage the Sandinista regime.

The sabotage proposals included: turning up late for work; calling in sick; leaving lights and taps on; hoarding food; making false hotel reservations; dropping typewriters; threatening the boss by phone; pulling down electricity cables; and leaving metal tacks on roads to perforate tyres. The manual also gave step-by-step instructions for starting a fire and making a Molotov cocktail.

The CIA and the Pentagon war

Contra attacks were backed up by direct CIA assaults on infrastructure: oil storage tanks, pipelines, ports, communications centres and military depots. As part of the propaganda strategy, these CIA attacks were made to look like the work of the Contras. The mining of Nicaraguan harbours caused an international outcry in 1984; declassified documents now show that this operation was carried out by the CIA under the direction of the National Security Council.[12] The Pentagon backed up the CIA's covert war by carrying out highly threatening military manoeuvres, involving thousands of US troops, on Nicaragua's borders and coastlines. The military build-up was deliberately designed by Pentagon psychological operations specialists to give the impression that the US was preparing to invade Nicaragua. 'One of the central purposes is to create fear of an invasion, to push very close to the border, deliberately, to set off all the alarms,' a US official wrote.[13] Declassified material unearthed by Peter Kornbluh at the National Security Archive shows that the Department of Defense also sent 'surplus' planes and military material to the Contras while a congressional ban on funding was in place, and sent special forces teams to back up the counter-insurgency force.

The economic embargo

On coming to office Reagan stopped all economic aid to Nicaragua and lobbied multi-lateral institutions to do the same. Nicaragua received no loans from the World Bank or the Inter-American Development Bank after September 1983. An economic embargo banning all US trade with Nicaragua was imposed in 1985. For a country which previously bought 70 per cent of its imports from the US, the impact was severe. Food shortages led to empty shelves in the shops. The Nicaraguan currency, the cordoba, became worthless as hyperinflation spiralled to over 1000 per cent. Heavily indebted, Nicaragua failed to pay its oil suppliers, Mexico and Venezuela. When they cut off supplies, Nicaragua was forced to rely on oil from the Soviet Union.

Congress and the Contras
Congress banned military aid for the Contras in 1984 after the CIA illegally mined Nicaraguan ports. The Reagan administration continued to fund the Contras illegally (see 'The Iran–Contra affair' below) and stepped up its propaganda efforts at home in order to persuade Congress to change its mind. In 1986, both Houses of Congress, the House of Representatives and the Senate, approved US$100 million of aid for the Contra War. After the Irangate scandal erupted in late 1986, Congress approved no more military aid for the Contras, but it continued to approve 'non-lethal' aid until the Sandinistas fell in 1990.

The US Congress Approves Contra Aid

This poem was written by the priest Ernesto Cardenal, who was the minister of culture in the Sandinista government.

The senator sings out his speech in his baritone voice
beautifully modulated. Up and down the scale
like playing a trumpet arpeggio with frequent runs,
    now it's a clarinet,
        the long concatenation of tangled words
           exquisitely articulated in every syllable
    syl-la-biz-ing
neatly the difficult bits of his bad prose
with virtuoso diction.
The next speaker
        in language florid
          high flown, grandiloquent
quoting large chunks of James Monroe by heart
as if reciting
        not looking at the script,
raising his voice (and face)
        and suddenly dropping
to a deep bass.
    He sits down sweatily
acknowledging the not very warm applause.

    Bertilda washes her son's wounds,
and says: 'Early this morning I was going to make coffee

and I saw them beating a boy in the street
so I shouted: 'Contras!'
    The boys started shooting,
there were just two of them
    and about a hundred contras.'
    The boys were her son and nephew.
'What did I feel? I felt nothing, I just thought:
If they kill them they'll have to kill me.
    I loaded three rounds for my nephew
    because my boy was hurt.
I tied up my two-year-old so she couldn't run about.'

Again:
Heady cocktail of timbre and tone modulations
with anastrophes,
    prosopopoeias here and there
        ingenious paronomasias
and sonorous anaphoras.
    His tropes resound in the decorated chamber
and the decorations echo them back,
few present in the chamber at the time
but his peroration addresses a multitude
        (hence the applause) ...

'Thirty million in humanitarian aid for the contras'
    'No sir, thirty eight!'
        One of the humanitarians titters.
Another bangs the table as if trying to break it
big two-handed swipes like swinging a bat
'There is no graver problem today [*bang*]
and I shudder to speak of it [*bang*]
than the danger [*bang*]
of communism in Central America [*bang*]'

        They killed my uncle,
and his son Ramon, both died fighting.
    Ramon's six year old boy
they murdered in his bed,
he was asleep and they shot him.
He was wounded and asked to see his dead father.
He stroked his face and said:
    'Look, they've made a hole here'.
        And just then the child died too ...

E. Cardenal, *Nicaraguan New Time*, London, Journeyman, 1988. Translated by Dinah Livingstone.

The Sandinista Revolution

Reagan's image of a grey totalitarian state was a lie. *Sandinismo* is best described as a blend of nationalism, Marxism and Christianity – three priests inspired by liberation theology were members of the cabinet. One of the first acts of the Sandinistas was to abolish the death penalty. None of Somoza's associates or torturers were executed, making it possible for many former National Guardsmen to escape and join the Contras. Although Nicaragua was increasingly forced to rely on Soviet trade, a communist system was never imposed. Throughout the Sandinista decade two thirds of the economy remained in private hands. The only property taken over by the state was the assets of the former dictator and, later, large uncultivated estates. In fact, for many peasants, the pace of land reform was too slow. The Sandinistas improved health and education for the poor. A mass literacy campaign was launched in 1980, in which 100,000 volunteer teachers taught half a million Nicaraguans to read and write, reducing the illiteracy rate from over 50 to 13 per cent. The World Health Organization praised the Sandinistas' immunization and preventative healthcare campaigns. Health clinics were built in isolated villages, a stark contrast to the Somoza years when the rural poor had almost no access to doctors. As a result, polio was eradicated and the incidence of malaria, diarrhoea, measles and whooping cough fell, giving Nicaragua some of the best health indicators in the Third World. One of the more quixotic measures of the Sandinistas was the setting up of poetry workshops across the country, giving the newly literate the chance to emulate celebrated Nicaraguan poets like Gioconda Belli and the great Rubén Darío.

One of the first sticking points with the Carter administration was the failure of the Sandinistas to hold immediate elections. The Sandinistas postponed the elections because they believed that mass participation in the revolution had given them legitimacy and because they wanted to focus on national reconstruction. They also feared that elections might exacerbate divisions within the FSLN's own ranks. In the first four years of the revolution thousands of people joined mass organizations such as trade unions, women's groups and youth groups, and these were given representation on the Council of State. In February 1984, the Sandinistas announced that general elections would be held the following November. Under heavy pressure from the United States, the largest right-wing opposition group, the *Coordinadora Democrática*, boycotted the elections on the basis that there had not been enough time to prepare a campaign. Declassified documents now show that the Coordinadora's presidential candidate, Arturo Cruz, was on the payroll of the CIA.[14] Cruz was well respected in Washington and was known in the US Congress as the moderate face of the opposition. The elections went ahead with six small opposition parties taking part; 74 per cent of the electorate voted. The Sandinistas won 63% of the vote and took 61 of the 90 seats in the National Assembly. The United States, which did not send election observers, condemned the elections as a fraud. But other international observers, including the European Parliament, said they were legitimate.[15]

The Reagan administration claimed that, 'in the American continent, there is no regime more barbaric and bloody, no regime that violates human rights in a manner more constant and permanent, than the Sandinista regime'.[16] All major human rights organizations, however, agreed that the Sandinistas did not routinely violate the fundamental rights of its citizens and did not engage in torture, disappearances or abduction. The advocacy organization Americas Watch described Reagan's claims as 'misleading' and 'deceptive'.[17] When the Contra War began, the Sandinistas imposed a state of emergency, but their restrictions on civil rights were comparable with those imposed by Western countries during times of war. The International Red Cross reported in 1988 that there were 3,500 political prisoners in Nicaragua, most of whom were former national guardsmen or Contras.[18] Between 1983 and 1986 special tribunals convicted 846 suspected Contras.[19] The state of emergency was lifted in 1988 and the special tribunals were abolished. All those accused of Contra activity were given an amnesty and in 1989 some 1,894 former national guardsmen were released from prison. All remaining political prisoners were released before the 1990 elections.

During the state of emergency, the Sandinista government first censored, then closed for fourteen months the main opposition newspaper, La Prensa. One other publication, Iglesia, a monthly journal published by the Catholic Church, was banned. The most serious abuse committed by the Sandinista government was its forced evacuation of Misquito people from the Atlantic Coast and the Honduran border. Fourteen thousand Misquito and Sumo people were forced to leave their villages and resettle inland in 1982 after Contras began recruiting among the indigenous population.[20] In the mid-1980s, the Sandinistas passed an autonomy act and allowed the evacuees to return home. The Misquito Coast is also the site of the most serious abuses by the Nicaraguan security forces; according to the OAS Inter-American Commission on Human Rights, Sandinista soldiers were responsible for the deaths of up to 150 Misquito people in separate incidents in the Rio Coco region.[21]

The Iran–Contra affair

The Iran–Contra scandal, which erupted in 1986, revealed that the Reagan administration had violated the law in two ways: it had illegally sold arms to Iran and it had used the proceeds illegally to fund the Contras. Anti-aircraft missiles were sold to Iran in a failed attempt to win the release of American hostages in Lebanon.[22] The revelation shocked both the public and Congress, as the hardline Reagan administration had repeatedly vowed it would refuse to negotiate with terrorists or sell arms to the anti-US government of the Ayatollah Khomeni. The sale of arms flouted the Arms Export Control Act and broke the US arms embargo on Iran – funding the Nicaraguan Contras was also illegal from 1984 to 1986 because Congress had imposed a ban. Two investigations were carried out into the Iran Contra affair, one by Congress and another by the Independent Counsel, which led to the prosecution of fourteen government officials and private citizens. Both inquiries found that Ronald Reagan had approved of arms sales to Iran. And both reports regarded Reagan as responsible for the overall policy on the Contras because he had ordered his officials to keep 'the body and soul' of the Contras together during the congressional funding ban. However, the inquiries could not prove he knew that the proceeds from the Iranian arms deals were diverted to the Contras. Both investigations complained of government obstruction; thousands of documents were shredded, many of those who testified suffered mysterious memory lapses, and seven officials were convicted of perjury, obstruction or giving false information to Congress.[23] Among the guilty were the following:

- *Robert McFarlane, National Security Adviser, 1983–85*
  Pleaded guilty to four counts of withholding information from Congress. Pardoned by George Bush senior.
- *Oliver North, National Security Council, Deputy Director for Political Military Affairs.*
  Convicted of altering and destroying documents; accepting an illegal gratuity, and aiding and abetting in the obstruction of Congress. Conviction reversed on appeal, on the technical grounds that immunized testimony given to Congress had prejudiced the criminal trial.
- *John Poindexter, National Security Adviser, 1985–86*
  Convicted of conspiracy, false statements, destruction and removal of records and obstruction of Congress. Conviction reversed on appeal on technical grounds.
- *Elliott Abrams, Assistant Secretary of State for InterAmerican Affairs (1985–89)*
  Pleaded guilty to withholding information from Congress. Pardoned by George Bush senior.
- *Clair E. George, CIA Deputy Director of Operations, 1984–87*
  Convicted of false statements and perjury before Congress. Pardoned by George Bush senior.
  Alan D. Fiers Jr, head of the CIA's Central American Task Force, 1984–86
  Pleaded guilty to withholding information from Congress. Pardoned by George Bush senior.
- *Richard V. Secord, retired airforce major general*
  Pleaded guilty to making false statements to Congress.

The Independent Counsel also indicted Defense Secretary Caspar Weinberger on four counts of false statements and perjury, and indicted the high-ranking CIA officer Duane Clarridge on similar charges. Both men were pardoned by President George Bush senior before their cases went to trial.[24] Four business associates of Oliver North were convicted of money crimes. No one was charged with violating the Export Arms Ban or the congressional Contra funding ban because these were not criminal statutes. The congressional report suggested that Oliver North may simply have been the CIA's chosen 'fall guy'.

It concluded that

The Committees cannot even be sure whether they heard the whole truth or whether [CIA Director] Casey's 'fall guy' plan was carried out at the public hearings. But enough is clear to demonstrate beyond doubt that the fundamental processes of governance were disregarded and the rule of law was subverted.'[25]

Illegal propaganda

The Reagan administration unleashed an unprecedented propaganda campaign to win support for the Contra War. On the evening of March 16 1986, just as Congress was preparing to vote on Contra aid, Ronald Reagan broadcast a televised address from the Oval Office using a map of Latin America that gradually turned red as the President warned of the 'malignancy' of communism emanating from Nicaragua.[26] A government is of course free to put its views to the public, but the Iran–Contra congressional investigation concluded that the Reagan administration went further, using covert propaganda techniques that violated the law:

> During the period when the Administration was denying to Congress that it was involved in supporting the Contras' war effort, it was engaged in a campaign to alter public opinion and change the vote in Congress on Contra aid. Public funds were used to conduct public relations activities; and certain NSC staff members, using the prestige of the White House and the promise of meetings with the President, helped raise private donations both for the media campaigns and for weapons to be used by the Contras....
>
> The program was conducted by an office in the State Department known as the Office of Public Diplomacy for Latin America and the Caribbean...[This Office] produced and widely disseminated a variety of pro-Contra publications and arranged speeches and press conferences. It also disseminated what one official termed 'white propaganda'; pro-Contra newspaper articles by paid consultants who did not disclose their connection to the administration....

The congressional report noted that: 'By law appropriated funds may not be used to generate propaganda "designed to influence a member of Congress" and by law ... appropriated funds may not be used by the State Department for covert propaganda activities.' The director of the Office of Public Diplomacy was a Cuban-American named Otto Reich. Although he was censured by Congress and the Comptroller, Reich was later rewarded with high-ranking positions in the George W. Bush administration.

Drugs

The smear campaign against the Sandinistas included the false claim that they were drugs traffickers. Reagan claimed:

> The link between the governments of such Soviet allies as Cuba and Nicaragua and international narcotics trafficking and terrorism is becoming increasingly clear. These twin evils – narcotics trafficking and terrorism – represent the most insidious and dangerous threats to the hemisphere today.[27]

One of the documents appended to the Irangate report is a strategy paper written by two fundraisers hired by Oliver North. In it the fundraisers write that their publicity should link the Sandinistas to drugs because 'the chance to have a single issue which no one can disagree with is irresistible'.[28]

In reality it was the Contras who were involved in drugs trafficking – and the United States knew it. A Senate inquiry headed by Senator John Kerry reported:

It is clear that individuals who provided support for the Contras were involved in drug trafficking, the supply network of the Contras was used by drug trafficking organizations, and elements of the Contras themselves knowingly received financial and material assistance from drug traffickers. In each case, one or another agency of the US government had information regarding the involvement either while it was occurring or immediately thereafter.[29]

Even more damning was the revelation that US government funds had been given to drugs traffickers.

The Subcommittee found that the Contra drug links included ... payments to drug traffickers by the US State Department of funds authorized by the Congress for humanitarian assistance to the Contras, in some cases after the traffickers had been indicted by federal law enforcement agencies on drug charges, in others while traffickers were under active investigation by these same agencies.[30]

The Kerry report concluded that Reagan's war in Nicaragua had, in fact, undermined counter-drugs efforts in Central America, 'weakening an already inadequate law enforcement capability in the region which was easily exploited by a variety of mercenaries, pilots and others involved in drugs trafficking'.[31]

El Salvador

Contemporary observers had believed that El Salvador, not Nicaragua, was more likely to have a revolution. The country was ruled by an alliance of the military and coffee oligarchy, whose trenchant defence of their wealth left most of the nation in poverty. El Salvador's popular movement, made up of well-organized peasant groups, large trade unions, students and professionals, was far more developed than Nicaragua's. Many priests, inspired by liberation theology, recognized that El Salvador was thirsting for change and worked with the popular movement. Five guerrilla groups united to form the Frente Farabundo Martí para la Liberación Nacional (FMLN) in 1980. The CIA certainly believed that revolution was likely, as this declassified intelligence report of 1980 shows:

All of the symptoms associated with impending revolutionary upheaval are present in El Salvador today. Barring major outside intervention, the present social, economic and political order will collapse or be overwhelmed by the revolutionary left during the next year or two.[32]

There were, of course, differences between El Salvador and Nicaragua. In Nicaragua (and Cuba) a single corrupt dictator lost the support of virtually the entire population, including sections of the elite. In El Salvador, by contrast, the oligarchy remained remarkably united and, though the death squads made a mockery of their democratic pretensions, the holding of elections in the mid-1980s gave governments a veneer of legitimacy. But perhaps the greatest factor in the defeat of El Salvador's popular movement was the intervention of the United States.

To prevent another Nicaragua, the United States gave military aid, military

The Murder of Archbishop Romero

The Archbishop of San Salvador, Oscar Arnolfo Romero, was killed by a single bullet while saying Mass at a small chapel in a cancer hospital in San Salvador on 24 March 1980. The previous day, during his sermon at the Cathedral of San Salvador, Archbishop Romero had appealed to soldiers and police officers to stop the repression.

Originally a conservative cleric, Romero became the government's most powerful critic, condemning torture and disappearances and calling for justice for the poor.

Within two months, the US embassy had evidence that the death squad leader Roberto D'Aubuisson was responsible for the murder and that his squad had links to the security services. But the US professed ignorance about the murder and took no action.

Years later, the UN Truth Commission found that D'Aubuisson had indeed ordered Romero's assassination. Neither D'Aubuisson nor his associates were ever arrested for the crime. The first judge investigating the case received death threats and fled the country. In 1988 the Salvadoran Attorney General requested the extradition from the United States of Captain Alvaro Saravia, one of those accused of planning the assassination. But the Salvadoran court threw out the extradition request.

No one has been convicted for the murder of Archbishop Romero.

'… I would like to make a special appeal to the men of the army, and specifically to the ranks of the National Guard, the police and the military. Brothers, you come from our own people. Your are killing your own brother peasants when any human order to kill must be subordinate to the law of God which says, 'Thou shalt not kill'. No soldier is obliged to obey an order contrary to the law of God. No one has to obey an immoral law. It is high time you recovered your consciences rather than a sinful order. The Church, the defender of the rights of God, of the law of God, of human dignity, of the person, cannot remain silent before such an abomination. We want the government to face the fact that reforms are valueless if they are to be carried out at the cost of so much blood.

In the name of God, in the name of this suffering people whose cries rise to heaven more loudly each day, I implore you, I beg you, I order you in the name of God: stop the repression …'

Archbishop Romero, speaking at San Salvador Cathedral, 23 March 1980. The homily is reprinted in Romero, *Martyr for Liberation: The Last Two Homilies of Archbishop Oscar Romero of San Salvador*, London, Catholic Institute for International Relations, 1982.

training and intelligence assistance to one of the most oppressive states in the world, a country whose 'murders, disappearances and other violations of human rights' were condemned by the United Nations General Assembly.[33] Despite the international revulsion caused by the murder of Archbishop Romero and four US churchwomen, El Salvador became the second-largest per capita recipient of US military aid in the world. Death squads acted with impunity. By 1983 more than 11,000 people had been killed or 'disappeared' by the security forces and their allies.[34] By the end of the decade a total of 75,000 people had been killed in the civil war and one million had been forced to flee their homes.[35] Peace accords were signed in 1992. The military was purged as part of the peace settlement, but no officers were prosecuted for human rights abuses because the government passed an amnesty law. Today, the country's land and wealth remain in the hands of a few. Arena, the right-wing party founded by the death squad leader Roberto D'Aubuisson, has won four consecutive elections and ruled the country for the past twenty years (since 1989).

The military oligarchic state

The military held power in El Salvador for most of the twentieth century, while an economic oligarchy, the so-called 'fourteen families', controlled the land, commerce and the banks. In the early 1970s, Christian Democrats allied with Social Democrats and Communists mounted a serious electoral challenge to the military regime, but were kept from office through fraudulent elections. This refusal to allow a genuinely popular candidate, José Napoleón Duarte, to take office, led to a radicalization of the opposition. Several guerrilla groups were formed in the 1970s, and popular organizations, peasants' groups, student and teacher organizations and trade unions continued to agitate for reforms. The army responded with repression.

Reformist military officers led a coup against the military old guard in October 1979. They promised elections, land reform and civil rights. But hardliners soon won control of the junta and rather than bringing the violence under control, they intensified the repression. The Carter government gave aid to the junta even when it became clear that it was even more repressive than the regime it had overthrown. The aid was maintained despite a plea from Archbishop Romero of San Salvador, who wrote to President Carter in February 1980 urging him to withhold military assistance.[36] One month later the archbishop was murdered. Still the Carter administration took no action. Death squads and the security services killed with impunity. In total, there were 9,000 politically motivated deaths in 1980.[37] El Salvador had descended into hell.

American church workers murdered

Three American nuns and one Catholic lay worker were arrested by the National Guard after leaving El Salvador's international airport on 2 December 1980. They were taken to waste ground, where at least two of the women were raped. All four women were shot dead at close range. The deaths caused revulsion in the United States, and President Carter suspended military aid. However, the aid was restored less than one month later when Ronald Reagan took office.

Five national guardsmen were convicted of the murders in 1984, but those accused of ordering the killing never stood trial.

Reagan's administration was informed by his embassy that the investigation was flawed, but his officials nevertheless assured Congress that the inquiry was proceeding satisfactorily. Assistant Secretary of State Thomas Enders repeated the Salvadoran line that no high-ranking officers were complicit. 'The available evidence suggests that the five former National Guardsmen now scheduled to stand trial acted alone. Indeed, there is actually some positive evidence that there was no complicity higher up.'[38] Secretary of State Alexander Haig even tried to rationalize the murders by suggesting – although there was no evidence to support this – that the women's vehicle had jumped a roadblock and that 'there may have been an exchange of fire'. When asked if he was suggesting the women had fired on the government forces, Haig tried to laugh the matter away, 'I have not met any pistol-packing nuns in my day, Senator.'[39]

The United Nations Truth Commission found sufficient evidence to state that the killings been planned in advanced, that the national guardsmen had been acting on the orders of a superior, and that high-ranking officers, including the Director General of the National Guard, covered up the facts and obstructed the investigation.

The guerrilla 'final offensive'

The FMLN, which had a left-wing nationalist ideology similar to that of the Sandinistas, launched a final offensive in January 1981. They failed to take power because the strong and united Salvadoran oligarchy enjoyed considerable middle-class support, while the popular movement had been weakened and cowed by the repression. The Christian Democrats, who joined the military junta, played a crucial role in giving legitimacy to the regime. Although the FMLN had failed to take power, the insurgents nevertheless still had considerable popular support and retained control of large swathes of the countryside.

Reagan in power

Within a month of Reagan taking office in January 1981, the State Department issued a paper entitled 'Communist Interference in El Salvador' in which it alleged that the Soviet Union and Cuba had given the guerrillas large quantities of sophisticated weapons. Secretary of State Alexander Haig briefed the press about a Soviet–Cuban 'four-phased operation' in which Nicaragua, then El Salvador, Honduras and Guatemala would be 'seized'.[40] The hawkish administration considered only a military solution to the El Salvador 'problem', and military experts saw the country as the ideal testing ground for the new Low Intensity Warfare theory. The US trained, advised and supplied the Salvadoran military, working closely with it at all levels, despite clear evidence of its collusion with death squads.

The death squads

The death squads were a nightmarish presence in El Salvador. With names such as White Warriors Union and Secret Anti-Communist Army, these clandestine groups

The Invasion of Grenada

Six thousand US marines and paratroopers invaded the Caribbean island of Grenada in October 1983. Ten thousand more US troops aboard taskforce ships were on hand to provide reinforcements if required. It was the largest US invasion since the Vietnam War and the first US military intervention in an English-speaking Caribbean country. Reagan described the tiny island, whose population was just 110,000, as a 'Soviet–Cuban colony being readied as a major military bastion to export terror and undermine democracy'.

The New Jewel Movement, a left-wing nationalist alliance, had taken power in a popular bloodless coup in 1979, replacing the corrupt US-backed Eric Gairy, who had ruled Grenada on and off since the 1950s. A People's Revolutionary Government was established which, in addition to the New Jewel Movement, included independent professionals, trade unions and some business leaders. Maurice Bishop, a charismatic radical lawyer, was the undisputed leader of the 'revo', as the Grenadian revolution was known.

The new government made health-care and secondary education free for the first time. The state played a larger role in the economy, but 60 per cent remained in the hands of the private sector. The government tried to diversify the economy and increase food production for local people. Thousands of people joined literacy campaigns, labour brigades, youth organizations and popular militias. This so-called 'popular democracy' replaced parliamentary elections. Grenada was not without its critics: human rights groups condemned both restrictions on the press and emergency powers allowing detention without trial.

The greatest concern of the US was Grenada's independent foreign policy. Grenada traded and sought loans from Europe, the Soviet bloc and Cuba.

Nearby Cuba sent doctors, teachers and construction workers. Within a month of Bishop assuming power, the US ambassador sent him a note saying, 'We would view with displeasure any tendency on the part of Grenada to develop closer ties with Cuba.' Bishop responded:

> From day one of the revolution we have always striven to have and develop the closest and friendliest relations with the United States, as well as Canada, Britain, and all our Caribbean neighbours ... But no one must misunderstand our friendliness as an excuse for rudeness and meddling in our affairs, and no one, no matter how mighty and powerful they are, will be permitted to dictate to the government and people of Grenada who we can have friendly relations with and what kind of relations we must have with other countries ... We are not in anybody's back yard, and we are definitely not for sale.

This defiance sealed Grenada's fate once the Carter administration ended and Reagan took power. For Reagan, Grenada was 'an exporter of revolution' and the new international airport was a planned Soviet missile base. This was denied

→ by its funder, the European Economic Community (EEC), as well as the British company, Plessey Airports, carrying out much of the technical work.

The US began a series of naval manoeuvres. In August 1981, it launched the largest naval exercise conducted by Western forces in peacetime since the Second World War. Some 120,000 troops, 250 warships and 1,000 aircraft carried out a mock battle with 'Soviet' ships, and there was also a mock invasion of a Caribbean island. During another exercise, in March 1983, US craft came within six miles of the Grenadian coast giving many the impression that the US was rehearsing for a real invasion.

Within Grenada, the leadership of the New Jewel Movement descended into acrimonious infighting. A hardline faction arrested and then murdered Maurice Bishop, to the horror of most Grenadians. The hardliners formed a Revolutionary Military Council and declared martial law. Six days later, on 25 October 1983, US troops invaded to restore 'law, order and democratic institutions' and to evacuate US citizens (even though the Grenadian government had agreed to let them leave voluntarily). Four hundred troops from six Caribbean countries were also part of the invasion force but did not take part in the fighting. The US troops met with little resistance because most Grenadians did not support their own hardline military rulers. Within one week, the island was subdued. Some 45 Grenadians, 29 Cubans and 18 US soldiers had died (mostly from friendly fire).

'It's a lovely piece of real estate,' said US Secretary of State George Shultz when he arrived in Grenada in February 1984. Since the invasion, Grenadians have elected pro-US prime ministers. The revolutionaries' rudimentary welfare state has been dismantled, state assets have been sold off and efforts to diversify the economy have been abandoned. Today Grenada is still an exporter of primary products – nutmeg, bananas and cocoa – and 32 per cent of the population live below the poverty line.

Sources: *Grenada Whose Freedom?*, London, Latin America Bureau, 1984; J. Ferguson, *Grenada Revolution in Reverse*, London, Latin America Bureau, 1990, and C. Sunshine and P. Wheaton, *Death of a Revolution: An Analysis of the Grenada Tragedy and the US Invasion*, Washington, EPICA, 1984.

of armed men targeted anyone they considered 'subversive'. They made public examples of their victims by displaying their tortured or dismembered bodies. Communiqués or placards warning others were left with the bodies or, in some cases, the letters 'EM' (the acronym for *escuadrón de la muerte*) were carved on the victim's skin. Most of the death squad members were off-duty police and military officers. Some death squads operated directly from within the military. The Reagan administration was well aware that the Salvadoran state was colluding with death squads because its own embassy had been sending reports saying just that. Instead of taking action against the Salvadoran military, the Reagan administration decided as one of its first acts was to fire the US ambassador to El Salvador, Robert White, who had become a vocal critic of the regime. In congressional hearings and media briefings, the Reagan administration claimed that responsibility for the violence in El Salvador lay with extremists on the left and right, not the security services. But the administration knew this was fiction: a CIA report written at the request of the State Department, for example, showed that the death squads were deeply entrenched in the state structure.[41] The briefing paper identified a death squad operating out of both the National Police and the National Guard and stated that there was strong evidence that the Treasury Police also ran a death squad. The United States was also informed by its own ambassador that exiles in Miami were funding death squads, but once again took no action.[42] The United Nations Truth Commission report states:

> It must be pointed out that the United States tolerated, and apparently paid little official heed to, the activities of Salvadoran exiles living in Miami, especially between 1979 and 1983. According to testimony received by the commission, this group of exiles directly financed and indirectly helped run certain death squads. It would be useful if other investigators with more resources and more time were to shed light on this tragic story so as to ensure that persons linked to terrorist acts in other countries are never tolerated again in the United States.[43]

D'Aubuisson: father of the death squads

The most notorious death squads were those run by Roberto D'Aubuisson. He was described in one US embassy dispatch as 'the father and leader of the death squads'; 'bloodthirsty, insane and a pathological murderer' and the 'real power in the country'.[44] Yet the United States had a long-standing relationship with him.

D'Aubuisson had studied at the School of the Americas in 1972 while he was an officer in the Salvadoran army. He went on to work as an intelligence officer for the National Guard and during that time 'assisted the US embassy, especially the military attaché, with information', according to a declassified cable from the US ambassador.[45] He was expelled from the military in 1979 for human rights abuses, including torture, illegal detention and the killing of prisoners; he went on to direct a number of death squads, using classified information from the intelligence services to identify targets. In 1980 he was arrested for plotting a coup. Documents found in the raid, which were seen by the US embassy, linked D'Aubuisson to the murder of Archbishop Romero, but he was never charged with that or any other crime.

D'Aubuisson went on to found the right-wing Arena party in 1981. He had considerable political talent. One US briefing described his popular touch:

> As a tactician, campaigner, a speaker and a stump politician he is almost unsurpassed … His main strengths [are] … his charisma, his rapport with the people and his ability to communicate. His use of common, everyday street language combined with vulgarities and his unpretentious style are extremely appealing to the working and *campesino* classes, especially compared to the more polished, intellectual approaches taken by other political leaders.[46]

'Anybody who thinks you're going to find a cable that says that Roberto D'Aubuisson murdered the archbishop is a fool'

Elliott Abrams was a State Department official during the Reagan years, who was prosecuted for lying to Congress during the Irangate scandal but was later given a high-ranking post by George W. Bush.

Abrams once told reporters: 'Anybody who thinks you're going to find a cable that says that Roberto D'Aubuisson murdered the archbishop is a fool'. In fact, declassified material held by the National Security Archive now shows there were dozens of US cables outlining evidence of D'Aubuisson's involvement, including correspondence from two US ambassadors, Robert White and Deane Hinton. Most damning is a secret memorandum written by Elliott Abrams himself in 1985, in which he writes: 'Based on two independent sources of information ... we believe it is highly likely that Roberto D'Aubuisson was an active participant in and very possibly at the head of the meeting during which Archbishop Romero's murder was planned.'

Sources: '12 years of tortured truth on El Salvador. US Declarations During War undercut by UN Commission Report', *Washington Post*, 21 March 1993; 'Documents Captured at the Time of D'Aubuisson's Arrest', Confidential Cable, from US Ambassador Robert White to Department of State, 20 June 1980, National Security Archive, EL00671; 'Assassination of Archbishop Romero', Confidential Cable from Ambassador Deane Hinton to State Department, 21 December 1981, National Security Archive, EL00731; 'Rightist Doings', Secret Cable from Ambassador Deane Hinton to State Department, 14 August 1981, National Security Archive, EL00721; 'Entry of Roberto D'Aubuisson into the US', Secret, Action Memorandum, 2 August 1985, from Elliott Abrams to Ambassador Michael Armacost, National Security Archive, EL00886.

D'Aubuisson was appointed president of El Salvador's Constituent Assembly in 1982, after his Arena party won the highest number of seats. D'Aubuisson ran a death squad in association with the Constituent Assembly's head of security, a former dentist called Dr Pedro Regalado. The US was aware of this because it was noted in a CIA report commissioned by the State Department to brief Secretary of State George Schultz.[47] According to the CIA's report, D'Aubuisson's death squad worked together with a death squad operating within the National Police. The liaison man was another Arena Constituent Assembly member, Oscar Mendez.

US ambassador Deane Hinton met D'Aubuisson at a garden party hosted by the Vice-President of ARENA in December 1981. During a conversation with Hinton, D'Aubuisson claimed that US intelligence in Miami had given him information about a list of 'communist traitors' whose names D'Aubuisson had made public as targets for elimination.[48]

Despite visa restrictions D'Aubuisson visited Washington numerous times. He was a guest of the American Legion and the right-wing American Security Council at an event in July 1980 that was attended by congressmen and several former US military officers.[49] He met presidential envoy Vernon Walters and Assistant Secretary of State Langhorne C. Motley in July 1984. Later that year he was fêted at a private dinner on Capitol Hill hosted by right-wing conservative groups. D'Aubuisson was presented with a plaque praising his 'continuing efforts for freedom in the face of communist aggression which is an inspiration to freedom-loving people everywhere'.[50] Among the hosts of the event were Gun Owners of America, the United States Defense Committee, the American Foreign Policy Council, the Young Americans Foundation and the *Washington Times*. D'Aubuisson's greatest supporter in Washington was the Republican senator Jesse Helms, who publicly defended him on numerous occasions.

The Reagan administration distanced itself from D'Aubuisson after 1984 because he was suspected of plotting to kill US ambassador Thomas Pickering. His estrangement ended when Vice-President Dan Quayle visited D'Aubuisson in El Salvador in June 1989. The following month D'Aubuisson was invited to attend the Fourth of July celebration at the US embassy. D'Aubuisson died of throat cancer on 20 February 1992.

The former US ambassador to El Salvador Robert White articulated a damning critique of the Reaganites' relationship with D'Aubuisson:

> Shortly after President Reagan took office, this administration ... began the process of rehabilitating ex-Major D'Aubuisson. No longer was he a pariah ... In a very real sense, the Reagan administration created Roberto D'Aubuisson, the political leader.
>
> Yet from the first days in office, the Reagan White House knew, beyond any reasonable doubt, that Roberto D'Aubuisson, in addition to other crimes, planned and ordered the assassination of Archbishop Oscar Arnulfo Romero ...
>
> The Reagan White House took on a great responsibility when it chose to conceal the identity of Archbishop Romero's murderer and not to use the evidence gathered by the Embassy to write a finish to the political futures of ARENA and the ambitions of Roberto D'Aubuisson.[51]

Massacres and propaganda
One of the tactics of the Salvadoran armed forces in the countryside was to terrorize the civilian population in order to erode the guerrillas' base of support. A number of horrific massacres were carried out, which were documented in the United Nations Truth Commission report. In one incident, the entire population of El Mozote village was murdered. The UN provided a harrowing account. It described how the men were tortured and executed in the morning. Then:

> ... around noon, they began taking out the women in groups, separating them from their children and machine-gunning them. Finally, they killed the children. A group of children who had been locked in the convent were machine-gunned through the windows.[52]

The State Department claimed no knowledge of massacres in El Salvador and intimated that they were guerrilla propaganda. The El Mozote deaths were particularly sensitive because the accused soldiers came from the US-trained Atlacatl battalion. Thomas O. Enders, Assistant Secretary of State for Inter-American Affairs, noted while giving evidence to Congress that reports of the massacre were 'originally put out by Radio Veneceremos, the insurgent radio'. He then read out a cable from the US embassy:

> Although it is not possible to prove or disprove the excess of violence against the civilian population of Mozote by government troops, it is certain that the guerrilla forces which established defensive positions in Mozote did nothing to remove the civilian populations from the path of the battle ...[53]

The Reagan administration's distortion of the facts in El Salvador was so glaring that Congress commissioned a report in 1993, comparing US government testimony with the findings of the UN Truth Commission. It found significant discrepancies between the two. According to the congressional report:

> The Truth Commission found that 85% of the violence was attributed to government armed forces, the related security forces, or right wing death squads. Administration testimony, however, while generally recognizing the existence of such violence, often characterized the guerrillas as the major sources of politically motivated killings.[54]

The UN report was critical of the guerrillas, particularly their practice of executing non-combatants, such as opposition mayors or 'informers'. However, according to the testimony the UN received, just 5 per cent of the accusations of serious violence were attributed to the FMLN, a very different picture to that painted by the Reagan administration.

Reagan's electoral strategy

Reagan's strategy was to send large amounts of military aid to ensure that the army defeated the insurgents, but also to encourage some semblance of democratic rule to make US involvement in El Salvador more palatable to Congress. Elections for a Constituent Assembly were held in 1982. The Left boycotted the vote; the Right in any case made it clear that it would not tolerate the Left's participation and that anyone campaigning for them would become a target for the death squads. The United States hoped that a moderate would win the elections, but to its dismay Arena, D'Aubuisson's party, won the largest number of seats. US officials rapidly negotiated a deal whereby D'Aubuisson became the head of the Constituent Assembly but did not become the provisional president of El Salvador.

To ensure a more favourable outcome in the presidential elections of 1984, the US poured money into the campaign of the Christian Democrat Napoleon Duarte. USAID, the US aid and development organization, bankrolled the electoral process, providing funds for drawing up an electoral register and printing ballot papers. The US got the desired result: Duarte won 53.6 per cent of the vote, compared with 46.4 per cent for D'Aubuisson. Before Duarte's election, Congress had become increasingly reluctant to approve military aid for El Salvador, forcing Reagan to rely on emergency drawdowns. Once Duarte became president, Congress approved every request for economic and military assistance. Under Duarte, the level of political violence subsided, mainly because the military had by now broken the back of popular resistance. Yet El Salvador remained a frightening place. The death squads

US Training of Death Squads

Throughout the 1980s, the Reagan administration insisted that the US armed forces did not have links with death squads. This declassified cable shows that as late as 1990, US military trainers were training a death squad linked to an army unit. The cable reads as follows:

'1. Secret – Entire Text

2. Reference message A indicates Colonel Elena Fuentes,* Commander of the first brigade, is permitting the use of his brigade's civil defense training program as a cover for the recruitment, training and possible dispatch of paramilitary civilian death squads ... I tasked mission elements to ascertain what was going on in the first brigade.

3. The first result was to be told that indeed there was a semi-official civil defense unit with the name 'Los Patrioticos' being trained at the first brigade. I was also told that if we wanted to know what the unit did, the embassy need only query the brigade's US military advisers since they were involved in training the group ...

4. Taken aback I asked my MILGP [military group] commander to query his first brigade [illegible word] to determine if he or any other US MILGP personnel were involved in any way with 'Los Patrioticos'.

5. I have been informed that my worst fears are realized. Such a unit trains once a week at the first brigade. MILGP trainers have participated in the last two training sessions (subjects: Zeroing and Assembly/Disassembly of Weapons). Additional info includes:

- The unit not only trains but participates in routine patrolling and augments the brigade in periods of crisis
- The majority of the participants are upper-middle and upper-class male professionals many of whom carry the M14 Brigade issue as well as personal weapons
- The unit has trained the brigade for one and a half years.

6. My MILGP Commander has given me a memorandum outlining the extent of US involvement with the civil defense force over the years, on the basis of which he recommends that we continue to assist the First Brigade train 'Los Patrioticos'. He argues that to cut off our participation would give credibility to unproven accusations, signal further withdrawal from our relationships with the ESAF [El Salvador Armed Forces] and in general be a 'slap in the face' of Elena Fuentes and the ESAF. He points out his belief that it is the presence of the US advisers that allows the monitoring of type and tone of training in all areas. He also argues that we are already 'a little pregnant with the training that has taken place' ...

7. On being informed of our trainers' involvement with this unit, I ordered the MILGP Commander to withdraw whatever support was being provided effective immediately ...'

* Francisco Elena Fuentes was the commander of the first infantry brigade of the Salvadoran army, which was notorious for human rights abuses.

Source: Secret cable from the US Ambassador William G. Walker to the US State Department, 29 October 1990, National Security Archives, EL01215

continued to act with impunity, and on average there were more than 350 political killings a year for the rest of the decade.[55]

War and peace
The hawks in the Reagan administration were determined to defeat the guerrillas militarily and would not countenance the idea of peace talks; when Assistant Secretary of State Thomas Enders – no dewy-eyed liberal – proposed talks between the rebels and the Salvadoran government, he lost his job.[56] The years of intensive military aid and training paid off by 1984, when the balance of forces turned against the guerrillas. The FMLN could no longer hold on to their territory and were forced to rely on hit-and-run actions. Although the rebels did not have the strength to take power, the military still could not defeat them. With Reagan in power there was little prospect of peace and the war dragged on for eight more years.

By 1989, both sides in El Salvador recognized that they faced a stalemate and began tentative talks. When these collapsed, the FMLN launched another 'final offensive'; the ultimate failure of this offensive convinced the rebels to take peace negotiations seriously. The two sides began talks through mediators; this marked the start of a two-year process overseen by the United Nations, and in 1992 resulted in a peace agreement. 1989 was also the year of a horrific 'last-gasp' attack by the death squads. Six Jesuit priests, their housekeeper and her daughter were brutally murdered in the Catholic University in San Salvador. The murders hardened US public sentiment against US policy in El Salvador, particularly when it was revealed that the Salvadoran military had colluded in the killings. The new administration of George W. H. Bush came under pressure from Congress to make aid to El Salvador conditional on peace talks. Although Bush came to office promising to continue Reagan's policy and initially resisted congressional pressure, slowly US policy changed towards supporting the peace talks, which were in any case already now a reality.

Garrison Honduras

Honduras was the archetypal 'banana republic'. A tiny Central American country, Honduras was ruled by an alliance of landowners and the military; foreign fruit companies enjoyed a preponderant influence. The military was a powerful autonomous force that had a veto on all governments, and between 1957 and 1981 the military ruled directly. After the Nicaraguan revolution, the Carter administration saw Honduras as an ideal ally to prevent the spread of continental revolution. It sought to strengthen the armed forces of Honduras as a bulwark against the neighbouring insurgencies, while at the same time gently pushing for a transition to a civilian regime. Honduran politicians had also been clamouring for a return to elected rule, and in 1980 a constituent assembly was elected. Despite the opposition of Reaganite hardliners Jeane Kirkpatrick and Vernon Walters, who sympathized with the Honduran Right's view that civilians could not be trusted to run the country, presidential elections were held in 1981.[57]

Ambassador Negroponte

The declassified correspondence of the US ambassador to Honduras, John Negroponte, shows he was a key player in the Contra War. He implored CIA director William Casey to give the Contras more arms and gave advice on how the US President should present the Contra War to a restive Congress. When Congress voted in 1984 to ban aid to the Contras, Negroponte met the Honduran president to urge him to continue backing the illegal Contra War.

Negroponte opposed the Contadora peace initiative, a peace plan for Central America launched by four Latin American countries in 1983, which the Reagan government eventually derailed. In one cable to Washington, Negroponte wrote, 'A negotiated outcome would be a Trojan horse not unlike the 1962 missile arrangement which facilitated consolidation of the Cuban revolution.' In another memo he objected that the Contadora peace process could lead to 'effectively shutting down our special project' – a reference to the Contra War.

Negroponte defended the Honduran military despite its abuses of human rights. One of his key allies was the Honduran armed forces chief, General Gustavo Alvarez, an extreme right-wing officer who was trained at the School of Americas and Fort Benning. Negroponte lauded Alvarez's 'commitment to constitutional government' just five months before the general was removed from his post for 'authoritarian tendencies'.

Sources: 'Contradora Process: Next Steps', Memo from John Negroponte to Department of State, CIA and NSC, May 21 1983, National Security Archive, The Negroponte File, Electronic Briefing Book, No 151; 'Ambassador's August 7 Meeting with Honduran President Suazo and Presidency Minister Carlos Flores', Cable from US Embassy Tegucigalpa to Department of State, August 8 1984, National Security Archive, The Negroponte File, Electronic Briefing Book, No 151, Part 2, 'Next Steps in US/Nicaraguan Dialogue', Cable from Ambassador John Negroponte to Department of State, May 19 1983, National Security Archive, The Negroponte File, Electronic Briefing Book, No 151. D. Schulz and D. Sundloff Schulz, *The United States, Honduras and the Crisis in Central America*, Colorado, Westview Press, 1994, p. 73; 'General Alvarez on the Democratic Process', Cable from Ambassador John Negroponte to Department of State, 13 October 1983, National Security Archive, The Negroponte File, Electronic Briefing Book, No 151.

Under Reagan, this new democracy became a militarized state. Human rights violations actually rose under civilian rule because the military became even more powerful as a result of an unprecedented influx of US military aid. Because it bordered on Nicaragua and El Salvador, Honduras was seen by the US as a vital strategic asset and the perfect place from which Nicaraguan counter-revolutionaries could launch their assault. Contra training camps were built all along the Nicaraguan border, as well as US garrisons, supply dumps and air bases. More than one thousand US troops were stationed there and large-scale joint exercises were carried out with the Honduran forces. Military aid rose twentyfold between 1980 and 1984, from US$4 million to US$78.5 million, while economic aid tripled to US$168 million.

Subsequently, the Honduran truth commission found that 184 people were 'disappeared' by the armed forces between 1980–92. Secret unmarked graves have since been found in six Honduran provinces. Government excavators also found human remains beneath El Aguacate, a military base built by the United States to train Contra forces.[58] The base had been used as a detention and torture camp.

Genocide in Guatemala

The United States shaped Guatemalan history and guided it towards the abyss of genocide in the 1980s. The US-inspired overthrow of President Arbenz in 1954 ended any hope of peaceful reform. The coup eliminated the political centre and pushed Guatemala inexorably towards political polarization and war. For the next thirty years, Guatemala was ruled by generals who came to power either through *coups-d'état* or, more commonly, through fraudulent elections. Guerrilla groups emerged in the 1960s to fight for social change. Guatemala was a favoured ally of the US in these years, receiving military training, equipment, intelligence and counter-insurgency advice. President Carter cut off military aid in 1977 and despite vigorous attempts by Reagan, Congress refused to reinstate it, ensuring that the US aid ban remained in place during one of the darkest periods of Guatemalan history, the systematic destruction of Mayan villages in 1982–83. It was not until 1985 that Congress formally approved a restoration of military assistance. For the next five years the US supported the Guatemalan counter-insurgency effort and aided the military, even though the Guatemalan armed forces continued to murder political opponents with impunity. In 1990, Congress cut military aid once again, but the CIA continued to fund human rights abusers. Peace accords were signed in 1996.

Resistance and reaction
Half the population of Guatemala were indigenous Mayans, who had suffered racial discrimination, exclusion, and poverty since the Spanish Conquest. The guerrillas were part of a broad opposition movement and had considerable support in Mayan villages. Successive governments had waged counter-insurgency campaigns in the countryside and engaged in selective repression in the cities, but the government of General Romeo Lucas García (1978–82) took the terror to new levels. Political executions by the army and state-sponsored death squads rose from 1,371 in 1979 to 3,426 in 1981. Reagan was nevertheless determined to prevent the insurgents from taking power and to avoid Guatemala becoming the next fallen domino in the region. He sought to restore relations with the repressive Lucas government. 'Given the extent of the insurgency and the strong communist support worldwide for it, the administration is disposed to support Guatemala,' said John Bushnell, acting Assistant Secretary of State, in May 1981.[59] A month later the Department of Commerce granted export licences for the sale of US$3.1 million worth of trucks and jeeps to the Guatemalan military. In secret meetings with the Guatemalans, US officials promised to send aircraft and restore training programmes.[60]

General Efraín Ríos Montt led a coup in March 1982, and under his leadership the scorched-earth policy was extended across the country. In one of the worst episodes in Guatemalan history, hundreds of villages were burnt and their inhabitants were either killed or forced to flee. The United Nations Commission for

Historical Classification later described these as 'acts of genocide'. At the height of this deadly campaign, Reagan met with Montt and declared that Montt was 'totally dedicated to democracy.'[61] Reagan tried to persuade Congress to lift the aid ban, lamenting that Ríos Montt 'had been given a bum rap' on human rights. The Reagan administration sent economic aid and approved US$6 million of military helicopters and spare parts for Ríos Montt's government, although this was delayed for a year after two USAID workers were killed. Declassified documents now confirm that in order to get round the congressional ban, the Reagan government persuaded Israel to send military assistance to Guatemala.[62] This was arranged by Colonel Oliver North and Constantine Menges of the National Security Council. Among the items they asked Israel to supply were helicopters, rifles, machine guns, communications equipment, uniforms and training in 'psychological warfare, counterinsurgency tactics and propaganda'. The Israelis sent so many weapons that the US grew concerned about losing its own market for arms in Guatemala.

The CIA

The full extent of the CIA's role in Guatemala is yet to be revealed. The CIA remained active in the country throughout the period of the military aid ban. The few CIA documents from this period that have been declassified are heavily censored, making it impossible to get a clear picture of the CIA's actions. However, a report by the US Intelligence Oversight Board (IOB), covering the years 1984–95, gives some indication of their role.

> Several CIA assets [agents] were credibly alleged to have ordered, planned or participated in serious human rights violations such as assassinations, extrajudicial execution, torture or kidnapping while they were assets – and that the CIA's Director of Operations headquarters was well aware at the time of the allegations.[63]

The CIA continued to give funds to assets after the second ban on military aid in 1990. Among their paid assets was Colonel Julio Roberto Alpírez, who was present during the torture of at least one victim and who helped to cover up the murder of US citizen Michael Devine.[64]

Death toll

The toll of death and suffering of the 34 year counter-insurgency war (1962–96) makes sombre reading. The Commission for Historical Clarification estimated that 200,000 people were killed or disappeared and that up to one million people were forced to leave their homes.[65] Massacres were carried out in 629 villages. Most of the victims were Mayan indigenous peoples; half of the massacres included collective killings of women and children.[66] The Commission found that state forces (the army, police, intelligence services, and Civil Defence Patrols) were responsible for 93 per cent of the human rights violations committed during the war. It also criticized the United States for its role:

> The CEH [Comisión para el Esclarecimiento Histórico – Commission for Historical Clarification] recognizes that the movement of Guatemala towards polarization,

militarization and civil war was not just the result of national history. The Cold War also played an in important role. Whilst anti-communism, promoted by the United States within the framework of its foreign policy, received firm support from right-wing political parties and from various other powerful actors in Guatemala, the United States demonstrated that it was willing to provide support for strong military regimes in its strategic backyard. In the case of Guatemala, military assistance was directed towards reinforcing the national intelligence apparatus and for training the officer corps in counterinsurgency techniques, key factors which had significant bearing on human rights violations during the armed confrontation.

Anti-communism and the National Security Doctrine formed part of the anti-Soviet strategy of the United States in Latin America. In Guatemala, these were first expressed as anti-reformist, then anti-democratic policies, culminating in criminal counterinsurgency.[67]

Peace and justice

Elected government returned to Guatemala in 1986, but the military continued to murder opponents and wage war in the countryside. A human rights accord was signed by the military and the guerrillas in 1994. The terms of the accord allowed for a UN-sponsored commission to investigate human rights abuses in Guatemala. A clause inserted by the government, however, protected individuals named in the report from prosecution. As the grisly task of exhuming mass graves began, the scale of the atrocities became clear. Final peace accords were signed in May 1996. Although a small number of officers were purged and an even smaller number were prosecuted, the military has not been subject to the overhaul required to ensure that human rights will be protected in the future. Guatemala today is a country awash with weapons, a country steeped in violence and poverty, and still trying to come to terms with the horrors of the war.

Reagan's Legacy

Ronald Reagan changed history in Central America. A chance to create more just societies, to overturn decades of military abuse, extreme poverty and injustice was missed. In Guatemala and El Salvador, a generation of reformers and revolutionaries were murdered: trade unionists, students, professionals, peasants and clergy. The insurgencies in those countries, though flawed, were not small extremist sects but forces that won widespread support in countries where peaceful opposition was almost impossible. The revolution in Nicaragua, which was more pluralistic than Cuba, was forced onto a war footing. Its social reforms were blighted by the cost of the war and economic embargo. Today Central America remains poor, unequal and haunted by memories of the horror. US politicians, meanwhile, debate how to stop the flow of migrants seeking a better life in the North.

7

The End of the Cold War
1989-2001

The collapse of the Soviet Union in December 1991 left the United States as the world's undisputed military superpower. Ideologically the US was unassailable, since the failure of communism appeared to vindicate those who promoted capitalism and free enterprise. The fall of dictatorships across the Eastern bloc underlined the supremacy of the democratic system. Yet governments also appeared weaker in the face of growing corporate power and rapidly advancing communications, which allowed global stock markets to bring an economy to the brink of collapse. This was the era of the mega-transnational in which corporate mergers created ever-larger giants. Paradoxically, just as the US appeared to be at the peak of its power, it faced growing economic competition from a united Europe and from Japan and the Asian economies. The free trade agenda promoted vigorously by the US government in the 1990s reflected the needs of US corporations. In order to compete with the low-priced Asian goods flooding the US market, US companies sought cheap labour abroad to make their products, which were then sent back to the United States tariff-free; this search ignited the boom of the maquiladora – assembly-production plants – in Mexico and Central America.

All Latin American governments were democratic by the mid-1990s. Dictator-ships had fallen across South America – Argentina (1982); Brazil (1985–89) and Chile (1990) – as people's protests tarnished the military's veneer of invincibility and the debt crisis of the 1980s shattered their reputation for efficient economic management. Peace agreements were signed in Central America. Although the collapse of the USSR may have demoralized the Salvadoran and Guatemalan guerrillas, Soviet aid to the insurgencies was never significant and did not determine the outcome of the civil wars. Those wars ended because the Central American militaries, aided by the Reagan administration, emasculated the popular movements and fought the guerrillas to a stalemate. Similarly, although the Sandinistas were disorientated by the end of the Cold War, the key factors in their electoral defeat were war and hardship, for which the United States was largely responsible. The Sandinistas' defeat added to the ideological turmoil of the Latin American Left. Sweeping ambitions of revolutionary transformation in South America had already been snuffed out by the grim repression of the military regimes. Torture and disappearances were etched onto the memories of a generation. New 'social movements' organized around single-issue demands emerged, but the Left's horizons had been drastically reduced. The debt crisis, hyperinflation and unemployment of the 1980s had further weakened the trade unions and grassroots organizations, while the failure of populist presidents to tame inflation added to the sense that there was no alternative to free market capitalism. The centrist governments of the 1990s all implemented the same US-promoted neoliberal policies of privatization, deregulation and the opening of markets to foreign competition.

As vice-president, George Bush senior had had a similar outlook to Ronald Reagan and had supported his belligerent policies. But a new approach was called for in the post-Cold War era. The Bush administration, after some foot-dragging, supported peace deals in Central America – not because the external (Soviet) threat had disappeared, but because revolutionary upheaval in El Salvador and Guatemala was no longer likely. This new enlightenment was not extended to Cuba, where policy hardened, emboldened by the faith that without its Russian benefactor the Cuban revolution would soon implode. Economic matters became a priority under the Bush administration, particularly the promotion of free trade and the opening up of Latin American markets. A pragmatic resolution of the debt crisis, in which private creditors wrote off debt and new bonds were issued, was one of the administration's first acts. International financial institutions such as the IMF and World Bank, which had dispensed loans in Latin America during the debt crisis, grew more and more influential. And new topics appeared on the agenda, notably drugs trafficking, the environment and migration. The amount of cocaine entering the United States rose steadily in the 1980s, and powerful drugs cartels emerged in Colombia. But the drugs trade was also used by the US, as a pretext to intervene against insurgencies in Peru and Colombia and to build up a new military presence in Latin America, now that the threat of communism was no longer plausible. Narco-trafficking remained the primary pretext for military intervention until the 'war on terror' was launched by George W. Bush a decade later. On the whole, though, the threat from the Left had receded across the continent and docile pro-market governments were in power. Latin America ceased to be a priority for the United States; instead the Middle East and the former Soviet Union dominated foreign policy. The single major intervention in Latin America during George Bush's presidency took place in Panama.

The Invasion of Panama

The invasion of Panama was the largest US military operation since Vietnam and was the twentieth time US troops had been sent there. Twenty-six thousand troops were involved in the attack that began just after midnight on 20 December 1989. The invasion was a violation of international law and was condemned by the OAS, but many Panamanians welcomed the troops which were removing a hated dictator from office. Manuel Antonio Noriega had been a longstanding ally of the United States and the CIA's highest-ranking paid asset in Latin America. The United States had not only tolerated Noriega, whose crimes included international drugs trafficking and gunrunning, as well as internal repression, but awarded him honours and enlisted his help in foreign policy operations, including the illegal Contra War against Nicaragua.

Noriega, the illegitimate son of a domestic servant, had grown up in poverty in the care of his godmother. As a teenager he studied at the Instituto Nacional, a Panamanian high school, where he got involved in left-wing politics. Noriega went on the US payroll at an early stage of his career. US intelligence paid him twenty-five dollars a month to report on his fellow students, according to his biographer Luis Murillo.[1] Noriega won a scholarship to a military academy and on graduating in 1962 joined the Panamanian military. He rose rapidly through the ranks and was recruited as a paid informant of the CIA. He took three courses at the School of the Americas, in military intelligence and jungle operations. In 1968 a nationalist military officer, Omar Torrijos seized power. A year later a group of officers tried to oust Torrijos in a counter-coup. Noriega remained loyal to Torrijos, a move that made his career. When the conspirators were defeated, Noriega was appointed head of military intelligence, which made him an extremely valuable asset to the CIA.

Under Torrijos, Panama became a major money laundering centre. Strict banking secrecy was imposed and banking taxes were abolished, making Panama the perfect location for tax dodgers and other criminals. Noriega began to launder money for the Medellín cartel, the largest drugs cartel in Colombia, in the late 1970s. He later allowed the cartel to build cocaine processing plants in Panama. Noriega opened multi-million-dollar bank accounts, some of which he used to bribe Panamanian politicians, turning the country into a 'narcokleptocracy'. Torrijos died in an air crash in 1981, after which Noriega became the real power in Panama, ruling first through puppet presidents and later directly.

Despite clear evidence of his involvement in narco-trafficking, he remained an informant of the CIA and, ironically, the US Drug Enforcement Administration (DEA). Noriega often gave the DEA tip-offs about drugs traffickers who were competing with him, which enabled him to consolidate his control over the Panamanian trade. Noriega also shared DEA information with traffickers with whom he was friendly, according to a US senate investigation.[2] For example, he advised other drugs smugglers whether their planes were on a DEA watch list. The DEA regarded Noriega as a valuable collaborator and rewarded him with numerous letters of commendation. DEA Administrator Jack Law wrote to Noriega on 27 May 1987, just a year before he was indicted by the US Justice Department, stating: 'DEA has long welcomed our close association and we stand ready to proceed jointly against international drugs traffickers whenever the opportunity arises.'[3]

As well as drugs trafficking and money laundering, Noriega was involved in gunrunning, buying arms from Cuba and selling them on to Salvadoran rebels. He also sold visas, passports and residence permits to Chinese, Libyan and Cuban migrants

Noriega, Drugs and the United States

A Senate inquiry headed by John Kerry found that the United States had known about Noriega's drugs trafficking and money laundering since the late 1970s, but had done nothing because he was a useful intelligence asset and latterly because the Reagan administration required his cooperation in the war on the Sandinistas. Below are extracts of the Senate's findings.

'The saga of Panama's General Manuel Antonio Noriega represents one of the most serious foreign policy failures for the United States ... It is clear that each US government agency which had a relationship with Noriega turned a blind eye to his corruption and drug dealing, even as he was emerging as a key player on behalf of the Medellín Cartel.'

'By the time General Noriega was indicted [in 1988] the United States government had received substantial information about criminal involvement of top Panamanian officials for nearly twenty years and done little to respond.'

- The US Drug Enforcement Administration received the first reports linking Noriega and narcotics before 1978.
- By early 1980s, the CIA knew Panamanian officials were laundering money for drugs traffickers.
- Between 1970 and 1987, Noriega's name appeared in 80 Drug Enforcement Administration files.
- An investigation by the Senate SubCommittee for the Western Hemisphere in 1986 provided ample evidence of drugs trafficking.

Dr Norman Bailey, a National Security Council staff member from 1981 to 1983 also gave evidence:

'Bailey stated that at the time he was at the NSC there already existed "available to any authorized official of the US government ... a plethora of human intelligence, electronic intercepts and satellite and overflight photography that taken together constituted not a 'smoking gun' but rather a twenty-one cannon barrage of evidence" of Noriega's involvement in criminal activity and drugs ...

Clear and incontrovertible evidence was, at best, ignored and at worst, hidden and denied by many different agencies and departments of the Government of the United States in such a way as to provide cover and protection for [Noriega's] activities while, at the same time, assuring that they did the maximum damage to those very interests that the officials were sworn to uphold.'

→

→ *The Former US Ambassador to Costa Rica, Francis J. McNeil, gave evidence to the Kerry committee:*

'McNeil characterized Noriega's relationship with American intelligence agencies as too "cozy", leading our intelligence agencies to depend on him and Panamanian intelligence for handouts and treating Noriega as an allied service. McNeil stated that as a consequence the US took a 'see no evil approach' to Noriega.'

Noriega's role in Reagan's Contra War

- Noriega met Colonel Oliver North in June 1985. He agreed to train Contra troops and give them free movement in and out of Panama
- Noriega also gave US$100,000 to the Contra's southern front.
- Noriega met CIA Director William Casey on November 1 1985 to discuss Nicaragua and other matters. Casey did not raise the issue of drugs trafficking.
- Noriega met National Security Council director, Admiral John Poindextor, on 17 December 1985. Drugs trafficking was not discussed.
- Noriega met Oliver North, with Poindextor's approval, in London in September 1986, to draw up a list of targets for sabotage in Nicaragua.

'Noriega recognized that so long as he helped the United States with its highest diplomatic priorities ... the United States would have to overlook activities of his that affected lesser US priorities. In the mid 1980s, this meant that our government did nothing regarding Noriega's drug business and substantial criminal involvement because the first priority was the Contra war.'

Source: 'Drugs, Law Enforcement and Foreign Policy: A Report Prepared by the Subcommittee on Terrorism, Narcotics and International Operations of the Committee on Foreign Relations', United States Senate, December 1988 (Kerry Report)

trying to enter the United States and sold high-tech equipment to the Soviet Union. Even though these activities ran counter to the interests of the United States, Noriega remained a trusted confidant of the intelligence services. George Bush senior himself had numerous personal conversations with Noriega. They first met at a lunch in the Panamanian embassy in Washington in December 1976 when Bush was Director of the CIA. Soon after taking the job as CIA chief, Bush was confronted with the 'singing sergeants' scandal – Noriega had bribed US officers serving in Panama to give away US state secrets. To avoid a fuss, the Pentagon gave the men an honourable discharge. Bush took no action, made no complaint and maintained the CIA's links with Noriega. The dictator remained a valuable contact when Bush was vice-president. Another of Noriega's associates was CIA Director William Casey. Noriega visited the CIA headquarters in Langley and Casey's home on numerous occasions.[4]

Why Did the US Turn Against Noriega?

Noriega's help in the Contra War became less vital to the Reagan administration once Congress approved aid for the Contras in 1986. The Panamanian dictator became a growing embarrassment for the White House in 1986, when a Senate inquiry and high-profile articles in the *New York Times* revealed details of his drugs trafficking, gunrunning, spying and money laundering. Noriega's reputation sank further when he ordered his henchmen to attack the US embassy and consulate, after the US Congress passed a resolution backing a return to civilian rule. Reagan responded by suspending aid and eliminating Panama's sugar quota. US officials held secret talks with the Panamanians in 1987 to discuss the dictator's resignation but Noriega, like Somoza a decade earlier, refused to go. Noriega was indicted for drugs trafficking by the US Justice Department in February 1988. A month later the US backed a coup against him, but the plot was bungled and Noriega survived.

Another ongoing concern of the United States was the security of the Panama Canal. Under an agreement signed by presidents Carter and Torrijos in 1977, the United States agreed to withdraw from the Canal Zone by the end of 1999 and gradually cede control to Panama in the intervening years. Ten per cent of US trade passed through the canal and the US wanted to ensure it did not fall into anti-American hands. The US became increasingly concerned that Noriega had failed to appoint a new administrator for the joint US–Panama canal commission.[5] There were also domestic reasons for Bush to take action. Just months after Bush took office, Noriega defied US opinion by declaring the results of Panama's presidential elections void. Bush had already been widely criticized for his tepid backing for the Tiananmen Square students and anti-communist protesters in the Eastern Bloc. Countering the 'wimp factor' also played a part in Bush's calculations.

The White House gave four reasons for the invasion of Panama, codenamed Operation Just Cause: protecting American lives, enforcing the Panama Canal Treaties, restoring the democratic process, and bringing General Noriega to justice.

Operation Just Cause

Operation Just Cause relied on overwhelming force. Thousands of special forces and paratroopers joined the 13,000 troops already stationed in US bases in Panama. US forces quickly overpowered the Panamanian Defence Force, which was subdued within hours. Twenty-three US soldiers and three US civilians were killed; the number of Panamanian casualties has still not been verified. According to the Pentagon, 314 troops and 202 civilians were killed. The Panamanian Commission for the Defense of Human Rights in Central America (CODEHUCA) estimated the number of civilian casualties at 2,000, and the Independent Commission of Inquiry (a group of US human rights organizations and individuals including former US Attorney General Ramsey Clark) said estimated civilian deaths ranged from 1,000 to 4,000. One of the reasons for the high number of civilian casualties was the shelling by US forces of a slum area situated next to the headquarters of the Panamian Defence Force. No warning was given to the residents of El Chorrillo, which was home to 30,000 people. Shells set the rickety wooden houses alight and much of the shantytown was levelled. The fire also gutted several residential apartment blocks.

General Noriega took refuge in the Vatican embassy in Panama City. He was arrested by US forces a week later. Without any extradition proceedings, he was taken to Florida and tried by a district court. A jury found him guilty of eight counts of drug-related offences and he was sentenced to forty years' imprisonment, although this sentence was later reduced to thirty years.

The Clinton Years

When he took office in 1993, Bill Clinton may have had the glamour of John F. Kennedy, but unlike his Democratic predecessor he had no grand reformist plan for Latin America to match Kennedy's Alliance for Progress, Carter's human rights crusade, or Roosevelt's Good Neighbor policy. An opportunity to recast US relations with Latin America after the Cold War was lost. Latin America was a very low priority; instead the Middle East, the Balkans and domestic affairs took up the President's time. Clinton was the first president since Calvin Coolidge not to make a tour of Latin America in his first term of office, and no Latin America specialists were appointed to the higher echelons of his foreign policy team.[6] In opposition, Clinton had advocated an idealist foreign policy and deplored Bush's pragmatism, but once in office he adopted Bush's policies. For example, in opposition he criticized Bush for advocating a North American Free Trade Agreement (NAFTA), but once elected Clinton approved NAFTA, and the free trade agreement between Mexico, the US and Canada came into force on 1 January 1994. With florid rhetoric at a Pan-American summit in Miami, Clinton then promised to make the whole of the Americas a free trade area. But although this aim won the backing of the Republican leadership, many Democrats opposed it on environmental and labour-standards grounds. Clinton found it impossible to win congressional approval to fast-track trade negotiations with Chile, let alone other Latin American countries, and the much-vaunted free trade bloc came to nothing.

The only significant action towards the region that had a Clintonesque stamp was the intervention in Haiti in 1994, in which the marines reinstalled the ousted elected president Jean-Bertrand Aristide. But on the whole, Clinton allowed hardliners in Congress and the national security establishment to set the agenda for Latin America. As part of a cynical (but successful) manoeuvre to win votes in Florida, Clinton pursued an even more hardline Cuba policy than his predecessor, backing both the Torricelli Act (1992) and the Helms-Burton Act (1996), measures that strengthened the economic embargo and which were both condemned internationally. Similarly, Clinton allowed hawks to set the agenda on drugs policy and Colombia. The US military and national security apparatus were largely responsible for drawing up Plan Colombia, nominally an anti-drugs initiative, but one with an obvious counter-insurgency aim. Throughout the Clinton years,

Congress banned US military aid for counter-insurgency purposes in Colombia because the Colombian military had such a poor human rights record and because the US did not want to get sucked into a Vietnam-style conflict. As more and more military aid was poured into Colombia, making the country the world's third-largest recipient of US military aid, officials used tortuous terminology to assure Congress that the weapons would not be used against Colombian guerrillas. (This pretence was dropped after 9/11, when George W. Bush passed a measure allowing US military aid in Colombia to be used against 'terrorists'.)

With the exception of Colombia, Latin America was generally believed to be quiescent during the 1990s. US-friendly, pro-market governments held power. But the revolt by the Zapatistas, timed to coincide with the inauguration of the Free Trade Area of the Americas on 1 January 1994, presaged events to come. The Zapatistas, poor indigenous farmers from southern Mexico, spoke out against monolithic, monocultural global capitalism, and called for a 'world in which there is space for many worlds'. Little by little, protests against poverty and neoliberalism sprouted in different parts of the Americas. Bolivian protestors successfully reversed water privatization and the Brazilian landless occupied hundreds of acres of land. By the next decade, social movements had grown so powerful that pro-market presidents were forced to flee ignominiously from Bolivia, Ecuador and Argentina. Outspoken, left-wing and nationalist presidents were elected across the region.

The Zapatistas: Let Us Introduce Ourselves

Let us introduce ourselves.
We are the Zapatista National Liberation Army.
For ten years, we lived in these mountains, preparing to fight a war.
In these mountains, we built an army.
Below, in the cities and plantations, we did not exist.
Our lives were worth less than those of machines or animals.
We were like stones, like weeds in the road.

We were silenced.
We were faceless.
We were nameless.
We had no future.
We did not exist.

For the powers that be, known internationally by the term 'neoliberalism',
we did not count,
we did not produce,
we did not buy,
we did not sell.

→

→ We were a cipher in the accounts of big capital.

Then we went to the mountains to find ourselves and see if we could ease the pain of being forgotten like stones and weeds ...

This is who we are.
The Zapatista National Liberation Army.
The voice that arms itself to be heard.
The face that hides itself to be seen.
The name that hides itself to be named.
The red star who calls out to humanity and the world
to be heard, to be seen, to be named.
The tomorrow to be harvested in the past.

Behind our black mask,
Behind our armed voice,
Behind our unnameable name,
Behind us, who you see,
Behind us, we are you.

Behind we are the same simple and ordinary men and women,
who are repeated in all races,
painted in all colors
speak in all languages
and live in all places.
The same forgotten men and women.

The same excluded,
the same untolerated,
The same persecuted.
We are you ...

From the mountains of the Mexican Southeast.
The Indigenous Clandestine Revolutionary Committee.
General Command of the Zapatista National Liberation Army.
Planet Earth.

Source: Opening Remarks at the First Intercontinental Encuentro for Humanity and Against Neoliberalism, 27 July 1996, Chiapas, Mexico. Reprinted from *Our Word Is Our Weapon: Selected Writings of Subcomandante Insurgente Marcos*, edited by J. Ponce de León, London, Serpent's Tail, 2001, p. 101.

The Zapatistas

Thousands of indigenous men and women marched into San Cristóbal de las Casas, the capital of the southeastern Mexican state of Chiapas, on 1 January 1994. The Zapatistas, claiming to speak for all the world's excluded, occupied San Cristóbal and six other towns. The Mexican military cracked down, bombing villages and killing more than two hundred people in subsequent days.[7] But the Zapatistas had captured the imagination of the Mexican public, who protested against the repression. Within twelve days the Mexican government had agreed to a ceasefire. The army remained in Chiapas, however, waging low-intensity warfare, including surveillance flights and harassment at checkpoints. The military launched two major offensives, in 1995 and 1999, dispatching thousands of troops to try to dismantle the autonomous communities, the self-governing villages and communities that supported the Zapatistas. Throughout this period the Zapatistas remained armed but did not carry out offensive actions, such as the bombings and sabotage favoured by other Latin American guerrilla groups. The Mexican military's campaign showed no such restraint and was supplemented by paramilitary attacks on peasants in the Chiapas region. Acting with the tacit approval of the local police, the paramilitaries were responsible for dozens of kidnappings and murders, and over 4,000 people fled their homes.[8]

The Zapatistas are a novel guerrilla group. They do not aim to take power. They are armed but rarely use their weapons. They have devoted their energy to political acts of dialogue and consciousness-raising, carried out with a light-footedness and wit that is largely attributable to their enigmatic leader, Sub-comandante Marcos. A former university professor, the pipe-smoking and balaclava-clad Marcos won a worldwide audience by publishing his communiqués, stories and poems on the Internet, despite being holed up in a remote jungle community with few connections to the outside world. The Zapatistas have sought to bring together popular movements from Mexico and abroad. Six thousand Mexicans attended a National Democratic Convention in Chiapas in 1994 and 3,000 international activists attended an 'intergalactic' meeting 'for Humanity and against Neoliberalism' two years later. When the Zapatistas held a dialogue with the Mexican government in 1996 they invited several hundred experts, including academics and indigenous leaders, to put forward their views. The result was a bill of rights for Mexico's indigenous people, known as the San Andrés Accords. The Zedillo government (1994–2000) later rejected the Accords, and a much-watered-down version was finally approved by President Vicente Fox in 2001. The Zapatistas have marched to Mexico City twice (in 1997 and 2001), each time receiving a tumultuous welcome from ecstatic crowds. The Fox government (2000–06) dismantled several military bases around Chiapas and freed many Zapatista prisoners, but paramilitary actions against the communities continue.

The United States and the Zapatistas

Of all the counter-insurgency campaigns in Latin America, one might have expected the United States to have been most involved in the one just over its border. But the Mexicans have always been very reluctant to permit a US military presence in their country; as the historians Jorge Domínguez and Rafael Fernández de Castro point out, 'For much of the twentieth century, there has been only one source of credible threat to Mexico's international security: the United States.'[9] Since the 1911 revolution, the Mexicans have tried to preserve their independence and neutrality by buying military equipment from a wide range of countries and by refusing to accept large amounts of US military aid, training and advice. This changed in the 1990s. Mexico began to accept more US aid and take part in joint operations, but the level of military collaboration has never been as great as the US would like.

US military aid for Mexico in the 1990s was officially earmarked for combating drugs trafficking, but a report by the US Congress General Accounting Office found that some of this US military equipment was diverted to combat the Zapatistas.[10] The level of US military aid and sales rose sharply after the Zapatista uprising in 1994. Mexico bought 28 armed personnel carriers and 73 military aircraft from the US in 1994–95, on top of 60 UH-60 helicopters it had purchased from the US in 1992.[11] US military training assistance (IMET) rose from less than half a million dollars in 1995 to US$9 million in 1998, and the numbers of Mexican officers being trained in the US rose to 757 by 1997, a historic high. The US offered still more assistance to its southern neighbour. When a new guerrilla force, the Popular Revolutionary Army (EPR), emerged in 1996 in the Mexican states of Guerrero and Oaxaca, the US ambassador, James Jones, offered the Mexicans 'whatever they need' to combat the 'terrorists'. Confident that they could contain the insurgents themselves, the Mexicans declined the offer.

The Zapatistas accused the US government of aiding the counter-insurgency war in Chiapas. In his 'Letter to the American People' (1995), Marcos wrote:

> By providing war material support – military advisors, undercover actions, electronic espionage, financing, diplomatic support, CIA activities – the US government has begun to get involved in the Mexican government's dirty war against the Zapatista population. Little by little, it is getting involved in an unequal war ...[12]

Anecdotal evidence suggests some US presence in Chiapas, but the documents declassified so far do not show that the US security services have played a major role. Instead US agents kept a close eye on how the Mexicans were dealing with the conflict. A secret briefing paper by the US Defense Intelligence Agency written just five days after the uprising assesses the risks:

> While the insurgents are not strong enough to face the Mexican army, neither is the army capable of eradicating the rebels in hiding ... A stand-off with recurring violence could frighten foreign investors and embarrass the government, affecting the presidential elections in August.[13]

The intelligence community was aware that the Mexican authorities had detected 'subversive activity' in Chiapas in 1992, two years before the revolt, so were not taken completely unaware by the rising. Some of the documents discuss how to encourage the Mexican military to cooperate more with the US. A report written by a political officer in the US embassy in 1995 outlines the issues:

> We will need to deal with the traditional Mexican policy of non-intervention which makes the foreign ministry and military establishment alike opposed at this time to any form of joint hemispheric defense force … We must recognize that, on these issues, the Mexican military remains an extremely conservative institution which looks skeptically on issues of international cooperation. However, we remain optimistic of the possibilities of success in persuading our Mexican (and civilian) counterparts of the wisdom of closer contacts with the US bilaterally and other hemispheric partners in multinational fora.[14]

The threat posed by the Zapatistas was in any case primarily political and not military. And the political and economic alliance between the Mexican and US governments during these years could not have been stronger: the NAFTA free trade treaty was signed in 1994, and the US provided a US$20 billion rescue package when the Mexican peso collapsed a year later. The Clinton administration was also notably weak on condemning human rights abuses in Chiapas. The consequence of this increased political, economic and military cooperation was that Mexico's long-cherished nationalist strategy of neutrality was eroded.

The Invasion of Haiti

The United States has a long history of intervention in Haiti, including the longest occupation by US marines of a Caribbean or Latin American country (1915–34). In the years after the Second World War, stability was maintained by the brutal anti-communist dictator François ('Papa Doc') Duvalier who was backed by presidents Johnson and Nixon. Papa Doc, a US-educated doctor, used black nationalism and voodoo to court the impoverished black population. His enemies were suppressed by his sinister secret police, the Tonton Macoutes, who were evoked vividly in Graham Greene's 1965 novel *The Comedians*. Papa Doc bequeathed power to his nineteen-year-old playboy son, Jean-Claude Duvalier ('Baby Doc'), in 1971. Baby Doc's dictatorship was supported by presidents Ford and Reagan. When domestic opposition to Baby Doc's regime began to grow in the mid-1980s and his corruption, brutality and involvement in drugs trafficking became embarrassingly overt, the Reagan administration withdrew support and urged him to abdicate. In 1986, amid political turmoil Papa Doc was airlifted out of the country on a US cargo plane. For the next four years the country was ruled by a series of military-backed presidents until 1990, when a left-wing priest, Jean-Bertrand Aristide, was elected president with over 70 per cent of the vote.

Aristide espoused liberation theology, the faith that the Church should be on the side of the poor. He was a critic of Haiti's military-backed elite and its supporters in

Washington. When he took office, tensions in the country were high, and he failed to stop his supporters carrying out revenge attacks on collaborators of the fallen dictatorship. He was overthrown in a coup led by General Raoul Cédras in September 1991, just nine months after his election. The Bush administration, which had little sympathy for Aristide's radicalism, nevertheless granted him asylum and made half-hearted efforts to restore democracy, imposing a trade embargo and freezing Haitian state assets in the US. But the most pressing problem was the thousands of Haitians fleeing the island in boats. Bush ordered the US Coast Guard to intercept the refugees and repatriate them to Haiti. This treatment of impoverished black Haitians contrasted with US policy towards Cuban refugees, who were automatically given political asylum if found at sea. Bush was accused of racism and double standards. Among his sternest critics was Bill Clinton, who accused Bush of playing 'racial politics' and said, 'I wouldn't be shipping those poor people back.'[15]

Clinton, as in so many other policy areas, performed a *volte face* on taking office. He made it even harder for Haitian refugees to gain entry to the US, and a naval blockade was imposed around Haiti to try to prevent any more poor and desperate Haitians from leaving. When this failed, Haitians were detained at the US naval base in Guantánamo Bay, Cuba. In Haiti, Clinton sought to negotiate a peaceful transfer of power and encouraged the UN to pass a motion calling for the return of Aristide. The US sent a warship to try to pressure the Haitian military to abide by the UN ruling, but the regime sent armed thugs to the docks and the White House ordered the ship to withdraw, in a humiliating climb-down. At home, Clinton was under pressure from the left wing of his Democratic Party, from the Congressional Black Caucus, and from human rights groups and Aristide's own well-organized supporters in Washington, who compared the policy of repatriating Haitians with the returning of Jews to Nazi Germany.[16] They reminded Clinton of his campaign promise to restore democracy to Haiti. However, Clinton was also aware that there was little public support for an invasion, particularly after the Somalia debacle. He turned again to the UN, which imposed a trade embargo in May 1994. Over the summer, the screws were tightened on Haiti; flights from the US to the island were banned, travel visas were outlawed and the assets of Haitian nationals in the US were frozen. Whilst planning for an invasion, Clinton sent a last-minute delegation – comprising Jimmy Carter, Colin Powell and Senator Sam Nunn – to negotiate with General Cédras. The mission persuaded the general to step down. So when twenty thousand US troops landed in Haiti on 19 September 1994, they met with no resistance. Within a month Aristide was reinstated as president.

Operation Restore Democracy was a clear short-term success, but Clinton was nevertheless accused of vacillating and showing indecision in the run-up to the invasion. He had been tied by a campaign promise to restore democracy, but was reluctant to get bogged down in a military adventure with ill-defined aims – something that had proved so disastrous in Somalia. Clinton was also hampered by a national security apparatus that did not support his aims in Haiti. After the fall of Baby Doc, the CIA had funded the pro-authoritarian organizations that sought to prevent Aristide gaining power, according to leaked intelligence and congressional sources.[17] The CIA reportedly funded the Front for the Advancement and Progress of Haiti (FRAPH) a paramilitary death squad, and the army's intelligence gathering organization, National Security Intelligence (SIN). Moreover, individuals paid by the CIA helped to organize the 1991 coup against Aristide, according to the *New York Times* and other newspapers. The chairman of the US Senate Intelligence Committee rejected these allegations in 1993, saying the CIA did not conspire against Aristide or try to discredit him.[18] The full facts about CIA activities will not be known until the documentation is declassified, but the CIA's antipathy to Aristide was well known. The CIA's chief analyst for Latin American affairs, Brian Latell, briefed Congress in 1993 that Aristide had psychological problems. A year earlier, Latell had praised Haiti's dictator, Raoul Cédras, as one of 'the most promising group of Haitian leaders to emerge since the Duvalier family dictatorship was overthrown'.[19]

Cuba

Cuba policy under Clinton was subordinated to domestic concerns, so while the President personally may have been in favour of taking a more nuanced approach, his administration ended up passing the most hardline piece of anti-Cuban legislation for decades – the internationally condemned Helms-Burton Act. Even before he became president, Clinton demonstrated that Cuba policy would be sacrificed to short-term electoral considerations. The Cuban-American vote is concentrated in two key states, Florida and New Jersey. Robert Torrecelli, a Democrat congressman for New Jersey, introduced the Cuba Democracy Bill just before the 1992 election. The law tightened the embargo by banning subsidiaries of US companies from trading with Cuba. Clinton supported the bill in order to outflank the Republicans from the right.

The balseros crisis
On taking office, Clinton faced an immigration crisis. Tens of thousands of Cubans were fleeing the island on rickety homemade rafts to escape the economic crisis that followed the collapse of the Soviet Union. For forty years US policy had been to grant asylum to Cubans found at sea. Faced with 30,000 *balseros* or 'raft people' approaching US shores, this policy was hastily changed. The US began to intercept the refugees at sea and send them back to Cuba. In a historic move, the Clinton administration directly negotiated an immigration deal with Cuba in September 1994. The US agreed to take 20,000 Cubans a year, while the Cuban government agreed to try to prevent people leaving the island illegally. (Cubans are still granted entry if they make it to US shores, which has resulted in distressing scenes of the US Coast Guard firing water-hoses at incoming vessels to prevent them from landing.)

In the early days of the Clinton administration there were signs that Cuba policy might become more flexible. The Torrecelli Law (1992) had two tracks: one tightened the embargo, but a second sought to strengthen links with Cuban civil society by making travel and communication easier. This 'people to people' approach – the exercise of so-called 'soft-power' – was seen as an alternative way of undermining Castro's one-party rule. Clinton announced a series of measures in 1995 including the opening of news bureaux in Cuba; the expansion of cultural exchanges and US non-governmental activities in Cuba; and a relaxation of travel restrictions. Numerous delegations of academics, religious leaders, business executives and politicians visited Cuba in the early Clinton years. Cuba had started to open its economy to foreign investment and many US companies were keen to investigate the potential opportunities, should the US embargo be lifted. Between 1994 and 1996, representatives of at least 174 US companies travelled to Cuba, including executives from AT&T, First Boston Bank, Gillette, Johnson & Johnson, Merck, Marriott and Reebok.[20]

The Helms-Burton Act

Hopes of a thaw in US–Cuban relations were dashed by two events. First, in 1994 the Republicans won a majority in Congress. Far from relaxing the embargo, the Republicans wanted to tighten the noose and introduced the hardline Helms-Burton Act, named after the two congressmen who sponsored it – Jesse Helms and Dan Burton. At first it appeared that Clinton might resist Republican pressure to approve Helms-Burton, but the shooting down of a US plane by the Cuban air force in February 1996 made that politically impossible. For two years, Brothers to the Rescue, a group of right-wing Cuban-Americans, had been flying planes over the waters separating Florida and Cuba searching for *balseros* fleeing the island. The group had also air-dropped anti-Castro leaflets in Cuba. After a number of warnings that they were violating Cuban airspace, the Cubans shot down a plane, killing four Cuban-Americans, three of whom were US citizens. Less than a month later, in March 1996, Clinton signed the Cuban Liberty and Democratic Solidarity (Libertad) Act, as the Helms-Burton Act was formally known, declaring 'We will not tolerate attacks on United States citizens.' Both the Torrecelli and the Helms-Burton Acts were passed in an election year.

The Helms-Burton Act tightened the embargo in a number of ways, but the most controversial clauses were those that targeted foreign companies. One clause made it possible to sue, in US courts, foreign companies that traded in former US assets that had been expropriated after the 1959 revolution. This clause potentially violated international law and prompted the European Union to make a complaint to the WTO. A compromise was reached in which the clause (known as Title 3) would become law but the president would waive its application every six months. Another highly controversial measure was Title 4, which stated that any foreign individual trafficking in expropriated property would be denied a visa to the United States. Among the other measures in Helms-Burton were US opposition to Cuba's membership of international financial institutions, restrictions on the movements of Cuban diplomats in the US, increased anti-Castro US television and radio broadcasts to Cuba, and a clause preventing the US government from recognizing a transitional government that included either Fidel Castro or his brother Raúl.

Plan Colombia

Colombia is a divided country. Like all Latin American countries, a small elite owns most of the wealth. Unlike many of its neighbours, Colombia has been a democracy for most of the twentieth century, but a closed oligarchic political system and a ruthless military have been used to ensure that the privileges of the elite were never threatened. During the 1940s a reformist politician, Jorge Eliécer Gaitán, challenged the wealthy landowners and urban capitalists and spoke up for the workers. An inspiring orator, he drew huge crowds of the poor onto the streets. Gaitán was shot dead by an assassin in 1948. His murder sparked off the *Bogotazo*, a wave of mass rioting in the capital, Bogotá. In the countryside, it was the start of five years of rural conflict, known simply as *La Violencia* (1948–53), in which 200,000 people died. *La Violencia* was in part a civil war between Liberals and Conservatives, and in part an uprising by peasants against landlords. These rebellions were put down by the military, and the landowning elite re-established their dominance. A chance at reform had been missed. In some areas of the country, radical liberal peasants did not lay down their arms but set up self-governing 'resistance communities'. It is from these armed peasant communities that the modern-day Revolutionary Armed Forces of Colombia (FARC) guerrillas descend.

Colombia's two main oligarchic parties, the Liberals and Conservatives, established the National Front in 1957, a pact in which they agreed that they would alternate power. Although the formal agreement ended in the 1970s, no other parties have ever formed a government. Colombia became the showcase for US foreign policy in Latin America in the 1960s. Its civilian governments contrasted with the brutal dictatorships spreading over the rest of the hemisphere. The peaceful image of Colombia was in fact a mirage; rural conflict continued and Colombia's four main guerrilla groups were founded in this period. The United States helped draw up a comprehensive counter-insurgency plan and poured US military aid and special forces into Colombia, but failed to snuff out the guerrillas.

The formation of the FARC

The FARC was formed by communists and dissident Liberals in 1966 and developed a strong base of peasant support in the south and southeast of Colombia. For many years, they were the only authority, and at times they were even welcomed by landlords who had grown tired of rural banditry. Although the FARC has links with the Communist Party, it was fundamentally a peasant army, which gave it a highly pragmatic attitude. Its philosophy was best described as nationalism blended with radical agrarianism – agrarian reform was its main concern. During the 1980s, the FARC formed a political party, Unidad Popular (UP), and stood for elections. More than three thousand UP candidates were murdered by death squads; their fate has made the FARC extremely sceptical about the prospects for peaceful political change.

The FARC and drugs
In the 1970s thousands of peasants migrated to southern Colombia in search of land. Here they found that the only crop from which they could make a living was coca. The FARC at first disapproved of coca growing but, pragmatic as ever, soon began to tax the trade in coca paste (not cocaine). Although they were not trafficking drugs, this lucrative business enriched the FARC. During the 1990s, the FARC began to trade in coca paste and, according to UN sources, some fronts also became involved in small-scale international cocaine trafficking (see Chapter 9). However, the FARC do not control the drugs trade in Colombia. The guerrillas' other main source of income is kidnapping for ransom, a practice that has brought it widespread condemnation and loss of support among the Colombian Left.

Other guerrilla groups
The National Liberation Army (ELN) was set up by middle-class students, intellectuals and radicalized clergy in 1964 and had a nationalist, pro-Cuba line. The ELN never established themselves among the peasantry to the same degree as the FARC, but won considerable support among oil workers, students and left-wingers in northern Colombia. The ELN also kidnaps for ransom and became known for its tactic of blowing up oil pipelines. The ELN was almost wiped out by a paramilitary offensive in the 1990s and the remnants are now engaged in exploratory peace talks with the Uribe government. A pro-Maoist guerrilla group, the Popular Liberation Army (EPL), was founded in 1967. It has never formally laid down its arms, but barely exists today. A fourth guerrilla group, the Nineteenth of April Movement (M19), was founded in 1973 by left-wing middle-class nationalists. M19 demobilized in 1990.

The paramilitary death squads
Landowners set up armed groups to defend themselves from guerrilla extortion in the 1970s. From the beginning, these armed groups worked closely with the police and army. The paramilitary death squads did not just target guerrillas but all 'subversives', in which category they included peasant activists, trade unionists, left-wing students and human rights workers. In the late 1970s a broad-based popular movement emerged in Colombia, demanding political and economic reform. The most reactionary elements of the establishment were not prepared to countenance reform, so turned to the death squads. There have been more than 50,000 political killings since 1982, and death squads have been responsible for most of these murders, according to the Colombian Commission of Jurists.[21]

The crisis of the 1990s
Colombia became the top priority for the US security establishment in the 1990s. In the words of General Charles E. Wilhelm, the head of the US Armed Forces Southern Command, it had become 'the most threatened nation' in the region.[22] The Colombian government had lost control of large swathes of territory. The FARC had expanded from a small regional force to a nationwide insurgency, growing from

3,600 fighters in 1986 to 20,000 by 2001. There are several reasons for the FARC's growth. Land concentration had stimulated peasant migration to the isolated southern lowlands and the subsequent boom in coca cultivation enabled the FARC to build up a base of support among the new migrants and a source of income from taxing the coca trade. State repression against the popular movement may have also added to their appeal. A deep economic recession in the 1990s exacerbated hardship and added to the pool of possible recruits for all armed groups. The paramilitaries also expanded. The largest paramilitary network, the United Self-Defence Forces of Colombia (AUC) grew from 1,800 fighters in 1990 to 11,000 in 2001. Its operational capacity was increased by the logistical support and free passage frequently awarded to it by the Colombian military. The paramilitary death squads targeted all those who spoke out for reform or peace, making Colombia a terrifying place to live in.

The US transforms Plan Colombia
Exhausted by violence, Colombians elected Andrés Pastrana as president in 1998, on his promise to hold peace talks with the FARC. Pastrana withdrew government troops from a large area in southern Colombia the size of Switzerland, a move that was a *de facto* recognition of the FARC's strength. Pastrana launched Plan Colombia in 1999. The original Spanish-text Plan Colombia advocated an integrated peace plan, with moderate social reforms. It recognized that coca cultivation was a social phenomenon and that peasants needed support to switch to alternative crops. The US took this document, rewrote it entirely and turned it into a plan for war.[23] The English-language US version, published a year after the original version, makes 'strengthening the Colombian state' the top priority. Drugs trafficking was not mentioned in the original document, but in the US version it becomes the root cause of Colombia's problems, and eight paragraphs are dedicated to it in the preamble.

The United States advocated a military solution for what was essentially a social problem. Although before his election Clinton had recognized that drugs were a social problem, it became clear he had chosen the military path when he appointed Barry McCaffrey as 'drugs czar'. General Barry McCaffrey was a former head of the Southern Command, responsible for all US forces in South America, and had also been honoured as a hero of the Gulf War. The real aim appeared to be defeating the guerrillas rather than ending the drug trade. Plan Colombia comprised US$1.3 billion of aid, of which 77 per cent was military aid. The package included 18 Blackhawk and 42 Huey helicopters, radar systems, reconnaissance aircraft, and money to build military bases in the Andean region. On top of the Plan Colombia aid, the US Congress approved a further US$330 million of ordinary military aid, making a grand total of US$1.1 billion for the years 2000–01 – the highest amount any Latin American country has ever received.

The peace process collapsed in 2002. Substantive talks had never got off the ground. President Pastrana was accused of being too weak and allowing the guerrillas to dupe him. The FARC used the demilitarized zone to recruit and train new forces and continued to kidnap civilians throughout the peace process. Critics argued that the FARC had never taken the peace process seriously and simply used the

Breakdown of Plan Colombia Aid

	%
Military aid	57
Police aid	14
Law enforcement	6
Alternative development	9
Human rights	7
Aid to displaced people	4
Judicial reform	2
Peace promotion	1

Source: Center for International Policy, Washington

demilitarized zone to consolidate their control of the south. What is certainly true is that once the US became involved in Plan Colombia, the FARC became highly suspicious of the government's motives. What was the purpose of building up a stockpile of US military hardware, they must have asked themselves, if not to launch a future offensive against the guerrillas? The extreme Right were also working against peace. The paramilitaries, working in concert with the armed forces, continued to murder social activists with impunity. The failure of the government to act against the paramilitaries further convinced the FARC that it was not safe to lay down their arms and enter the political process.

In addition to strengthening the Colombian armed forces, the US version of Plan Colombia advocated the aerial spraying of pesticides on Colombia's coca farms. These chemicals killed not only coca plants but also food crops and animals. There is evidence that fumigation has harmed human health as well. Fumigation does not, however, reduce the supply of coca, since desperately poor peasants simply leave their poisoned plots and set up new coca farms deeper in the Amazon basin. US drugs policy is looked at in more detail in Chapter 9, but, in short, Plan Colombia derailed the Colombian peace process, exacerbated the civil war, poisoned large tracts of land, endangered human health, and failed to reduce by a single gram the amount of cocaine entering the United States.

George W. Bush and the 'War on Terror'

I am concerned about what appears to be a growing instability in the region ... An election can present an opportunity for those with extremist views to exploit themes of nationalism, patriotism and anti-elite or anti-establishment rhetoric to win popular support – especially in young and vulnerable democracies ... In many parts of the region – distrust and loss of faith in failed institutions have also fueled the emergence of anti-globalization and anti-free trade elements that incite violence against their own governments and their own people.

General John Craddock, Commander, US Southern Command, 25 April 2006[1]

[Some] countries in Latin America continue to appear to be running against the tide of history. Venezuela continues to be led by a Castro admirer and is aggressively importing weaponry out of proportion to his needs and recklessly provokes the United States. Bolivia has a new government that may be on the tipping point in regard to their relationship with the United States. Several countries remain unstable or may become so soon, with Haiti and Cuba being of prime concern ...

We are also concerned about the unconventional threats in your area [Latin America], including extremist groups and supporters of Islamic terrorist groups. As we've seen, so called 'ungoverned spaces' can become safe havens for terrorists. In addition to the terrorist groups we are also concerned about the possible shipment of weapons of mass destruction through your Area of Responsibility [Latin America].

Duncan Hunter (Republican), Chair, House Armed Services Committee,
16 March 2006[2]

Did the attacks on New York's Twin Towers and Washington on 11 September 2001 change Bush's foreign policy? All the elements of what would become known as the Bush doctrine – aggressive unilateralism, the willingness to take pre-emptive military action and the desire to reassert US global authority – had been espoused by neoconservatives long before. As early as 1991, Paul Wolfowitz, Lewis 'Scooter'

Libby and Dick Cheney, all of whom became key players in the Bush administration, wrote a paper entitled 'Defense Policy Guidance' advocating both the use of military might to prevent the rise of potentially hostile powers and the use of pre-emptive force against states suspected of developing weapons of mass destruction. The New American Century, a neoconservative think-tank whose supporters included Donald Rumsfeld, Richard Perle, John Bolton, and Wolfowitz, was founded in 1997. They dismissed Clinton's emphasis on multilateralism, humanitarian intervention and peacekeeping as 'globaloney' and called instead for an aggressive unilateral policy, starting with the removal of Saddam Hussein. Some historians have even suggested that Reagan's wars in Central America prefigured the war in Iraq: both were forceful interventions aimed at pre-empting the establishment of 'unfriendly'governments. But 11 September 2001 certainly assured the ascendancy of the neoconservatives within the Bush administration. Before 9/11, Bush had expressed a willingness to act unilaterally to defend vital US interests, but afterwards this 'defensive' stance was transformed into an evangelical mission to spread US military power, influence and values – an ambition which sounded distinctly like empire-building, backed by a grandiose missionary zeal. As Bush put it, 'Our mission is to rid the world of evil.'

In Latin America, Bush's priorities were originally much like his predecessor's: the promotion of free trade agreements in line with large corporations' need for new markets and cheap labour; the protection of oil supplies (the US imports more oil from the Americas than it does from the Middle East); and the promotion of stable, pro-market and pro-US governments. Drugs, migration and Cuba all remained themes that played well domestically. Latin America had not been a priority for US policy makers since the Cold War, and 11 September 2001 reduced its importance even further.

11 September, in fact, led to a notable drift between the outlooks of Latin America and the US. Poverty, unemployment and social problems were the main concerns of Latin Americans, while the US became preoccupied by security, terrorism and drugs. Most Latin American governments were alarmed when the US ignored the will of the UN and went ahead with the invasion of Iraq. The torture of Iraqi prisoners, the legal limbo of the Guantánamo Bay prison camp, and secret rendition flights also worried Latin American governments, which wanted the hegemonic power to their north to obey international law. A dispute over the International Criminal Court illustrated this tension.[3] Twelve Latin American governments refused to grant US military personnel immunity from the court's jurisdiction on their soil. In response, Washington, at various times between 2003 and 2006, suspended all non-drugs-trafficking-related military aid to those states (Barbados, Bolivia, Brazil, Costa Rica, Ecuador, Mexico, Paraguay, Peru, St Vincent and the Grenadines, Trinidad and Tobago, Uruguay and Venezuela).

Under George W. Bush, the Pentagon played a much greater role than the State Department in shaping US foreign policy. The alarmist forecasts of military men replaced the diplomats' more nuanced picture of Latin America. 'This region can hardly be considered benign,' warned General John Craddock, Commander of

Southern Command in 2006.[4] 'The transnational terrorist, the narco terrorist, the Islamic radical fundraiser and recruiter, the illicit trafficker, the money launderer, the kidnapper and the gang member all have access to and leverage an unprecedented freedom of movement.'[5] The mention of Islamic radicals was particularly misleading because even the Pentagon admitted that there was no evidence of Islamic terrorist activities in Latin America, with the exception of the mysterious bombings of an Argentinian Jewish cultural centre in 1994 and the Israeli embassy in Buenos Aires in 1992. Defense Secretary Donald Rumsfeld sounded the same note as Craddock when he warned of 'a combination of violent gangs, drug traffickers, smugglers, hostage-takers, terrorists ... seeking to destabilize governments' and 'take advantage of borders and ungoverned areas'.[6] While Latin American governments worry about crime, this image of their countries as an ungoverned terrain harbouring menacing villains was crude and irrelevant to their more pressing concerns about jobs, trade and living standards.

After 11 September 2001, Latin American elites who had a common interest in signing trade and investment deals felt, if not snubbed, then overlooked. This was clearly the case with Mexico. On 6 September 2001, the Mexican president, Vicente Fox, visited the White House. He was told by George Bush that Mexico was the US's most important partner in the world (a novel statement which might have raised some eyebrows in Britain). There were high hopes of building on the 'success' of the North American Free Trade Agreement (NAFTA). The two governments planned to thrash out a common agreement on migration and to work closely on security issues. But just five days later, Washington's gaze had moved to another continent. Serious talks with Mexico never took place. Relations deteriorated when Mexico opposed the Iraq war at the UN, but the most bitterly divisive issue was migration, which now became part of the US domestic debate on terrorism. The border with Mexico was suddenly not only a gateway for illegal immigrants seeking work, but a dangerously unprotected flank in the 'war on terror', a porous border through which hundreds, if not thousands, of terrorists could creep into US territory. The lowest point in Mexican–US relations came in 2006, when Congress and the president approved – without consulting the Mexicans – the building of a 700-kilometre wall along the border.

If there was a rift between the conservative Mexican government and the Republican George Bush, an even greater gulf was to be expected between the US and the new governments of the Left. While the top minds of the Pentagon and State Department concentrated on the Middle East, nationalist and left-leaning countries were elected to power in Venezuela (1998, 2006), Chile (2000, 2006); Brazil (2002, 2006), Argentina (2003, 2007), Uruguay (2004), Bolivia (2006), Nicaragua (2006), Ecuador (2006) and Paraguay (2008). Two decades of free market policies and IMF deals had brought little but increased poverty and joblessness. Revolts against the Washington Consensus had erupted across the continent in the 1990s and early 2000s. The Zapatistas took up the cause of Mexican indigenous communities squeezed by globalization. Bolivians built burning roadblocks against the sale of natural resources to the US, and Argentinian pensioners hammered on

The Spectre of Brazil's President Lula

'In Brazil, there is a presidential run-off election ... At present, the leading candidate is Mr Luiz Inácio Lula da Silva, who is a pro-Castro radical who for electoral purposes has posed as a moderate ... There is a real prospect that Castro, Chávez and Lula da Silva could constitute an axis of evil in the Americas which might soon have nuclear weapons and ballistic missiles ...'

Letter from Henry J. Hyde (Republican), Chairman of the House International Relations Committee to George W. Bush. 24 October 2002, http://newsmax.com.archives/articles/2002/10/28/124037.shtml

'If the pro-Castro candidate is elected president of Brazil, the results could include a radical regime in Brazil re-establishing its nuclear weapon and ballistic missile programmes, developing close links to state sponsors of terrorism such as Cuba, Iraq and Iran and participating in the destabilization of fragile neighboring democracies. This could lead to 300 million people in six countries coming under the control of radical anti-US regimes and the possibility that thousands of newly indoctrinated terrorists might try to attack the United States from Latin America.'

Source: Constantine C. Menges, former National Security Council member, quoted in 'Blocking a new axis of evil', *Washington Times*, 29 August 2002

the doors of banks, cursing the IMF. Guatemalan Mayan indigenous peoples joined with trade unionists in protest against the Central American free trade area. Thousands took to the streets to protest against austerity measures, privatizations, free trade agreements or pension cuts in Ecuador, Brazil, Panama, El Salvador, Nicaragua, Costa Rica and Honduras. Popular protest culminated in the flight of presidents from Argentina (2001), Bolivia (2003) and Ecuador (2005).

It was apt that the wave of new governments was described as a pink (rather than red) tide sweeping Latin America. Far from being communists, many of the new office-holders were highly pragmatic. The Socialists in Chile, for example, had been part of the governing coalition since 1990 and continued to implement neoliberal policies of tightly controlled public spending, privatization and free markets, ameliorated by targeted welfare programmes. Presidents Tabaré Vázquez of Uruguay and Luis Inácio Lula da Silva (universally known as 'Lula') of Brazil, both of whose parties were socialistic in origin and outlook, followed this model of fiscal responsibility coupled with social benefits. Although some US Republicans made dire predictions that Lula would form part of a pro-Cuban 'axis of evil' (see box), after his election Washington worked hard to differentiate what it saw as the moderate governments of Brazil, Chile and Argentina from the so-called 'radical populists' in Venezuela and Bolivia. Argentina's Néstor Kirchner was slightly more combative than either Lula or Chile's Michelle Bachelet, telling President Bush at the Summit of the Americas in 2005, 'I'm not obsequious, like many of the politicians you are used to listening to.'⁷ Coming to power in the midst of a severe financial crisis, Kirchner forced the IMF and foreign creditors to write off debt and renationalized a small number of failing services, but on the whole Washington did not regard his government as a threat. To an extent, Argentina, Brazil and Chile were facilitators for Washington in Latin America – they sent troops to Haiti, for example, and cooperated with Washington's investigations into terrorist activity in the tri-border region of Paraguay, Argentina and Brazil. But they certainly did not swallow the Bush agenda wholesale. The South Americans refused to back a 'free trade area of the Americas' and instead enlarged their own trading block, Mercosur. To the chagrin of Washington, the OAS condemned the 2002 anti-Chávez coup in Venezuela (see below), while Brazil, Argentina and Chile steadfastly refused to join a US-led common front against Venezuela, Bolivia or Cuba.

The Radical Populists

It was in the confrontation with Venezuela that the marriage between Cold War paranoia and neoconservative aggression was most evident. The United States has historically shown little tolerance of independent-minded nationalist regimes in Latin America, and George W. Bush's appointment of old faces from the Reagan era – many of whom had been involved in the Iran-Contra scandal – suggested that, right from the start, his administration planned to take a hard line against radicals. 11 September 2001 merely hardened neoconservative determination to confront so-called 'rogue' states. Venezuela had been governed by an elected left-wing nationalist, Hugo Chávez, since 1998. Producing scenes reminiscent of Chile in 1973, in 2002 Washington backed a short-lived coup against Chávez. When this failed, the US continued to fund the opposition within Venezuela and sought to isolate Chávez internationally. Chávez was irksome to the US not just because Venezuela was its fourth-largest oil supplier, but because he had toured the world seeking to construct a Third World anti-Bush alliance. Chávez was dubbed a 'radical populist' by the Pentagon, a label that was also attached to Evo Morales, the president of Bolivia, elected in 2005. Morales is a former peasant activist who is friendly with both Chávez and Fidel Castro. Washington also suspected Rafael Correa, who was elected president of Ecuador in November 2006, of being a radical populist. Correa, a left-wing economist, said he would not renew the US lease on the Manta military base in his country, and, following the example of Chávez and Morales, he held elections for a constituent assembly to write a new constitution. Daniel Ortega, the president of Nicaragua, was also put in the radical populist category, although the former Sandinista guerrilla is now a far more moderate and less principled leader than he was in the 1980s.

A definition of radical populism was given by General James Hill, former Chief of the Southern Command.

> Traditional threats [to the United States] are now complemented by an emerging threat best described as radical populism, in which the democratic process is under-mined to decrease rather than protect individual rights. Some leaders in the region

are tapping into deep-seated frustrations at the failure of democratic reforms to deliver expected goods and services. By tapping into these frustrations ... the leaders are at the same time able to reinforce their positions by inflaming anti-US sentiment.[8]

Neoconservatives were also worried that the radical populists, and in particular, Hugo Chávez, would breathe new life into the Cuban regime, just as the Bush administration was making detailed plans for a post-Castro scenario.

While much of the Pentagon's rhetoric was devoted to the new threat of radical populism, the largest US military intervention in Latin America remained that in Colombia. Colombia received more military aid than the rest of Latin America put together. Hundreds of US servicemen and private contractors became embroiled in the war against left-wing guerrillas. One of most important consequences of 11 September 2001 was George W. Bush's decision to allow military aid to be used against 'terrorists' in Colombia, a move that the Pentagon had long desired but that had been politically unpalatable. With the help of the US, Colombia's president Alvaro Uribe succeeded in pushing the insurgents out of the cities and securing major highways, but the guerrillas still controlled large swathes of the countryside in southern Colombia. Meanwhile, right-wing paramilitaries had de facto control of much of the north of the country. Colombia's human rights record remained the worst in South America and on some counts – the murder of trade unionists, for example – the worst in the world.

Before examining in more detail some of the countries in which the Bush administration was most active, it is worth both highlighting the key individuals and organizations that played particularly controversial roles and taking a closer look at the US military presence in the region.

Who Makes US Foreign Policy?

As already mentioned, George W. Bush seemed to go out of his way to appoint men who had earned their spurs in the Irangate scandal. The most controversial of these was the right-wing Cuban-American Otto Reich, chosen in part as payback for the Cuban-American community's support for Bush in the presidential election, which proved so crucial to his win. Congress refused to ratify Reich's appointment as Assistant Secretary of State for the Western Hemisphere because of his role in Irangate, so Bush used his presidential veto to put Reich in the post for a year. He then appointed Reich as his special envoy to Latin America and gave him a seat on the National Security Council. Reich dived straight back into his old role of aiding reactionary forces in Latin America. He kept in close contact with the supporters of the coup in Venezuela and refused to listen to the pleas of the American ambassador in Haiti who warned that the elected president was likely to be overthrown. Elliott Abrams, another Iran–Contra veteran, and Roger Noriega, a hardliner who succeeded Reich at the State Department, also applauded the coups in Venezuela and Haiti.

Who Was Who in the Bush Administration (2001–09): the Reaganites Return

Otto Reich, Assistant Secretary of State for the Western Hemisphere (2001–02), Special Envoy to the Western Hemisphere (2002–03)
Reich, a Cuban-American, was director of the Office of Public Diplomacy (1983–86), which produced propaganda about the Contra War and El Salvador during the Reagan years. The US Comptroller General criticized Reich's Office of Public Diplomacy for 'prohibited, covert propaganda activities'. He was also censured by the Congressional General Accounts Committee and the Congressional Iran–Contra committees. Reich also worked as a lobbyist for the rum company Bacardi, whose distilleries were taken over by the Cuban state after the 1959 revolution.

Elliott Abrams, National Security Council member (2001–09) and Special Adviser to President George W. Bush
Abrams pleaded guilty to withholding information from Congress during the Iran–Contra Scandal, and oversaw Contra operations in Central America. In 1986 he travelled to London under an assumed name to solicit US$10 million from a representative of the Sultan of Brunei to purchase arms for the Contras. During the Iran–Contra scandal, he was forced to apologize for misleading Congress about soliciting funds from third countries and was pardoned by George Bush senior.

John Negroponte, US ambassador to the UN (2001–04); Director of National Intelligence (2005–09)
As ambassador to Honduras. (1981–85), Negroponte oversaw CIA and Contra operations in that country. After the US Congress banned official US assistance in 1984, he encouraged the Honduran government to continue supporting the Contras.

Robert Gates, Defense Secretary (2006–09)
Gates was Deputy Director for Intelligence at the CIA during the Iran–Contra scandal. The Independent Counsel who investigated the Iran–Contra affair criticized Gates, saying that, contrary to his testimony to a grand jury, Gates had known that proceeds from the sales of arms to Iran were diverted to the Contras.

Colin Powell, Secretary of State (2001–05)
Colin Powell is not a neocon, but nevertheless played a role in the Iran–Contra affair while serving as senior military assistant to Secretary of Defense Caspar Weinberger. In 1986 Powell, following orders from Weinberger, helped to arrange the transfer of missiles from the US army to the CIA for sale to Iran. He later said he was operating under a presidential order.

Sources: Digital National Security Archive, Iran-ContraAffair Collection, Glossary, Elliott Abrams, Colin Powell.

Noriega's replacement in 2006 was not an ideologue but a pragmatic State Department diplomat, Thomas Shannon. Some saw this as a sign that Condoleezza Rice was seeking to mend fences with Latin American governments that had been alienated by the neocons. Choosing Charles Shapiro as his deputy, however, suggested otherwise. The former ambassador to Venezuela had become notorious for fraternizing with the coup leaders throughout the three-day failed anti-Chávez coup of 2002. And any illusion that Bush was turning his back on the old Reaganites was dispelled when Iran–Contra veteran Robert Gates was named Secretary of Defense in 2006.

The International Republican Institute

The main tool of intervention in Latin America during the Bush era was the International Republican Institute (IRI), the international arm of the Republican Party. The IRI received generous grants from USAID, the US government aid agency, and the National Endowment for Democracy (NED), which is funded by Congress and the State Department. The IRI also received contributions from corporations such as Halliburton and Chevron. Among the companies represented on its board were Lockheed Martin, Chevron Texaco, AOL Time Warner and Ford. Its chair was right-wing Republican senator John McCain and its president was George Folsom, an investment banker who was a member of the Bush–Cheney transition team. IRI's vice-president was Georges Fauriol, a former colleague of Otto Reich at the Americas Forum and a member of the Center for a Free Cuba.

The New Strategy of the US Military in Latin America

The military had to rethink its strategy in Latin America after the end of the Cold War, since it could no longer justify its presence on the basis of fighting communism. It was also forced to reorganize its forces in the continent because, under a treaty with Panama, it agreed to remove all its bases by 31 December 1999. Panama had been the centre of the Southern Command operations and home to the School of the Americas since the Second World War. The School of the Americas moved to Fort Benning, Georgia in 1984. Southern Command, which is responsible for US forces in Latin America and the Caribbean, except Mexico, moved its headquarters to Miami, Florida, in 1997.

The new US military strategy in Latin America has been to operate from a larger number of small, Latin-American-owned bases across the continent. The US military has ten-year leases on four 'forward operating locations' in Ecuador, Curaçao, Aruba and El Salvador. US forces also have the right to use two other bases in Honduras and Paraguay (see map, p. 129) on an *ad hoc* basis. The US does not own these facilities but paid substantial sums to ensure they were adequately equipped for its needs. The US also uses radar and surveillance sites across the Americas. These smaller, more dispersed bases make US forces more mobile, more light-footed and more able to carry out covert operations. The secretive nature of contracts also makes it harder to ascertain exactly how many US troops are in Latin America at any

The US Military in Latin America

Southern Command
Miami, Florida.

School of the Americas
Fort Benning, Georgia. It was renamed Western Hemisphere Institute for Security Cooperation in 2001.

Forward operating locations (FOLs)
Owned and operated by the host country. Small numbers of US military forces, Drug Enforcement Administration, Coast Guard and Customs personnel are stationed at FOLs. US aircraft have the right to land.
* Manta, Ecuador. Ten-year lease signed 1999
* Aruba, Netherlands Antilles. Ten-year lease signed 2000.
* Curaçao, Netherlands Antilles. Ten-year lease signed 2000
* Comalapa, El Salvador. Ten-year lease signed 2000.

Enrique Soto Cano Air Force Base, Honduras
A semi-permanent Honduran-owned air base near Comayagua. The base is home to Joint Task Force Bravo, part of the US Southern Command. It currently has about 550 troops stationed there. During the Central American wars of the 1980s, over 2,000 US military personnel were stationed at the base. Joint Task Force Bravo carries out military exercises, humanitarian assistance, disaster relief and counter-drug operations. The Honduran Constitution does not allow a foreign military presence in Honduras. A 'handshake' agreement between the two countries allows Joint Task Force Bravo to remain there on a semi-permanent basis. The base is also home to the Honduran Air Force Academy.

Pedro Juan Caballero Air Base, Paraguay
A Paraguayan military base built entirely with US funds, the air base started operations in 2006. Located on the border with Brazil, 344 miles (550 km) northeast of the Paraguayan capital, Asuncion, it contains a heliport and state-of-the-art radar system and has accommodation for 100 military personnel.

Guantánamo Bay Naval Station, Cuba
The US navy has had a presence at Guantánamo Bay since 1903, when a treaty was signed by President Theodore Roosevelt and the Cuban President Estrada Palma. The lease on Guantánamo Bay is perpetual with no termination date. US forces remained despite the Cuban revolution in 1959. During the 1960s, US withdrawal from the base was one of Fidel Castro's five negotiation points, but in recent years Cuba has not made a point of claiming it.

In 2002, US Southern Command was given responsibility for the custody of 'war on terror' detainees at Guantánamo. In January 2002 a temporary detention facility, Camp X-Ray, was established, which was replaced by the more permanent Camp Delta in April 2002. Camp Delta has the capacity to hold

2,000 detainees. In January 2005, 545 detainees were being held. 850 US forces are stationed at Guantánamo.

Radar sites

Seventeen radar sites in Latin America are operated by US Southern Command. Six are ground-based radars in Peru (Iquitos, Andoas and Pucallpa) and three are in Colombia (San José del Guaviare, Marandúa and Leticia). The rest are mobile and operate from secret locations. The US navy also has built a new 'relocatable over-the-horizon radar' (ROTHR) in Puerto Rico to carry out surveillance of South America. It has two ROTHRs in Virginia and Texas watching over Mexico and the Caribbean.

Sources: Just the Facts defence database, maintained by Center for International Policy, Latin America Working Group and Washington Office on Latin America: www.justf.org. Also J. Lindsay-Poland, 'US Military Bases in Latin America and the Caribbean, Americas Policy Programme, Centre for International Policy, 2 August 2004; Alejo Livez, 'United States Eyes Triple Border', Latinamerica Press/Noticias Aliadas, 19 October 2006.

Military Bases and Radar Sites Used by the US in Latin America

time. The increased use of private military contractors adds to the murkiness of the picture. The disadvantage for the US of this strategy is that they are reliant on like-minded governments remaining in power in Latin America. President Correa of Ecuador, for example, has already promised to oust US forces from the Manta base, when the lease expires in 2009.

Counter-drugs operations are the pretext the US uses for leasing most bases and radar sites in Latin America. However, drugs trafficking is by no means the military's only concern in Latin America, as a quick glance at the US army war school's priorities for 2006 shows. Insurgencies, territorial security, political instability and the rise of populism and the Left are among its concerns. Colombia is by far the largest recipient of US military aid in the region, receiving 70 per cent of the total budget for Latin America. The amount of military aid Colombia received rose sharply with the start of Plan Colombia in 2000, and the Bush administration kept it at consistently high levels – an average of over US$500 million a year (2001–07), compared with US$87 million in 1997. US military aid to the rest of Latin America also rose under George W. Bush from an annual average of US$163 million in 1997–2000, to US$219 in 2001–07, a 34 per cent rise.

US Military Priorities in Latin America

'Evolving regional security matters in the Western Hemisphere
  a. US interests in Caribbean security issues
  b. Hemispheric security forces (military and police) and new threats
  c. Improving security ties with Brazil
  d. Lessons from the Colombian insurgency
  e. Transformation of the Colombian armed forces during war
  f. Reemergence of Sendero Luminoso
  g. Ungoverned space and implications for territorial security
  h. Military role in securing a stable Haiti
  i. Venezuela as an exporter of political instability
  j. Narco-funded terrorism networks
  k. Instability and disenfranchised indigenous and poor populations
  l. Implications of the rising threat of populism in the region
  m. Implications of the return of the Latin American Left
  n. Long-term implications of Chinese engagement in Latin America
  o. Implications of economic integration such as the Central America Free Trade Agreement (CAFTA) and Southern Common Market (MERCOSUR)
  p. Impact of the American Serviceman's Protection Act of 2000 (ASPA) on hemispheric security relations
  q. Maintaining the viability of hemispheric security forces during a time of declining budgets
  r. Implications for US security of a post-Castro Cuba.'

Source: US Army War College: *Key Strategic Issues List 2006*, edited by Dr A. J. Echevarria II, US Army War College, July 2006.

Top Ten Countries Worldwide Receiving US Military Training, 2004

Country	Number of trainees
Afghanistan	12,362
Colombia	8,756
Bolivia	1,975
Thailand	1,282
Israel	1,281
Egypt	1,241
Mexico	876
Argentina	647
Ukraine	612
Philippines	549

Source: 'Erasing the Lines: Trends in US Military Programmes with Latin America', a joint publication by Center for International Policy, Latin America Working Group Education Fund & Washington Office on Latin America, December 2005

Venezuela

You've got Chávez in Venezuela with a lot of oil money. He's a person who was elected legally just as Adolf Hitler was elected legally and then consolidated power and now is, of course, working with Fidel Castro and Mr Morales and others. It concerns me.

Donald Rumsfeld, US Defense Secretary, 2006[9]

On all fronts, the behavior of the Venezuelan Government is wanting. The Government of Venezuela has stated that it regards the US-led war on terrorism as a ruse for US imperial ambitions. It has refused to condemn narco-terrorist organizations based in Colombia, and has publicly championed the cause of terrorists in Iraq ...

Frank C. Urbancic, US Principal Deputy Coordinator for Counterterrorism, 2006[10]

The ebullient Venezuelan army colonel Hugo Chávez first came to national attention when he attempted a military coup in 1992. Coming from a nationalist vein within the army, Chávez, like many Venezuelans, had become increasingly disillusioned with the *Punto Fijo* system – a tacit agreement between the two main political parties to alternate power – a set-up that encouraged backroom dealing and corruption. Oil-rich Venezuela had enjoyed rapid economic growth in the 1960s and 1970s. US-style skyscrapers and gleaming shopping malls were built. But even in the boom years, *ranchitos* – little shacks – began to appear on the edges of Caracas as the rural poor were attracted to the city to find work. Two decades later, 2 million people lived in the sprawling hillside shantytowns surrounding the capital. A rise in bus fares in 1989 led to riots which were brutally put down by the armed forces. Up to a thousand people were killed by the security forces during the *Caracazo*, as the conflict became known. The *Caracazo* made a deep impression on Chávez, who believed the army should be on the side of the poor. Although his 1992 coup attempt was unsuccessful, a televised broadcast in which he conceded that he had failed '*por ahora*' (for now) not only made him a national figure, but raised hopes among many that he would make a comeback. After two years in prison, Chávez began to build a political movement, working with left-wing military officers, intellectuals and former guerrillas. In 1998, he won a landslide electoral victory and was elected President of Venezuela.

Chávez and the elite

Chávez spent his first years in power reforming the political structure. A constituent assembly was elected which wrote a new constitution. This constitution was approved by the population in a referendum in December 1999. Under its terms Venezuela was renamed the Bolivarian Republic of Venezuela in memory of Simon Bolivar, independence leader. Chávez was re-elected President in 2000. In his early years, Chávez's rhetoric was more radical than his actions. His broadsides against the pillars of the establishment – the Church, the rich, the media and the old political parties – angered the wealthy, and he has often been criticized for alienating the middle class unnecessarily. But for the poor this was part of his appeal. When you talk to Chávez supporters, in the shantytowns or rural villages, you will hear, again and again, the phrase, 'He talks like us.' The white elite, in contrast, regarded Chávez, who is of mixed race, as vulgar and coarse.

Chávez's first radical legislation came in November 2001, when 49 laws were introduced by decree. One of the most controversial centred on PDVSA, the state-owned oil company. Chávez believed the company had been run in the interests of a rich elite and that oil revenues should be used for the good of the nation. The decree outlawed the privatization of PDVSA, a sale that had been eagerly anticipated by US and Spanish oil companies. The decree stated that PDVSA should have a 51 per cent stake in all joint ventures with private companies and raised the amount of royalties those companies had to pay. Among the other 48 measures was a ban on privatizing social security and a land reform law, which allowed the government to expropriate idle and under-used farmland. The decrees convinced the elite that Chávez had to go because they not only sidelined corporate interests hoping to profit from the oil industry, but also directly attacked private property rights, a historical cause of coups from Guatemala to Brazil to Chile.

Relations with the United States

Chávez's relations with the Clinton administration were cool, but civil enough. The US's main concern was Chávez's campaign to raise international oil prices by strengthening OPEC, the organization of oil-producing countries. As part of this drive, Chávez visited Iraq's Saddam Hussein, a trip that elicited a testy response from the State Department: 'We do think it's a rather dubious distinction to be the first democratically elected head of state to meet with the dictator of Iraq.' Washington was also irritated when Venezuela refused in 1999 to allow US military anti-drug flights over Venezuelan airspace. However, Clinton's ambassador in Caracas did concede that Venezuela was a democratic country: 'Venezuela is an active partner in building an integrated hemisphere through the economy, through a consolidated democracy and through sustainable development.'[11]

Chávez's Personal Electoral Mandate

Presidential election	December 1998	Chávez (56%) Turnout: 64%
Presidential election (in line with new constitution)	May 2000	Chávez (59%) Turnout: 54%
Recall referendum	August 2004	Chávez (59%) Turnout:70%
Presidential election	December 2006	Chávez (63%) Turnout: 75%

Other elections

Referendum on whether to convoke constituent assembly	April 1999	88% vote yes
Elections for constituent assembly	July 1999	*Chavistas* win 91% of the vote.
Referendum to ratify constitution	December 1999	71% in favour
Elections for National Assembly (congress)	May 2000	*Chavistas* win a majority of the seats (but not the crucial two-thirds majority). Turnout: 56%
Elections for state governorships	May 2000	*Chavistas* win 15 out of 23 states.
Elections for state governorships	October 2004	*Chavistas* win 20 out of 22 states.
Elections for National Assembly	December 2005	*Chavistas* win all 167 seats, after the five main opposition parties boycott the poll. EU observers describe the elections as free and fair, but the OAS has some reservations. 25% turnout
Referendum on wide-ranging constitutional reforms, including the abolition of presidential terms	December 2007	Chávez loses by 49% to 51%

Clinton's White House may not have been unduly concerned by Chávez, but the International Republican Institute (IRI) was. As early as 1998 the IRI warned:

> US policymakers have yet to confront the possibility that the country may veer away from the democratic path being followed by most Latin American countries. The consequences of such a development would be profound: the United States imports more oil from Venezuela than from any other country [sic] and bilateral trade has been expanding rapidly in the 1990s. For these reasons, the travails of Venezuelan democracy bear watching.[12]

The IRI spent nearly half a million dollars on training Venezuelan political parties and working with groups drafting the constitution in 1999.[13] The National Endowment for Democracy (NED) gave a grant of US$246,000 to the opposition trade union confederation, the CTV.

Chávez and George Bush

Bilateral relations took a sharp turn for the worse with the inauguration of George W. Bush in January 2001. The White House strongly disapproved of a Chávez trip to Iran on OPEC (Organization of Petroleum Exporting Countries) business, and a visit by Fidel Castro to Caracas later that year. Chávez's condemnation of US intervention in Afghanistan (on his weekly television show he held up photos of Afghani child bomb victims) also angered the Bush administration. Secretary of State Colin Powell told Congress, 'We are not happy with some of the comments he has made with respect to the campaign against terrorism.'[14] The director of the CIA, George Tenet, was more succinct: 'He does not have US interests at heart.' As Chávez's enemies began preparing to launch a coup, reports began to appear in the press about Chávez's supposed links with Colombian guerrillas. Senator Jesse Helms claimed, 'Physical evidence ... establishes beyond any doubt, I think, that he is supporting narco-terrorists in Colombia.'[15] These allegations came from a now-declassified US intelligence document that was based entirely on an unsubstantiated report in the Colombian newspaper *El Tiempo*, and a letter published in a Venezuelan daily. This Secret Intelligence Assessment, prepared by Southern Command, was circulated among Washington departments and among members of Congress to influence opinion.[16]

The 2002 coup

The opposition in Venezuela was led by the business federation, Fedecámaras, and the trade union confederation, CTV. They called a national strike/lockout for 11 April 2002. On the morning of the 11th, a large opposition demonstration marched to Chuao, a rich area of Caracas. There they were exhorted by Fedecámaras leader Pedro Carmona and trade union boss Carlos Ortega to march to the presidential palace, Miraflores. A much smaller number of Chávez supporters had gathered outside the palace. As the opposition march approached the palace, they were confronted by the National Guard blocking their path. The National Guard fired tear gas into the crowd, demonstrators threw rocks, and as the march dispersed into nearby streets shots were fired killing several people, *chavistas* and opposition supporters both. *Chavistas* believe that snipers were placed in nearby buildings to cause deaths that would justify a coup, and there is some evidence to support this.[17] That evening a high-ranking naval officer appeared on television calling for a military insurrection: 'The President of the Republic has betrayed the trust of the people, he is massacring innocent people with snipers. Just now six people were killed and dozens wounded in Caracas.'

But this footage had been filmed much earlier in the day, before anyone had been killed. CNN journalist Otto Neustald later revealed that he had received a phone call the night before:

> On the 10th at night they called me on the telephone and said, Otto, tomorrow … the march will go toward the presidential palace, there will be deaths and then 20 military officials of high rank will appear and pronounce themselves against the government of Chávez and will request his resignation. They told me this on the 10th at night.[18]

Late in the evening of 11 April the chiefs of the National Guard, the army and the military high command announced that they no longer recognized the Chávez government. The president was taken into custody on a military base at four o'clock the next morning.

On 12 April, business leader Pedro Carmona swore himself in as president in Miraflores Palace. Applauded by the great and the good of the Venezuelan upper class, including leading opposition politicians, media moguls and military officers, he ceremoniously abolished the constitution and closed down the National Assembly and the Supreme Court. He then dismissed all elected mayors, state governors, the attorney general, the comptroller general, the human rights ombudsman and members of the national electoral council.

The unravelling of the coup

The coup appeared victorious, but it unravelled rapidly over the next two days for three main reasons: some parts of the army remained loyal to Chávez; the coup leaders were divided; and thousands of *chavistas* came out onto the streets to demand the reinstatement of their president. Carmona had made a fatal error in failing to share out the spoils of victory. The head of the army, General Vásquez Velasco, whose support was crucial to the success of the coup, had expected to be rewarded with a cabinet post but was overlooked. Similarly, trade union leader Carlos Ortega, a key figure in the coup, was left out of the cabinet. Meanwhile, as news of the coup spread to the shantytowns, thousands of Chávez supporters descended on Miraflores. 'The hills looked like a giraffe with moving spots,' one *Chavista* said, as the people made their way down the steep mountainside to get to central Caracas. The private media stations had reported that Chávez had resigned, but rumours began to circulate that Chávez had been in effect kidnapped. As support for the coup crumbled, the TV station reverted to playing cartoons and old movies and failed to broadcast pictures of Chávez supporters taking to the streets.

On the morning of Saturday 13 April, the commander of the parachute regiment in Maracay announced a rebellion against the coup. Later that day, spurred on by the crowds outside Miraflores, the president's own honour guard made their way up through the basement of the presidential palace and burst in on the coup leaders, who fled to their cars. At 3.45am the next morning Chávez was flown back by helicopter from his captivity on the island of La Orchila to the presidential palace. He was greeted by cheering crowds shouting: 'Oo, ah, Chávez no se va!', a new slogan for the movement, which translates roughly as 'Chávez isn't going anywhere!'

US Involvement in the 2002 coup

A number of official documents relating to the coup have been declassified by the US authorities as a result of a freedom of information request made by lawyer Eva Golinger and journalist Jeremy Bigwood.[19] These declassified documents show that the CIA knew a coup was being planned and did nothing to warn the Venezuelan government about it. They confirm that the US paid large sums to opposition parties and organizations in the run-up to the coup. They show that US officials met the coup plotters in Washington in the weeks before the coup. The public record shows that the US was quick to welcome Chávez's ousting and was one of the few countries to recognize the short-lived Carmona regime. The material declassified so far does not, however, prove that the US masterminded the coup. Yet circumstantial evidence suggests there is more to be discovered about US involvement. For example, in November 2001, coup leader Pedro Carmona had led a business delegation to Washington, where he met senior government officials in the State Department, the Department of Commerce and the Department of Energy, as well as some Congressmen.[20] Carmona made several more trips to Washington, including one a month before the coup. On numerous occasions Carmona met Otto Reich, Secretary of State for Western Hemisphere Affairs. Reich also met opposition trade union leader Carlos Ortega in Washington in February 2002.[21]

In the weeks leading up to the coup, the CIA circulated reports to the White House, the State Department and the Pentagon, noting that a coup was imminent. One briefing entitled 'Conditions Ripening for Coup Attempt', published four days before 11 April, gives a suspiciously accurate description of what actually unfolded on that day: 'Dissident military factions ... are stepping up efforts to organize a coup against President Chávez, possibly as early as this month ... To provoke military action, the plotters may try to exploit unrest stemming from opposition demonstrations ...'[22]

In the year before the coup, US funding for the Venezuelan opposition soared. Venezuela became Latin America's top recipient of National Endowment for Democracy (NED) grants, receiving almost US$900,000 in 2001. The money was given to opposition parties, trade unions, NGOs and Fedecámeras. Much of this money was funnelled through the International Republican Institute (IRI). A senior IRI officer visited Venezuela in February 2002 to meet Pedro Carmona and opposition party leaders. The IRI also funded Carmona's trip to Washington a month later.[23] The IRI's support for the coup became apparent on the evening of 12 April, when IRI president George Folsom heaped praise on the coup leaders:

> Last night, led by every sector of civil society, the Venezuelan people rose up to defend democracy in their country. Venezuelans were provoked into action as a result of

systematic repression by the Government of Hugo Chávez ... IRI also applauds the bravery of civil society leaders – members of the media, the Church, the nation's educators and school administrators, political party leaders, labour unions and the business sector ... We stand ready to continue our partnership with the courageous Venezuelan people.[24]

US officials maintained contact with coup leaders throughout the events of the weekend. On the evening of 11 April, Carmona met the coup leaders at the defence ministry headquarters at Fort Tiuna. Two US military mission officers, Colonel James Rodgers and Colonel Ronald McCammon, were present. The United States has denied that these two officers, or indeed any US officers, were present at the base at that time, but they were seen by several witnesses and also signed their names upon entering Fort Tiuna.[25] Also reportedly present was General Enrique Medina Gomez, military attaché at the Venezuelan embassy in Washington.[26]

The US ambassador, Charles Shapiro, met Pedro Carmona at the presidential palace on Friday 12 April. He emerged 'all smiles and embraces', according to one pro-Chávez congressman.[27] The US authorities admit the meeting took place, but say Shapiro used the opportunity to urge Carmona not to dissolve parliament. Carmona told the *Guardian* newspaper that Shapiro never gave him this advice.[28] The State Department admits that Shapiro had a number of other conversations with Carmona during the weekend. A declassified document advises State Department officials only to tell journalists '*if pressed*' that 'Ambassador Shapiro spoke with a number of Venezuelans involved in the events there, including then Interim President Carmona'.[29]

Otto Reich meanwhile admitted making 'two or three' phone calls to Gustavo Cisneros, a key backer of the coup and one of the richest men in Latin America. Cisneros owned one of the main Venezuelan TV stations, Venevisión, as well as numerous other business franchises including Coca-Cola and Pizza Hut. Carmona and other coup leaders met with Cisneros in the offices of Venevisión on the afternoon of the coup.[30]

There are other indications of US involvement. Wayne Masden, a former US intelligence officer, alleged that offshore US navy ships provided signal jamming and communications intelligence to the opposition during the coup.[31] Venezuelan air force logs confirm that US naval ships were in the area at that time. Another glimpse of possible US meddling is given by this anecdote told by Chávez himself. At a diplomatic party on 8 April, a US marine officer called David Cazares asked for a 'General González'. He did not realize that there were two Gonzalezes present, only one of whom, General Néstor González González, was involved in plotting the coup. Cazares was directed to the other general, a Chávez loyalist, and said to him, 'Why haven't you contacted the ships that we have on the coast and the submarine submerged in La Guaira? What has happened? Why has no one contacted me?'[32]

While these fragments of evidence do not amount to a smoking gun, there is no doubt that the US was happy to see Chávez fall. White House spokesperson Ali Fleischer, speaking on 12 April, gave *de facto* recognition to the new government and repeated the opposition's version of events, including the false claims that Chávez had resigned and that his supporters had killed ten people. The following day Roger Noriega, the US ambassador to the Organization of American States, harried OAS delegates for failing to condemn Chávez's 'undemocratic behavior'.[33] The OAS did not follow the US lead and instead condemned the coup. Even after Chávez was restored to power, US officials continued to blame the victim for the coup. Condoleezza Rice told a TV interviewer that Chávez must 'right his own ship, which has been moving, frankly, in the wrong direction for a long time'.[34]

The oil strike and the recall referendum

US support for the opposition increased after the coup, even though many of its members had shown blatantly anti-democratic credentials. Two months after the coup, an Office of Transition Initiatives was set up in the US embassy in Venezuela. The Office was funded by USAID and was a crucial source of support for opponents of Chávez as they tried a number of other ways to oust him.

The first was a national strike, in reality a lockout since the employers simply shut up shop, in December 2002 called by the business federation, the opposition trade unions and the PDVSA management (a highly paid group with a high degree of operational autonomy, and opposed to Chávez's interference in running the national oil company). The 64-day stoppage crippled Venezuela and is estimated to have cost the country over US$10 billion. Petrol ran out at the pumps and thousands of shantytown inhabitants had no gas canisters to cook on. Food supplies were scarce in the cities, and oil-rich Venezuela was forced to import fuel. Within two weeks of the strike's launch, the White House called for 'early elections', echoing the opposition's demand.

During the strike, privately owned television stations donated free air time to the opposition, broadcasting repeated commercials in favour of the strike. The adverts tried to create a sense of crisis by showing dramatic old footage of teargas-fogged street battles with the police. Alberto Ravel, the head of Globovision, admitted that he put his twenty-four-hour news channel at the aid of the opposition – abandoning all pretence of objectivity – 'because my country was in danger'.[35] A declassified document unearthed by lawyer Eva Golinger shows that a US-financed consultancy, DAI, gave media training to opposition groups to promote 'democratic and modern values, rupturing with the patterns of paternalism and populism'.[36]

If the opposition expected the shortages to lead to rioting, they miscalculated; since the coup the shantytown-dwellers had become highly politicized and were determined to sit out this latest attempt to unseat Chávez. As the strike dragged on past Christmas, support began to fizzle out. In a dramatic move, the army seized the ports, installations and tankers in January 2003 and with the help of blue-collar workers and retired managers slowly began to get the oil pumping again.

US corporate sabotage?

While the US authorities played a background role in the strike, funding the opposition and backing their demands, one US company played a more important part. Science Applications International Corporation (SAIC), a computer consultancy firm, had previously formed a joint venture with PDVSA to run the oil company's electronic systems. These systems controlled the company's computers, refinery equipment and other machinery. The joint venture was called INTESA. During the strike, INTESA managers changed the access codes and sabotaged the programmes, making it impossible at first for the government to get the refineries back to work safely. When INTESA refused government requests to give them the access codes, the government raided INTESA's offices and seized its equipment. SAIC (which owned 60 per cent of INTESA) has longstanding links to the US intelligence services and the defence industry. Among its former executives are the former director of the CIA and Defense Secretary Robert Gates, the former National Security Agency director Bobby Ray Inman and another former Defense Secretary, Melvin Laird.[37] SAIC's deal with PDVSA also meant that it had access to highly sensitive commercial and geopolitical information such as the size and location of all of Venezuela's oil deposits, its production capacity and storage facilities.

Referendum

The opposition's third attempt to remove Chávez was conducted in a more legitimate manner: a referendum. Under the terms of Venezuela's new 'Bolivarian Constitution', citizens may call a referendum to recall the president if they collect a sufficient number of signatures, equivalent to 20 per cent of the electorate. The opposition set up petition-signing tables across the country in December 2003. The electoral authorities eventually confirmed that enough people had signed the petition and a referendum was set for August 2004. To the opposition's surprise, Chávez won a convincing victory, gaining 59 per cent of the poll, or 5.8 million votes, 2 million more than he had received in the presidential elections in 2000. Seventy per cent of the electorate had turned out to vote. The results were verified by the Carter Center and the OAS. US funding for opposition groups soared in this period; in total nearly US$15 million was distributed by the embassy's Office of Transition Initiatives, USAID and NED over 2003–04. The group organizing the referendum, Sumate, also received generous funding.

Why did Chávez win the referendum?

In the run-up to the referendum, Chávez ran an impressive get-the-vote-out campaign, sending teams of supporters into shantytowns and villages across the country. He launched a voter registration drive, ensuring that the – mainly poor – citizens who were not on the electoral roll signed up. He also gave citizenship and voting rights to long-term immigrants. In total between 2 million and 3 million new voters were added to the rolls. But the most important factor in Chávez's victory was undoubtedly his ambitious social welfare programmes, funded by oil revenues. Millions of Venezuelans have benefited from schemes such as Mission Robinson – (a literacy drive which taught over one million adults basic reading and writing), Barrio Adentro ('Inside the Shantytowns'), which has put 13,000 Cuban doctors in the shantytowns, Mission Ribas (which enrolled 600,000 young school drop-outs into evening classes to finish their school education) and Mission Sucre (which gave poor students extra help to get to university). In addition, the government set up shops in poor areas, selling subsidized rice, beans and other necessities. While some condemned these 'Missions' as populist gimmicks destined to peter out once the oil price fell, they undoubtedly improved the lives of many and were the main reason for Chávez's strong support among the poor. Chávez, however, seemed to have overstretched himself when he called another referendum in 2007, asking the population to approve wide-ranging constitutional reforms, including the abolition of presidential term limits. The proposals were criticized not only by his opponents, but also by many of his own supporters. They also drew criticism from the UN. Chávez narrowly lost the vote.

Chávez and human rights
The United States has consistently condemned Chávez's human rights record. To put their complaints in context, in Venezuela there are no disappearances, no death squads, no political prisoners, no state-sponsored executions, as there are in Colombia, the country that receives the vast bulk of US military aid to the region. The United Nations has not, to date, written a full report on human rights in Venezuela. In 1996, before Chávez came to power, the UN sent a mission to examine allegations of torture and mistreatment by the security forces; it concluded that both were serious problems. The UN returned in 2002, after Chávez had become president. It welcomed clauses included in Chávez's 1999 constitution which strengthened human rights in a number of ways, but concluded that there were still 'numerous complaints of torture, cruel, inhuman and degrading treatment, abuse of authority and arbitrary acts committed by agents of State security bodies'.[38] The victims were not political prisoners but usually low-income male criminal suspects. These abuses by the state police forces predate Chávez, but still occur. The UN also noted 'complaints of abuse of power and improper use of force as a means of control, particularly during demonstrations and protests'. Heavy-handed police treatment of demonstrators occurred before Chávez, but since his accession to power this has been one of the most common complaints of the opposition and has also been noted by international human rights groups such as Human Rights Watch and Amnesty International. Fourteen people were killed during anti-government demonstrations in 2004.

Chávez has been criticized by Human Rights Watch for undermining the independence of the judiciary by packing the supreme court and lower courts with allies.[39] Human Rights Watch has also condemned his treatment of the media. It warned that the Law of Social Responsibility in Radio and Television, introduced in 2004 to regulate what broadcasters could show, 'poses a serious threat to freedom of expression'. It also condemned the 'politically motivated decision' not to renew a television broadcasting licence for RCTV, Venezuela's oldest channel, which had been highly critical of Chávez and supported the coup against him.

There is little doubt that Chávez runs a highly personalist regime: he is the real power in the country and appears to make policy on a whim, sometimes during his own TV show. The national assembly has become little more than a rubber-stamping body since the opposition decided to boycott the 2005 congressional elections. The political polarization of the country is such that there are very few independent institutions: the judiciary, professional bodies, business groups, and TV channels are either pro- or anti- the regime. On both sides there is a somewhat cavalier attitude to democracy – or at least a disagreement about which democratic institutions should be respected. Most of the Venezuelan elite were prepared to support a military coup to remove an elected leader, while Chávez supporters have a revolutionary zeal and an urgency in their desire to use state power to transform the country. But Venezuela is not Cuba. There is no death penalty; elections are regularly held, and Chávez has respected every result. Opposition parties are numerous and vocal, and there is freedom of association and vigorous public debate.

Chávez Addresses the United Nations

Chávez made headlines during his address to the United Nations in 2006 when he described George Bush as 'the devil'.

'Yesterday, the president of the United States, the gentleman to whom I refer as the devil, came here, talking as if he owned the world. Truly. As the owner of the world ...

The president of the United States, yesterday, said to us, right here, in this room, and I'm quoting, "Anywhere you look, you hear extremists telling you you can escape from poverty and recover your dignity through violence, terror and martyrdom."

Wherever he looks, he sees extremists. And you, my brother — he looks at your colour, and he says, oh, there's an extremist. Evo Morales, the worthy president of Bolivia, looks like an extremist to him.

The imperialists see extremists everywhere. It's not that we are extremists. It's that the world is waking up. It's waking up all over. And people are standing up.

I have the feeling, dear world dictator, that you are going to live the rest of your days as a nightmare because the rest of us are standing up, all those who are rising up against American imperialism, who are shouting for equality, for respect, for the sovereignty of nations.

Yes, you can call us extremists, but we are rising up against the empire, against the model of domination ...

And you can wonder, just as the president of the United States addresses those peoples of the world, what would those peoples of the world tell him if they were given the floor? What would they have to say?

And I think I have some inkling of what the peoples of the south, the oppressed people think. They would say, "Yankee imperialist, go home."'

United Nations, New York, 2006

Future relations with the US

The tension with Venezuela will continue so long as the US military and intelligence services share the neoconservative view that Chávez is the greatest threat in the Western Hemisphere. Geopolitically they are concerned by Chávez's supposed friendships with Iran, Syria, North Korea and Cuba. John Negroponte, National Intelligence Director, and Condoleezza Rice both raised these alleged international links in testimony to the US Congress, and an entire congressional hearing in 2006 was devoted to the subject of 'Venezuela: Terrorism Hub of South America?' During his testimony Frank Urbancic, Deputy Coordinator for Counterterrorism, listed Chávez's alleged links with 'terrorists, Islamic radicals and insurgents', which included 'narco-terrorist organizations in Colombia' and 'leftists in Ecuador' alongside Iraqi insurgents and Hizbullah.[40] Referring to Hizbullah, Urbancic asserted, 'Without question, US interests are put at risk by the decision of the virulently anti-American Venezuelan regime assiduously courting a nation – Iran – that so prominently sponsors a surrogate terror group.' He concluded, 'Unfortunately today in Venezuela we see a regime that is increasingly out of step with the world ... In sum, in the international community's fight against terrorism, Venezuela is a liability.'

Chávez's alliance with left-wing governments in Latin America is also regarded with suspicion. A pamphlet published by the US Army War College, called *Venezuela's Hugo Chávez, Bolivarian Socialism and Asymmetric Warfare*, claims:

> In connection with the creation of new people's democracies, one can rest assured that Chávez and his Bolivarian populist allies will be available to provide money, arms, and leadership at any given opportunity. And, of course, the longer dysfunctional, rogue, criminal, and narco-states and people's democracies persist, the more they and their associated problems endanger global security, peace, and prosperity...

The Army War College concludes:

> inaction [against Chávez] could destroy the democracy, free market economies and prosperity that has been achieved and place the posterity of the hemisphere at serious risk.

Finally, there is the perennial question of oil. Venezuela is the US's fourth largest oil supplier, providing 13 per cent of its oil. The Americas as a whole provide the US with 53 per cent of its oil imports, compared with 24 per cent from the Middle Eastern Gulf region. In a congressional hearing on 'National Security Threats' Negroponte warned senators that Venezuela was attempting to diversify oil exports away from the United States.[41] Chávez has indeed signed some minor deals with China and held discussions with India. But it is very expensive to transport oil to China, and the Chinese would have to invest heavily in building refineries that could refine the type of heavy oil Venezuela produces. China, in any case, may not be a viable long-term option for Venezuela, since it is exploring reserves closer to home in the South China Sea.[42] Importantly, Venezuela's position as an oil supplier gives Chávez some leverage over the US, which he might be unwilling to cede. As Chávez put it: 'If it occurs to the United States, or someone there, to invade us, they can forget about Venezuelan oil.'[43]

Venezuela, the US Army and Asymmetrical Warfare

A US army publication analyses the threat posed by Chávez.

'Chávez and Venezuela are developing the conceptual and physical capability to challenge the status quo in Latin America and to generate a "Super Insurgency" intended to bring about fundamental political and economic change in the region ...

Chávez may be a military *caudillo*, but he is no "nut case". He is, in fact, ... a "wise competitor." He will not even attempt to defeat his enemies on their terms. Rather, he will seek to shift the playing field away from conventional military confrontations and turn to nontraditional forms of assault on a nation's stability and integrity ...

Chávez understands contemporary asymmetric warfare. He understands that this type of conflict requires more than weaponry and technology. It requires lucid and incisive thinking, resourcefulness, determination, imagination, and a certain disregard for convention. The promulgation of such a concept requires a somewhat different approach to conflict than that generally used by the United States over the past several years ...

Chávez's asymmetric war challenge is, thus, straightforward. Colonel Thomas X. Hammes reminds us that this kind of war is the only kind of war the United States has ever lost.

Recommendations
Asymmetric and irregular opponents are not invincible. They can be controlled and defeated, but only by coherent, patient action that encompasses all agencies of a targeted government and its international allies ...'

Source: M. G. Manwaring, *Venezuela's Hugo Chávez, Bolivarian Socialism and Asymmetric Warfare*, Strategic Studies Institute of US Army War College, October 2005

Bolivia

The US military had been warning of the 'threat' of growing radicalization in Bolivia for some time before Evo Morales, a peasant activist, was elected President at the end of 2005. General James T. Hill, head of the US Southern Command, had told members of Congress two years previously, 'If radicals continue to hijack the indigenous movement, we could find ourselves with a narco-state that supports the uncontrolled cultivation of coca.'[44]

The following year, his successor as Southern Command Chief, General John Craddock, warned:

The unrest that has plagued Bolivia since 2003 still simmers below the surface of a deeply divided and disaffected population. Distrust and loss of faith in failed institutes fuel the emergence of anti-US, anti globalization and anti-free trade elements who incite violence against their governments and their own people.[45]

An Interview with Activist Evo Morales

This interview was carried out in 2003 before Morales was elected President and during mass protests against free market policies in Bolivia.

'You have said you want to turn Latin America into a new Vietnam for the USA. What did you mean by that?
The US's constant aggression towards other countries will cause more uprisings, a growing national consciousness and a greater determination to defend our natural resources.

If the government of the United States continues its aggression against the peoples of Latin America, it's certain that it will be defeated. The people are no longer scared by threats, terror or even acts of violence. The peoples of Latin America have lost their fear of the United States. That's why I'm absolutely certain Latin America will be a second Vietnam for the US.

Here in Latin America there is a systematic uprising of social movements. In Latin America we're good at getting rid of presidents but we're still not good at putting them in – just look at Ecuador, Peru, Bolivia, Argentina. We're in this process now. But from what I've seen, today's political leaders come from the social struggles, trade union struggles and not from the universities. Those who come from the universities just go on to be technocrats for the IMF.

Which US policies, in particular, are you opposed to?
The imposition, via the World Bank, of neoliberal economic policies. Neoliberalism is the reproduction of the capitalist system, savage and inhuman. Capitalism is no solution for humanity or planet earth. We are seeing the clash of two cultures: the culture of life and the culture of death. The culture of life, represented by indigenous cultures, and the culture of death, represented by the West. I am sure the culture of life is going to win this confrontation.

The culture of life is reciprocity; solidarity and, fundamentally, the redistribution of wealth. We should live in harmony with mother earth, not try to subordinate her. Western culture is individualist, egoistic, capitalist and concentrates wealth in a few hands. Concentrating wealth in a few hands is no solution for humanity ...

What's your alternative? You've talked about 'people's power' but what does that mean exactly?
All our natural resources should belong to the Bolivian state and the people should have the right to participate in the administration of the country. There should be no more privatizations ... Above all, our natural resources should not be in the hands of transnational companies ...

What do you mean by popular participation?
We want to elect a constituent assembly to create a new Bolivia without injustice, without inequality, without discrimination. We want to live together, in

→

➜ diversity, but with unity. We want a new multi-ethnic, pluri-cultural state, without exploiters or exploited, without marginalized or marginalizers.

Could you explain why you are against the Free Trade Area of the Americas (ALCA)?

ALCA should be renamed the Agreement to Legalize the Colonization of the Americas. Because that's what it is: colonization. The transnationals, with their genetically modified products, are going to capture our market and our farmers won't be able to sell their products. It's the law of the jungle: survival of the strongest ...

Do you think with Lula in Brazil, Chávez in Venezuela and uprisings in Ecuador and Argentina, that there is a new Left in Latin America?

There is a new Left based on social movements. A new Left without dogma. A new Left that is for life.

Bush's genocidal and bloody intervention in Iraq has led to a rise in anti-imperialist feeling around the world, not just Latin America. And it will continue to grow, as long as US aggression continues. The peoples of the world will oppose this interventionism, these policies of hunger and misery, these policies which concentrate land in a few hands and leave many landless, these policies of discrimination. It's a great uprising, a rebellion against these policies. I hope the World Bank and IMF can understand that in Bolivia and Latin America people are no longer willing to submit to these policies. They have to understand the damage they are causing to our countries.

What type of Latin America do you want?

One with dignity, identity and sovereignty based on its natural resources. Latin America in brotherhood.

Who do you most respect in the world today?

Fidel Castro.

How would you describe yourself politically?

As someone who is at the service of the people.

How would you define George W. Bush?

A bloodthirsty butcher without human conscience or concern for the poor.'

Evo Morales interviewed by the author in 2003

Paranoia reached new heights in a speech by Roger Pardo-Maurer, Deputy Assistant Secretary of Defense:

> I would like to draw your attention to what I regard as the objective of subversion that Cuba and Venezuela *are* working on as a joint project ... and that is Bolivia ...They are trying to steer this revolution towards a Marxist, socialist, if you like, populist state in the new Bolivarian model. This is their big project ... Bolivia is the set battle piece going on right now. It is not by any means inevitable that Bolivia should go to a Marxist, radical, anti-US, pro-Cuba, drug producing state. That is not inevitable. But the other side is working very hard to take it that way ...[46]

Morales was elected President of Bolivia in December 2005 with an emphatic mandate. He received 54 per cent of the vote – the first time in Bolivia's history that a candidate has received a majority in the first round. Morales was not simply a peasant leader, but a leader of coca-growing peasants. The coca leaf has been used by indigenous communities in the Andean region for centuries and is a traditional part of their culture. But the US regards coca leaf as a narcotic because it is the basis (after chemical processing) of cocaine. Morales is a self-educated indigenous Aymaran who was born into a poor family in the Bolivian highlands and started work at seven years old. He rose to national prominence as head of the militant coca unions which defended their crops from the army's militarized eradication campaign, a struggle in which many peasants were killed. Bolivia is the poorest country in South America and was not served well by neoliberalism; poverty grew dramatically in the 1990s. Mass social protest exploded at the end of that decade and Morales came to the fore as a natural leader. He narrowly lost the 2002 presidential elections – his campaign was given a boost when the US ambassador advised Bolivians not to vote for him. The victor in those elections, the pro-Washington González Sánchez de Lozada, was forced to flee to Miami just a year later, when protests against his pro-market policies made the country ungovernable. Morales had an ambitious vision: to build a new nation, governed by the indigenous poor majority, in which the wealth from Bolivia's natural resources would be taken back from the transnational corporations and used to benefit the poor. Nationalization, wealth redistribution and a new constitution were his campaign promises.

The US and Bolivia

The main source of conflict between the United States and Bolivia has been the question of coca (dealt with more fully in Chapter 9). For Bolivians, the coca leaf is a question of sovereignty. It is a traditional product and they believe the country has a right to grow it. The US equates coca with cocaine. There may be room for negotiation, though, because the Morales government has shown a certain amount of pragmatism. It is willing to cut the amount of coca grown in Bolivia, but say that eradication must be done by negotiation and not by force. The Bolivarians say traditional coca-growing communities should be allowed to produce sufficient coca leaf for domestic consumption, and they are also lobbying the UN to make coca leaf and coca products (coca tea, soap, etcetera) legal exports. At the same time Morales has reassured the US he will cooperate in other areas of counter-drugs policy, agreeing, for example, to assist with interdiction. The more sophisticated US policy makers know that an inflexible policy could push Bolivia further into the arms of Chávez. Yet they have to balance the possible benefits of a concessionary approach with the danger that Bolivia could set a precedent for other countries to opt out of the 'war on drugs'. This is particularly important because counter-narcotics has been the main pretext for a US military presence in Latin America since the end of the Cold War.

Perhaps the deciding factor will be whether the US is allowed to maintain close ties with the Bolivian military. Bolivia was the second-most important recipient of US military training and aid in Latin America during the ten years before Evo Morales came to power. Between 1998 and 2004, over 9,000 Bolivian soldiers were trained by the US military. Collaboration between the US and the Bolivian military not only allows the US considerable influence over drug policy, but also keeps it abreast in any potential conspiracies or coup plots. To US satisfaction, the military collaboration continued with Bolivia in the first year of Evo Morales's presidency, although there were signs that Bolivia wanted to loosen the ties; for example, Bolivia announced that it was withdrawing its personnel from the School of the Americas, as have Argentina, Uruguay and Venezuela.[47]

Another source of friction with the US is trade. Many Bolivians strongly oppose a free trade deal, which they regard as a form of semi-colonialism. They do, however, want to extend an agreement in which the US allows certain Bolivian products into the US tariff-free, in return for cooperation on anti-drugs policy. The value of Bolivian imports included in the so-called Andean Preferential Tariffs Agreement is of miniscule importance to the US economy but accounts for at least 80,000 jobs in Bolivia. Speaking during a trip to the United States in 2006, Morales adopted a conciliatory, yet composed tone:

> We have obvious differences, but we want to work out those differences. Even though we're an underdeveloped country, we're a sovereign country, a country with dignity … We want relations with all the countries that will be based on mutual respect … we want partners and not bosses.[48]

Morales's tone belies a crucial difference between the Bolivian and the Venezuelan position towards the United States. Chávez does not need trade deals with the US because he has a *de facto* one-way free trade deal: he can export as much oil to the country as he likes, tariff-free. Relatively impoverished Bolivia is in a much more precarious situation, which gives the US greater leverage.

Evo's revolution

In the first year of Evo Morales's presidency, the US toned down its rhetoric against him. The US can afford to await developments with Bolivia because it does not have a major economic stake in the country, as it does in Venezuela. No major US oil and gas companies are based there; the main foreign investors in Bolivia's gas fields are Brazilian and Spanish. Although indigenous Morales has the makings of an iconic figure, he does not yet have the international profile of Hugo Chávez. Morales, in fact, is faced with an exceptionally complicated domestic scene, and the US may decide that stepping back and allowing him to hang himself with his own rope may be the best policy. Not only does Morales have to negotiate with the myriad trade unions and social movements that make up his base (and as longstanding autonomous movements they are far less pliant than their counterparts in Venezuela), but he is also confronted by a powerful opposition led by agribusiness and ranchers in the rich Bolivian state of Santa Cruz. This powerful regional elite dominates the national media and controls most of the country's wealth. Their demand for autonomy could deprive the national government of much revenue.

Within months of coming to office, Morales met his campaign promise of holding elections for a constituent assembly. The assembly was beset by acrimonious division, however, and it took eighteen months to draft a constitution. The draft was finally approved during a controversial ceremony boycotted by the largest opposition group, in a building surrounded by government troops. The constitution was due to be ratified in a nationwide referendum in 2008, but because of political turmoil the vote was postponed. Instead, four regions of Bolivia held controversial referenda on autonomy in June and July 2008, which were in violation of the existing constitution and not recognized by the courts or the government. Morales responded by calling a recall referendum in August 2008 in which he, his vice-president and the regional prefects were to submit their mandates for validation by the electorate.

In its first year the Morales government also introduced an ambitious programme of social and economic reform. With great drama, troops were sent to the gas fields as Morales announced the nationalization of Bolivia's oil and gas industry. Bolivia's state-owned company now controls the reserves and will have a 51 per cent stake in any venture with a private company. Following months of wrangling, the foreign companies involved – Brazil's Petrobras and Spain's Repsol – agreed to pay higher royalties to Bolivia, although not as high as originally announced. The government also launched an education bond, paying poor families to send their children to school (a scheme that has had considerable success in Brazil). Free healthcare for women and children has been extended and a literacy campaign was launched, with Cuban help. Electricity charges for poor families were cut, while pensions and the minimum wage were raised. The high world price for gas, Bolivia's main export, helped to fund these measures. A land reform bill was passed by congress in 2006 which allows the state to expropriate underused or idle land. The government plans to redistribute 20 million hectares of land to poor peasants. Throughout Latin American history, land reform has been a source of conflict with both domestic elites and the United States, because it presents a direct challenge to property rights. The Bolivian landowning class are indeed strongly opposed to the land reform bill and will try to block its implementation, but it remains to be seen whether the US regards it as a significant threat.

Nicaragua

The prospect of former Sandinista guerrilla Daniel Ortega winning the 2006 Nicaraguan presidential elections horrified Washington, and US officials began trying to avert a Sandinista victory two years before the vote. Alarm bells first rang when Ortega's party, the Sandinista Front for National Liberation (FSLN) won a landslide victory in the municipal elections of November 2004. Dan Fisk, US Deputy Assistant Secretary of State, travelled to Nicaragua where he met leaders of right-wing parties, in the first of many US efforts to unite the right-wing opposition against Ortega. US ambassador Paul Trivelli, who was posted to Nicaragua in 2005, spent a year trying to cajole opposition parties into forming a united front. Trivelli, in clear violation of diplomatic protocol, repeatedly criticized candidate Ortega and called on Nicaraguans to vote for his opponents:

> In terms of the larger role, if the electoral machinery worked well and if the political landscape were level, the US ambassador, any other country, would sit on the sidelines and say: 'May the best man win.' In a country like Nicaragua that is obviously not the case.[49]

The ambassador's efforts to find a viable non-Sandinista candidate were backed up by US funds. The NED awarded grants of US$800,000 for electioneering work and opposition groups; the IRI received more than a third of those funds and made no secret of its antagonism towards the FSLN,[50] describing Ortega as a 'communist' and a 'former revolutionary dictator'. One initiative of the IRI was to organize a visit to Nicaragua for Jeane Kirkpatrick, Ronald Reagan's hardline adviser, who duly warned that democracy was 'in danger'. USAID also spent heavily on the Nicaraguan elections, awarding grants of US$1.87 million in 2006 and US$3.5 million in 2005.

The US not only opposed Ortega because of his revolutionary past; they were also unhappy about his criticism of the Central American Free Trade Area (CAFTA) and his friendship with Hugo Chávez. Ortega appeared on Chávez's television programme *Aló Presidente* and FSLN mayors signed a deal to receive cheap oil from Venezuela. As the election neared and Ortega maintained a lead in the polls, the US began to issue veiled and not-so veiled threats about the consequences of an FSLN victory. Writing in the Nicaraguan daily *La Prensa*, both the US Secretary of Commerce Carlos Gutiérrez and the deputy director of USAID Adolfo Franco warned that US aid could be in doubt if 'the former dictator' Ortega won the elections.[51] 'Some of Ortega's declarations worry us,' wrote Franco.[52] Ambassador Trivelli drummed the message home in an interview with the London *Financial Times*, in which he said the US would 're-evaluate' its relationship with Nicaragua if Ortega won. Four congressmen also lobbied to cut off Nicaraguan remittances (money sent home by Nicaraguans working in the US), if the wrong candidate won. These threats were highly reminiscent of the US blackmail in the 1990 elections, when voters knew that if they voted for the FSLN, the US embargo and the US's Contra War would continue and aid would remain frozen.

Nicaraguan voters were also bombarded with a barrage of propaganda. Jeb Bush, the brother of the president, took out a full-page advertisement in *La Prensa* warning of the dangers of an Ortega victory. Otto Reich wrote an anti-Ortega editorial for the same newspaper, and Roger Noriega, another former Assistant Secretary of State, wrote a similar article for the *Washington Post*. The notorious veteran of the Iran–

'Daniel Ortega is a declared enemy of the United States'

'The past and present of Daniel Ortega clearly indicate that he neither understands nor accepts the basic principles of freedom, democracy and the free market. Some say he has changed, that the years out of power have convinced him of the necessity for genuine democracy, for open markets, and for the maintaining of good relations with his neighbors and with the United States. This is what Ortega would want us to believe.

Daniel Ortega is an enemy of everything the United States represents. Further, he is a friend of our enemies. Ortega has a relationship of more than 30 years with states and individuals who shelter and condone international terrorism.'

Jeb Bush, in a full-page advertisement in *La Prensa*, 29 October 2006

'Like Adolf Hitler, the anti-American leftists in Latin America are using elections – not revolutions or military coups – to take and then solidify power. It's a tactic that seems to have escaped the striped-pants set in our State Department. Until this week's visit to the region by Defense Secretary Donald Rumsfeld, the State Department's response to the threatening leftward turn to our south – and a Sandinista return to power – has been both flat-footed and tone deaf.'

Source: Oliver North, 'Who Lost Nicragua', 6 October 2006. www.townhall.com

---

Contra scandal, Oliver North himself, visited Nicaragua days before the election, warning of the threat to democracy.

Despite the pressure, Daniel Ortega was elected President in November 2006. Ironically, although Washington hardliners cannot stomach an old Cold War foe coming to power and have put Ortega in the same radical populist camp as Chávez, Ortega is now impossible to confuse with the radical he used to be. Many of his former Sandinista comrades have broken with him and formed a new party. Ortega now says his inspiration is God, not Marx; to prove his point and to appeal to the Catholic vote, he backed a hardline anti-abortion law – which bans abortion in all cases even when a women's life in danger – just weeks before the elections. His running mate was a former negotiator for the Contra rebels, Jaime Morales Carazo, and he formed an alliance with a right-wing former president Arnoldo Alemán, who had been jailed for corruption.

Ortega's party has a minority in the congress, so he will have to make alliances to govern. His most likely partner is the right-wing PLC and its disgraced leader Alemán. Despite US fears, it is by no means clear that Ortega wants to pull out of the Central American Free Trade Agreement; instead he has made vague promises about reducing poverty and improving education. Ortega has made several overtures to the US since his election and there is clearly space for a rapprochement. If the White House fails to shake off its outdated Cold War mentality and shuns Ortega, it will only have itself to blame if the Nicaraguan president turns to the more welcoming embrace of Chávez and his friends.

Haiti: US Backs Another Coup?

President Jean-Bertrand Aristide left Haiti with his wife in the early hours of 28 February 2004 in a US chartered airplane and accompanied by US forces. At 11pm the night before, US ambassador James Foley had told the Haitian president that he could not guarantee his safety amid mass protests and a growing armed rebellion. Aristide maintains that he was kidnapped by the US and forced to leave. The US says he resigned and went willingly. Even if the latter is the case, the US helped to remove an elected leader from power, under pressure from armed revolt led by reactionary elements of the old military. The US Republican Party had a longstanding antipathy towards Aristide, a radical priest who preached against the wealthy. They had disapproved when Clinton sent the marines to reinstall him in 1994, and policy towards him hardened after George W. Bush came to power in 2001. The IRI, with the knowledge of key Bush officials, helped to destabilize the Aristide regime by working closely with opposition groups, including former military officers who had a known history of violating human rights. Aristide, however, also contributed to the violent and unstable atmosphere by creating vigilante gangs to intimidate his opponents.

Haiti Timeline

1975–86	Dictatorship of 'Papa Doc' and 'Baby Doc' Duvalier
1990	Jean-Bertrand Aristide is elected President.
1991	Aristide is ousted in a coup.
1994	Aristide is reinstalled by US marines.
1996	René Préval, an Aristide ally, is elected President.
2000	Aristide is re-elected President.
2001	Unsuccessful coup attempt against Aristide.
2004	Aristide leaves Haiti in a US-chartered plane, after mass protests and armed revolt.
2004–06	Haiti is ruled by an interim government backed by UN troops.
February 2006	René Préval is elected President.

Aristide returns to power, 1994

Aristide was restored to power by 20,000 US marines in 1994. Haiti is the poorest country in the Western Hemisphere and after three years of economic embargo the economy was in tatters. The Clinton government and international financial institutions offered Aristide loans and aid on condition that he implement a strict structural adjustment plan. Their demands included privatization of state enterprises, cuts in public spending, the laying off of 52,000 public employees, a rise in fuel prices and increased taxes. These measures hit the poorest section of the population –

Aristide's traditional base – and alienated his supporters. Official unemployment was over 60 per cent. Having lambasted the oligarchy for allowing the poor to live in inhuman conditions, Aristide found himself unable to raise welfare spending in a country where more than half the children suffered from malnutrition. Aristide later opened free trade zones producing toys, clothes and other consumer goods for the US market, reinforcing Haiti's position as the cheapest source of labour in the region. Despite these measures, Aristide never reached a rapprochement with the Haitian business elite, who distrusted his left-wing rhetoric and his mobilization of the poor. René Préval, an ally of Aristide, was elected President in 1996 because one of the conditions of Aristide's reinstatement by US forces was that he would not stand for two consecutive terms. Aristide himself was re-elected President in 2000. Although the presidential election was technically correct, the opposition boycotted the vote, resulting in a turnout of less than 15 per cent, which gave Aristide a less than emphatic mandate.

Aristide had dismantled the old, repressive army when he returned to power in 1994. A new army was not created and Aristide was reliant on the police force to enforce law and order. This was particularly difficult because many demobilized soldiers retained their arms, making Haiti a highly violent society. Unwilling to trust the police to defend his government, Aristide created a network of violent gangs, comprising party members and shantytown thugs. The *chimères* – 'monsters' – attacked and sometimes killed political opponents. They burned down the houses of their enemies and violently broke up opposition demonstrations. To many they were a macabre reminder of the Tonton Macoutes of the Duvalier era. As opposition grew, Aristide increasingly relied on his private 'army', particularly after an attempted coup against his government in 2001.

The opposition

The opposition to Aristide included even more professional purveyors of terror. The armed rebellion was led by Louis-Jodel Chamblain, Jean Pierre Baptiste and Guy Philippe. Chamblain and Baptiste were former leaders of FRAPH, the death squad run by the old Haitian military. Both had been convicted for their role in the Raboteau massacre in which twenty civilians were killed. Guy Philippe was a former police chief, cited by the UN for summary execution of suspects. Philippe was also involved in drugs trafficking. The political opposition was led by Democratic Convergence, an alliance of business leaders and supporters of the old regime, with strong US support and US AID funding. There was no formal link between the Convergence and the leaders of the armed revolt, but there appeared to be some coordination between them. The IRI, for example, ran a training session in 2002 for the Convergence at a hotel where two of the leaders were staying.[53] The US ambassador to Haiti, Brian Dean Curran, was so concerned by the IRI's activities that he warned Washington their behaviour 'risked us being accused of attempting to destabilize the government'.[54]

Ambassador Curran asked the White House to impose tighter controls on the IRI but was rebuffed. Instead the State Department and National Security Council formally expressed their support for Democratic Convergence. Assistant Secretary of

State, Otto Reich, speaking to the *New York Times*, admitted that the Bush administration policy was not one of reconciliation between the pro- and anti-Aristide factions. 'There was a change in policy that was perhaps not perceived by some people in the embassy,' he said, referring to Ambassador Curran – a Clinton appointee. 'We wanted to change, to give the Haitians an opportunity to choose a democratic leader.'[55] According to Ambassador Curran, Reich refused to act upon any of the urgent cables sent to him.

The other major opposition body was the Group of 184, an alliance of business organizations led by Andy Apaid, a factory owner, supporter of the old Duvalier dictatorship and opponent of Aristide's measures to extend workers' rights. At the end of 2003, mass protests by students and opposition groups convulsed Port-au-Prince, while an armed uprising was launched from the bordering Dominican Republic. The Caribbean economic community, CARICOM, proposed a compromise, in which a power-sharing body would hold power until parliamentary elections could be held. This plan was backed by the OAS, by President Aristide and initially by Colin Powell. But the opposition, scenting blood, refused. Refusing to heed calls from the Black Caucus in Washington for a military intervention, the Bush administration ordered ambassador Foley to give Aristide an ultimatum to leave the country. Just hours after Aristide's departure, the UN Security Council, at the behest of the US, Canada and France, passed a resolution recognizing the new interim government. CARICOM, however, refused to recognize the interim government and, together with the OAS, called for an investigation into Aristide's ousting. The investigation never happened.

After Aristide
UN peacekeeping troops were sent to Haiti after Aristide's flight, but were unable to prevent a bloodbath against supporters of the former president. According to a study by the British medical journal the *Lancet*, as many as 8,000 people were murdered in a 22-month period in 2004–05, and half of these deaths were political murders (some have criticized the methodology of this study).[56] Dozens of former military officers convicted of horrific human rights abuses, including death squad leader Louis Jodel Chamblain, 'escaped' from prison during this period. Elections were finally held in February 2006. René Préval, an ally of Aristide, won by a clear margin.[57] Aristide remained in exile in South Africa.

Cuba

After the collapse of the Soviet Union, Cuba no longer seemed a threat to the national security of the United States. The Cuba policy of both George Bush senior and Bill Clinton was almost entirely dictated by domestic electoral concerns. But George W. Bush was different; no president has wooed the Cuban-American lobby more assiduously than George W. – indeed Florida was crucial to his election as president – but domestic concerns have not been the only influence on his Cuba strategy. The neoconservatives in his administration grew increasingly agitated by what they termed the 'Venezuela–Cuba axis' and its destabilizing influence across Latin America. Once again, Cuba became an issue of national security. The neocons were also keenly aware of Castro's mortality and, even before he became ill and handed power to his brother Raúl, the Bush administration had drawn up a Transition Plan, which spelt out in incredible detail how the US might shape a post-Castro regime (see below).

To add to the pressure on Castro, Bush tightened up the embargo, restricting travel to the island and reducing the amount of money that exiles could send to their families. Visits to Cuba by academics, religious leaders, NGOs and business executives slumped during the Bush years. The Bush administration ignored the growing number of voices opposing the embargo. Many congressional politicians, both Democrat and Republican, argued that greater engagement with Cuban society might be a better way of undermining one-party rule. Some suggested that the embargo actually helped Fidel to stay in power by giving him someone to blame for his own mismanagement. Agricultural and tourism companies were keen to exploit business opportunities in Cuba. If Cuba had a market the size of communist China's, US corporate interests would probably have destroyed the embargo years ago, but the profits to be made in Cuba simply do not compare. The corporate anti-embargo lobby was not strong enough to overcome the neocons' ideological aversion to Castro and Bush's need to repay Cuban Floridians for their electoral support.

'Cuba is developing a biological weapons effort'

'Havana has long provided safe haven for terrorists, and has collaborated in biotechnology – including extensive dual use technologies with BW [biological weapons] applications – with state sponsors of terror...

The Bush administration has said repeatedly that we are concerned that Cuba is developing a limited biological weapons effort, and called on Fidel Castro to cease his BW aspirations and support of terrorism ... In early 2002, the intelligence community approved the following unclassified language on Cuba's BW efforts for an unclassified speech I was planning to give:

> The United States believes that Cuba has at least a limited developmental offensive biological warfare research and development effort. Cuba has provided dual-use biotechnology to other rogue states. We are concerned that such technology could support BW programs in those states. We call on Cuba to cease all BW-applicable cooperation with rogue states and to fully comply with all of its obligations under the Biological Weapons Convention.

... The Administration believes that Cuba remains a terrorist and BW threat to the United States. The Bush Administration continues to watch this rogue state very closely.'

John Bolton, Under Secretary of State for Arms Control and International Security, Testimony to the House International Relations Committee, 30 March 2004

Cuba and 11 September 2001

The attacks on 11 September presented the Bush administration with an opportunity for a rapprochement with Cuba. Fidel Castro strongly condemned the attacks and held a state-sponsored demonstration against terrorism. The Cuban government offered humanitarian aid, anti-anthrax drugs and airspace to US planes. These offers were rebuffed. Although Castro criticized the invasion of Afghanistan, he continued to make overtures towards the US, including offers of increased cooperation on migration, narcotics and terrorism. Castro was also notably quiescent on the question of Guantánamo Bay. The US has had an indefinite lease on the Cuban naval base since 1898 and historically this has been a strong source of resentment in Cuba. The Cubans, however, decided not to challenge the US decision to hold terrorist suspects at the base, although it later voiced qualms about the treatment of the prisoners. The fear of a US invasion largely explained Cuba's attitude. The invasion of Afghanistan and, particularly, Iraq had showed that the US was prepared to act unilaterally against so-called 'rogue states'. Cuban exiles in Miami were quick to draw the parallels, holding demonstrations in which they chanted 'Iraq Now! Cuba Later'.[58]

The Bush Administration Harbours Terrorists

Orlando Bosch and Luis Posada Carriles are Cuban exiles suspected of bombing a Cuban airliner in 1976, killing all 73 civilians aboard. Both men are resident in the US and George Bush's government refused to extradite them to Venezuela or Cuba.

They are suspected of numerous other terrorist attacks. The US Justice Department linked Bosch to 30 acts of terrorism, but he was pardoned of all US offences by George Bush Senior. Posada Carriles was imprisoned in Panama for attempting to assassinate Castro with 33lb of explosives, but was pardoned in 2004.

Declassified documents show that both Bosch and Posada Carriles were CIA assets. Posada Carriles was an informant and received CIA training in demolitions in the 1960s. He also took part in the CIA's bungled Bay of Pigs attack, although his ship never landed in Cuba.

The declassified records also show that the CIA had advanced warning of the attack on a Cuban airliner, but did not warn the Cuban government. A 1976 CIA memorandum entitled 'Possible Plans of Cuban Exile Extremists to Blow Up a Cubana Airliner' states 'A Cuban exile group, of which Orlando Bosch is a leader, plans to place a bomb on a Cubana airline flight.' Another declassified State Department document, which was sent to Henry Kissinger, notes a source overhearing Posada saying 'we are going to hit a Cuban airplane' and 'Orlando has the details', days before the plane was blown up off the coast of Barbados.

Sources: 'Luis Posada Carriles: The Declassified Record', National Security Archive Electronic Briefing Book No. 153. CIA Report, 'Possible Plans of Cuban Exile Extremists to Blow Up a Cubana Airliner', June 22, 1976. State Department, Bureau of Intelligence and Research, October 18, 1976, Memorandum, 'Castro's Allegations', To: The Secretary, From: INR Harold Saunders.

Biological weapons?

Soon after the attacks on the Twin Towers, the neoconservatives added Cuba to an expanded 'axis of evil'. In a speech entitled 'Beyond the Axis of Evil', Under Secretary of State John Bolton accused Cuba of seeking to obtain biological weapons. Cuba, Libya and Syria should be added to the list of rogue states, he said, adding that the Cuban threat to the US had been 'underplayed'. He went on to warn that 'States that sponsor terror and pursue WMD must stop ... Those that do not can expect to become our targets.'[59]

When questioned about the biological weapons claims, Colin Powell later clarified that Cuba did not actually possess such weapons but 'has the capability and capacity to conduct such research'.[60] Meanwhile, Assistant Secretary of State Dan Fisk told the press, 'Make no mistake about it ... Castro aids terrorism and aids terrorists.'[61] The accusation of harbouring terrorists was ironic, given the Bush administration's failure to take action against two convicted Cuban criminals, Orlando Bosch and Luis Posada Carriles (see box).

The Venezuela–Cuba axis

The claims of biological weapons and links to Islamic terrorists were clearly far-fetched; as former Southern Command leader Barry McCaffrey put it during a trip to the island in 2002, Cuba represented 'zero military threat'. The neoconservatives soon became concerned, however, about a more real, if nebulous, challenge: the political alliance between Venezuela's Hugo Chávez and Fidel Castro. The rise of the Left in Latin America had led to a resurgence of sympathy for Cuba. Chávez and Bolivia's Evo Morales, in particular, are admirers of Castro. At the same time cheap Venezuelan oil has provided a much-needed lift for the Cuban economy. Secretary of State Condoleezza Rice warned in 2006:

> There are clear signs the regime is using money provided by the Chávez government in Venezuela to reactivate its networks in the hemisphere to subvert democratic governments. The Castro regime's international meddling is done at the expense of the needs of the Cuban people.[62]

Roger Pardo-Maurer, Deputy Assistant Secretary of Defense, said that the two countries were championing a 'downright evil alternative' to the US model and had expansionist plans:

> With regard to Cuba ... They're back with a huge foreign policy and we need to be aware of that. As we all know, this foreign policy has to do with their association with Venezuela ... I want to ... give a sense of the scale of it because in talking with even very informed people, I find they're surprised at just how truly massive, how expeditionary this relationship is.[63]

Even General John Craddock, leader of the Southern Command and a career officer rather than an ideologue, saw geopolitical if not military dangers:

> I do not see Cuba as a military threat to the United States, I do not see Venezuela as a military threat to the United States, what I do see is an influence in Latin America

that creates, potentially creates instability and uncertainty, because in Cuba, obvious, it is a totalitarian state, a communist state, and in Venezuela it appears that demo cratic processes and institutions are at risk. That has great opportunity to create, again, instability and uncertainty throughout the region if those processes are exported. So we are concerned, and we believe the neighbors in the region should also be concerned.[64]

The Bush administration was so alarmed by the Venezuela–Cuba axis that national intelligence director John Negroponte appointed a new acting mission manager for Cuba and Venezuela to collect 'timely and accurate intelligence' on the two countries.

Planning for the Death of Castro

The death of Fidel Castro has long been an obsession of the White House and the Bush administration made detailed plans for the aftermath. For a long time Washington assumed that the regime would simply implode after Castro's demise, or as Pardo-Maurer put it: 'When the old man dies, this rotten apple will fall off the tree and roll our way.' The neocons became increasingly worried, however, that the alliance with Venezuela would enable the communist regime to endure beyond his death. Pardo-Maurer went on to paint the nightmare scenario:

Castro knows he's on his deathbed. He places the phone call, says 'Huguito, me muero' [I'm dying]. Hugo comes to Cuba. There is a touching death bed scene. Raúl and Chávez come out carrying the coffin. The revolution will live; the revolution will continue.

The Bush administration began to take action. In 2005 Caleb McCarry, a right-wing Republican fixer, was appointed Cuban Transition Coordinator. His job was to 'hasten the end of the dictatorship'. In the same year, the CIA added Cuba to its secret list of twenty-five unstable countries where US intervention might be required.

Transition plans

Bush's first post-Castro transition plan was published in 2004, and an updated version which specifically highlighted the threat of Cuba's alliance with Venezuela was released in July 2006 by Secretary of State Condoleezza Rice. The 2004 report is a 458-page document spelling out how a US government would help to shape a post-Castro regime. It aims to transform Cuba into a free market economy, to privatize the welfare state and dismantle the 'Communist' education system, including the provision of non-communist books in schools. Politically, it advocates free elections, the end of Communist Party rule and an overhaul of the police and judiciary. The report refers to an undefined 'transition government', with which the US would work and which would eventually call elections. The document is enormously ambitious, addressing every facet of Cuban society; most Cuba experts regarded it as highly unrealistic because the US does not have the influence there to impose it – at least not without the help of the marines.

While most of the document was an elaborate wish-list, the first chapter, 'Hastening Cuba's Transition', contained measures that the Bush administration could implement immediately. The most controversial of these were reduction in the amount of remittances exiles could send home and the tightening up of travel restrictions. Educational and tourist visits were also curtailed and the number of US visitors to Cuba slumped from 210,000 in 2003 to 40,000 in 2005. There was also increased financing for Cuban dissidents and the provision of US military aircraft to improve the transmission of Radio and TV Marti's anti-communist broadcasts into Cuba.

The Commission for Assistance to a Free Cuba, 2006
The updated 2006 report headed by Condoleezza Rice had an increased urgency. It warned that the Cubans had a 'succession plan' that must be thwarted and it highlighted the alleged dangers of Cuba's new alliance with Venezuela.

> Fidel Castro and his inner circle have begun a gradual but intrinsically unstable process of succession. The regime is unquestionably attempting to insulate itself from the consequences of Fidel Castro's incapacitation, death, or ouster. The regime continues to harden its edges and is feverishly working to forestall any opportunity for a genuine democratic transition on the island. The current regime in Havana is working with like-minded governments, particularly Venezuela, to build a network of political and financial support designed to forestall any external pressure to change. This state of affairs highlights the urgency of working today to ensure that the Cuban transition is genuine and that the Castro regime's succession strategy does not succeed.

The first few chapters cover the same subjects as the 2004 report: humanitarian aid, democracy and establishing a free market economy. Three new sections have been added, most notably: 'The Vital Role of Cubans Abroad', in which returned exiles are seen as key players in the reconstruction of Cuba. Two other chapters – 'The Role of the International Community' and 'Preparing Now to Support the Transition' – focus on encouraging other countries to isolate the Castro regime and support the US transition plans. The report earmarks a further US$80 million to be spent on propagandizing against Castro and funding opponents of the regime. Ominously, this report includes a 'Secret Annex' which has been classified for 'national security reasons', suggesting that the US has a secret military strategy for Cuba.

Fidel resigns
Fidel Castro resigned on grounds of ill health in February 2008, and his brother Raúl was duly elected president by the national assembly. The calm, controlled transition no doubt pleased a man who had seen ten presidents in the White House and outfoxed them all. The Cuban leadership insisted that communism would continue after Fidel, but a strangely timid choice of vice-president suggested that another transition would soon be necessary. Instead of choosing a young communist cadre who could lead Cuba in the twenty-first century, a 78-year-old hardliner, Machado Ventura, was picked. Cuba's admirers often concede that the population has gripes about the economy but claim they are happy with the political system. Yet it is

impossible to tell what people think when they cannot speak freely. While widespread dissent was not evident when Castro remained alive, it cannot be ruled out once he has left the scene. Many experts predicted that Cuba might follow the path of China, opening up the economy but maintaining the one-party state. Clearly the Bush administration hoped that the system would implode and that thousands of anti-communist exiles would return – backed, perhaps, by a 'peacekeeping' force. But in Cuba there is widespread distrust of the Miami exiles, and although many Cubans want change, no one wants to go back to the days of being 'America's playground'. Ninety miles away from the coast of the US, 'sovereignty' and 'dignity' are still words that have resonance in Cuba – a fact that any new US government should bear in mind.

Colombia

The US military became more and more embroiled in the Colombian counter-insurgency war during the George W. Bush years, but because most eyes were fixed on the Middle East there was little scrutiny of what US forces were doing in their own backyard. During the Clinton administration Congress, unwilling to get sucked into a Vietnam-style conflict, had put a number of conditions on military aid to Colombia, but after 11 September 2001 the political climate changed and it was possible for Bush to do what US politicians and military men had long thought necessary: allow US military aid to be used to fight the insurgency. Now US forces not only trained Colombian troops but began to provide logistical back-up during offensive operations, share radar and intelligence intercepts, and even carry out special operations themselves.

The military offensive was effective: left-wing guerrillas were pushed back to rural areas, major highways were secured and the cities were made safer. Militarily and politically, the guerrillas found themselves in a weaker position than they had been for two decades. Some commentators began to suggest that the FARC, or parts of it, might try to negotiate or even surrender. But ending the forty-year war will be no easy task because its underlying causes are social: land hunger, poverty and an exclusionary political system. A common misperception is that the drugs trade is the root of Colombia's problems. But the guerrilla war started long before the drugs traffickers came to Colombia, and although drugs money exacerbates the conflict, it is not the cause. Indeed, as Chapter 9 shows, the boom in the cultivation of illicit drugs crops stems from the same social problems that are the cause of the guerrilla conflict: rural inequality and poverty.

US politicians lauded the achievements of Colombia's President Alvaro Uribe; Condoleezza Rice stated to Congress that Colombia was 'becoming a success story'. General Peter Pace, Chief of Joint Staff, said the 'enormous success' of Colombia provided a model for Afghanistan to follow.[65] But Colombia is still suffering a humanitarian crisis: over 300,000 people fled their homes in 2005 – hardly a sign of a country at peace. Between 2 million and 3 million people have been forced to flee since the 1980s, according to UN figures, the highest level of internal displacement anywhere in the world apart from Sudan.[66] Colombia's human rights record is the worst in the Western Hemisphere. Although the number of political murders and disappearances has fallen, over 20,000 people have died in political violence, *excluding* combat deaths, since Plan Colombia was launched in 2000, and more than 11,000 since President Uribe came to power in 2002.[67] Worryingly, the proportion of abuses committed by the police and army has risen.

Uribe and the Patriot Plan
The failure of peace talks (1999–2002) left most Colombians disillusioned and exasperated with the armed groups. Right-winger Alvaro Uribe promised to re-assert the authority of the state and launch an offensive against the guerrillas. He had a landslide electoral victory in May 2002. Within a year, Uribe launched the Patriot Plan. This was a two-pronged assault, involving a 14,000-man military offensive against the guerrillas in southern Colombia and a repressive crackdown in major cities, involving mass detentions, to break the guerrillas' urban networks. The offensive in the south pushed the guerrillas back into rural areas, but they remained operational. Human rights groups highlighted the human cost of the military offensive, which led hundreds of thousands of civilians to flee their homes in the affected areas. The respected Colombian NGO the Consultancy for Human Rights and Displacement (Codhes) warned that the 'civilian population is trapped and becoming a spoil of war', and concluded that the Patriot Plan 'tends to aggravate the humanitarian and social crisis'.[68]

Meanwhile, the practice of mass arrests in the cities led to an upsurge in complaints about wrongful detention, abuse and even torture at the hands of the security forces. Uribe repeatedly granted the military temporary emergency powers, giving them *carte blanche* to override civil rights.

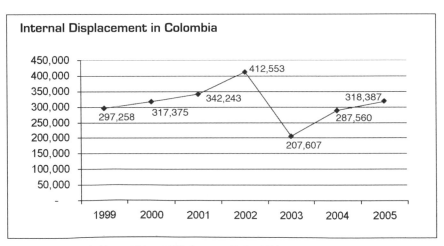

Source: Consultancy for Human Rights and Displacement (Codhes). Boletín informativo de la Consultoría para los Derechos Humanos y el Desplazamiento, issue 56, Bogota, February 2005. Figures for 2005 taken from Codhes press statement 'De la negación al desafío de la reparación: Informe CODHES 2005 sobre desplazamiento forzado interno en Colombia', 13 May 2006.

Who is Alvaro Uribe?

Alvaro Uribe Vélez is a hardliner who won landslide victories in elections for the Colombian presidency in 2002 and 2006. He is a lawyer who has studied at Harvard University and St Antony's College, Oxford. His father was a wealthy cattle rancher and was murdered by the FARC in 1983.

Uribe first came to public attention when, as a state governor in the 1990s, he promoted armed 'private justice and vigilance groups' (Convivir) to combat the guerrillas. So many of these private security groups evolved into paramilitary organizations that they were outlawed by the national government in 1999. Uribe tried to shed his extremist image in the 2002 elections, but the paramilitaries claimed him as 'their man'.

A declassified intelligence report written in 1991 by the US Defense Intelligence Agency (DIA) cites Uribe in a list of 'Narco-trafficker profiles'. It states Uribe was 'dedicated to collaboration with the Medellín Cartel', and was a 'close friend of Pablo Escobar', Colombia's most notorious drugs trafficker. The full citation reads as follows:

> Alvaro Uribe Velez – a Colombian politician and senator dedicated to collabora-tion with the Medellín cartel at high government levels. Uribe was linked to a business involved in narcotics activities in the US. His father was murdered in Colombia for his connection with the narcotic traffickers.
>
> Uribe has worked for the Medellín cartel and is a close personal friend of Pablo Escobar Gaviria. He has participated in Escobar's political campaign to win the position of assistant parliamentarian to Jorge (Ortega). Uribe has been one of the politicians, from the senate, who has attacked all forms of extradition treaty.

A press release issued by the Colombian president's office in 2004 took issue with a number of points in the declassified document. The press release stated that Uribe had no business dealings abroad, that his father had been murdered by the FARC and that Uribe had not opposed extradition. The statement did not, however, address the most damning allegations, that Uribe had collaborated with the Medellín Cartel and was a close friend of Escobar. Of course, US intelligence reports are not necessarily always accurate.

George W. Bush, welcoming Uribe to the White House in June 2006, said:

> President Uribe is a personal friend. I'm able to talk very frankly with him about a variety of subjects. I told him that one of the things I admire is he's a strong believer in democracy, human rights, human dignity. He's got a tough job in dealing with narco-terrorist groups in his country, but he's committed to dealing firmly with narco-terrorism. He's committed to helping reconcile past differences. He's committed to helping people get back into society. And I appreciate those commitments. He's committed to human rights.

Sources: *Narcotics – Colombian Narco-trafficker Profiles*, Defense Intelligence Agency, Intelligence Information Report, Confidential, 23 September 1991 (Date of Information 18 March 1991) 14 pp. Published by the National Security Archive. http://www.gwu.edu/~nsarchiv/NSAEBB/NSAEBB131/ index.htm. Text of the Colombian Casa de Narino press statement, 30 September 2004, reprinted on the National Security Website. http://www.gwu.edu/~nsarchiv/NSAEBB/NSAEBB131/index.htm. National Security Archive Press Release 'US. Intelligence Listed Colombian President Uribe among "Important Colombian Narco-traffickers" in 1991 ", 2 August 2004. White House press release, 'President Bush Welcomes President Uribe of Colombia to the White House', 14 June 2006.

Colombia: the US's loyal ally in Latin America

For neoconservatives in the Bush administration, unnerved by the rise of left-wing populists in Latin America, Uribe was highly valued as their most loyal ally in the region. The Colombian offensive against the guerrillas was timed perfectly to fit with the US 'war on terror'; ideologically, Uribe was close to George W. Bush. As we have noted elsewhere, Colombia receives over 70 per cent of all military aid to Latin America and is by far the world's largest recipient of all US military aid, outside the Middle East. One of the most controversial sums of military aid that Bush approved was US$98 million to defend an oil pipeline that had been repeatedly attacked by guerrillas. The pipeline was operated by the US company Occidental Petroleum – this was a clear case of the US defending its oil interests in the region. Oil may be an important factor in the US intervention in Colombia; oil is Colombia's top export earner and the country has known reserves of 2.6 billion barrels. Although this is a fairly small amount compared with Venezuela, the Colombian energy ministry thinks the country's reserves could be far higher (up to 37 billion barrels) – some of the best potential sites, however, are in territory controlled by the guerrillas. The southern Amazonian area – a FARC stronghold – is thought to be particularly rich in oil.

About half of US aid provided to Colombia between 1999 and 2003 was spent on creating an elite new 2,300-man battalion which operates in these FARC-dominated Amazonian states of Caquetá and Putumayo.[69] Much US funding has also gone on training and equipping five riverine battalions which operate in the most conflictive areas of Colombia (Putumayo, Guaviare, Guainía, Magadelena Medio and Urabá). The battalions are made up of 58 smaller 'riverine combat elements', trained by the US. Since 1999, the US has provided the Colombian army and police with 22 Black Hawk helicopters, 3 Bell helicopters and 80 Huey helicopters. It has also provided the Colombian air force with A-37 and A-47 combat planes, C-130 troop transporter aircraft and lightweight planes for spraying pesticides.

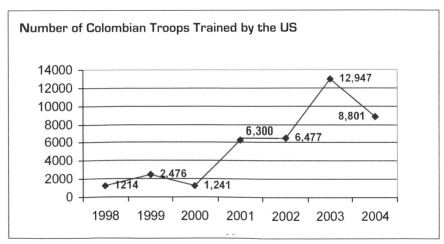

Number of Colombian Troops Trained by the US

Source: Just the Facts (defence database maintained by the Centre for International Policy, Latin America Working Group and Washington Office on Latin America) www.justf.org

US Military and Economic/Social Aid to Colombia ,1997–2007 (US$m)

	1997	1998	1999	2000	2001	2002	2003	2004	2005	2006	2007	2008	Total
Military aid	86.6	114.3	306.6	743.6	236.9	398.9	624.4	614.8	597.8	632.2	615.9	603.0	5,575
Economic/ social aid	0	0.5	8.8	231.4	1.4	115.5	136.7	134.5	134.7	132.2	132.2	139.5	1,167.4

Source: Center for International Policy

The US trains more soldiers from Colombia than from any other country apart from Afghanistan, and the number of trainees has risen sharply since Bush came to office. Over 34,000 Colombian soldiers were trained between 2001 and 2004. The most common course they take is light infantry skills, which include: combat in difficult terrains, map and compass reading, counter-insurgency tactics, camouflage, communications, marksmanship and ambush techniques.

US forces in Colombia

The Bush administration raised the cap on US personnel in Colombia to 800 US soldiers and 600 US private contractors. Private contractors are usually former US military personnel who are either employed directly by the State Department/ Pentagon or by private defence firms such as DynCorp and Northrop Grumman. The use of private contractors (perhaps more accurately named mercenaries) makes it hard to keep track of what US forces are doing in Colombia, because companies can plead corporate confidentiality. The number of private contractors employed by US defence firms is actually greater than 600 because the cap does not apply to non-US citizens (there are many Central Americans working in Colombia, for example).

US troops and private contractors carry out a number of functions, including operating radar sites, reconnaissance, transporting Colombian troops, and accompanying the air force on counter-narcotics missions in guerrilla-controlled areas, where the line with counter-insurgency operations is increasingly blurred. US personnel also provide logistical back-up to Colombian troops involved in the offensive in the south. They set up supply lines, ensuring the troops are provided with food and fuel. One of their most important functions is intelligence sharing. Information from US radars, surveillance flights, satellite photography, communications intercepts and human sources is shared with Colombian forces and used to plan counter-insurgency tactics.

The future of the FARC

The FARC are weaker, militarily and politically, than they have been since the 1980s. Thousands of their fighters have taken advantage of the Uribe government's demobilization scheme. The authorities claimed that 300 rebels a month were handing themselves in and while this was probably an exaggeration, it was clear that the FARC's numbers were falling. One estimate suggested that FARC membership had dropped to 10,000 in 2008, compared with 20,000 in 2001. US military aid contributed to their decline; in particular the technology to intercept radio, satellite and cellular phones, as well as other intelligence-gathering methods, helped the Colombian army carry out two spectacular coups: the bombing of a FARC camp in Ecuador in March 2008 which killed guerrilla leader Raul Reyes and, four months later, the rescue of fifteen hostages, including three US citizens and Ingrid Betancourt, a joint French and Colombian national who had been a candidate in the 2002 Colombian presidential elections. But there were also other factors. The death of the FARC's septuagenarian leader, Manual Marulanda, in March 2008 and the murder by his bodyguard of another FARC leader – the third member of the FARC's seven-man secretariat to die that year – disorientated the guerrilla group and produced divisions within its ranks about who should be the future leader. Perhaps most important, the political isolation of the FARC, both domestically and internationally, had been growing for many years. Its members had no overall vision for Colombia and little to say to people living in cities. Their practice of kidnapping civilians brought condemnation from both home and abroad; even President Hugo Chávez, once seen as a sympathizer, called on the FARC in June 2008 to end the war and release their hostages. The FARC returned to its roots as a peasant force, feeding off the poverty and hopelessness in the more isolated parts of the Colombian countryside. But as Colombian history shows, a peasant army, especially one with family connections in the community that go back many generations, can survive for years. And although the ideological glue holding the FARC together is far weaker than in the past – indeed a large proportion of its members are minors – the financing that the FARC receives via the drugs trade will allow the guerrillas to hold out longer than their dwindling numbers would suggest.

Paramilitaries demobilized?
Right-wing paramilitaries began to demobilize in 2003 after reaching agreement with President Uribe. Although the Justice and Peace Law (2005) was criticized for being too soft on paramilitaries, it led to a decline in political violence. Demobilized paramilitaries were exempt from extradition and from serving jail sentences longer than eight years and were allowed to keep enough of their 'legal assets' to 'live adequately' – a clause that allowed death squad leaders to hold on to the vast fortunes acquired through extortion and drugs trafficking. There is also evidence that the demobilization is only partial. Some 31,000 fighters were apparently demobilized, but only 16,000 weapons were handed in. An alarming analysis put forward by some experts is that this was not demobilization at all but a consolidation of paramilitary power.[70] Paramilitary networks, they say, had uncontested control in some parts of the north, including the states of Antioquia, César, Córdoba and Sucre, and ran the political structure like a mafia. They were so powerful that they now needed fewer armed men and could rely instead on a network of informants. To some extent this analysis is borne out by the observations of the United Nations High Commission for Human Rights, which wrote in its 2006 report:

> It should be pointed out that demobilization does not appear to have diminished either the influence or the control of paramilitary groups in their respective geographical areas. Rather, using parallel strategies based on pressure and threats, they

have been consolidated and in some cases extended in the economic, social and political fields.[71]

The extent of the paramilitaries' influence on the political establishment became clear in 2006–08, when the public prosecutor accused one third of Colombia's congressmen and congresswomen of having links with paramilitaries. Many local politicians also are being investigated by the prosecutor. President Uribe wants the international community to commend his imposition of 'democratic security', as he terms it. But the democracy is so flawed and the security so heavily weighed towards economic elites that 'democratic security' looks more like a new version of the concentration of land and resources that triggered the last round of Colombia's internal conflict fifty years ago.

Human rights
Colombia has the worst human rights record in the Western Hemisphere. The United Nations High Commission for Human Rights report for 2006 stated:

> The human rights situation was marked by a series of grave violations related to civil and political rights … It was possible to observe a pattern of extrajudicial executions and enforced disappearances, associated with violations linked to the administration of justice and impunity. Cases of arbitrary detentions, torture and other cruel, inhuman or degrading treatment were also recorded, as well as attacks on freedom of expression.[72]

The UN said that although the violations were 'not part of a deliberate State policy at the highest level', it had received numerous reports of abuses by the army and of collusion between the security forces and paramilitaries. The Colombian authorities often turned a blind eye to paramilitary activities, it said, and failed to take action against them once crimes were committed. It also received reports of massacres by the army.

The UN also condemned left-wing guerrillas for violations of international humanitarian law:

> The guerrilla forces, especially the FARC-EP and to a lesser extent the ELN, continued to perpetrate homicides, massacres, acts of terrorism, threats and attacks on the civilian population, hostage-taking, use of anti-personnel mines, recruitment of children and attacks on medical personnel and units.

Despite demobilizing, the right-wing paramilitaries are still responsible for a high proportion of political murders in Colombia, according to the Colombian Commission of Jurists. Paramilitaries committed 21 per cent of all political killings in 2006, compared with 49 per cent in 2001.[73] The armed forces were responsible for 14 per cent of all political killings in 2006, compared with 2 per cent in 2001. Left-wing guerrillas were responsible for 14 per cent. It was impossible to identify the perpetrators of the remaining deaths. Guerrillas are responsible for more than half of the kidnappings in Colombia.

Colombia: a success story?

The Bush administration presented Colombia as a success story, but the grisly catalogue of human rights abuses hardly suggests grounds for complacency. President Uribe, certainly, was popular in Colombia. A populace relieved at the decline of violence, in the cities at least, gave him another landslide victory at the polls in 2006. But while the US-backed hardline strategy weakened the insurgency, it has so far failed to achieve peace. Ending Colombia's endemic violence will be no easy task. Years of hatred and suspicion need to be overcome. Rural poverty, land hunger and unemployment need to be addressed. The Bush administration applied a rigid 'war on terror' approach rather than consider the complex reality of Colombia. It prioritized military objectives over solving social problems, and it encouraged Colombian hardliners to hold out for total victory. But while the young unemployed in isolated rural areas believe their best chance of food, clothing and shelter is joining a militia – whether in the service of the local elites or offering an insurrectionary road to a socialist society – the violence will be hard to end.

The Bush administration deployed the same heavy-handed, ideologically skewed approach across Latin America. It insisted on pursuing a corporate-backed free trade agenda that most populations had repeatedly rejected at the polls. It affixed the 'war on terror' to a region where it had little relevance, moulding characters in the region into exaggerated hate figures and conflagrating unnecessary wars of words with Chávez, Morales and Ortega. But the Cold War is over, Fidel Castro is no longer in power and the new US administration has an opportunity to take a fresh approach. It would be ironic, as Castro leaves the scene, if the US were to build up a new iconic enemy, Chávez, who could dominate and distort the inter-American agenda for decades to come.

Why US Drugs Policy Doesn't Work

Clara Gutiérrez has battered shoes, a wrinkled face, greying hair pulled back into a ponytail, and a stoic smile. She is forty-eight years old and has five children. She farms a small plot of land in southern Colombia, growing yucca, tropical fruit and coca leaf: the plant from which cocaine is eventually produced. Clara (all names of coca growers in this chapter are pseudonyms) and her husband had not planned to become coca farmers, but in this remote Amazonian region they soon found it was the only crop from which they could make a living.

For the past two decades US anti-narcotics policy has focused on such poverty-stricken peasants. Military aeroplanes spray pesticides onto their farms, killing food crops as well as coca. The noxious chemicals have killed animals, caused human illness, poisoned the water supply and may be doing irreparable damage to the environment in one of the most biodiverse regions of the world. The spraying is not even effective: coca cultivation in the Andean region rose 25 per cent between 1987 and 2006. In Colombia, the only country where the crops are sprayed with pesticides, coca cultivation has risen by over 500 per cent, a clear indictment of the 'fumigation' strategy. Meanwhile, despite record seizures of cocaine across the world, the street price of cocaine has fallen in New York and London, showing that more, not less, cocaine is getting in.

Why Do Peasants Grow Coca?

US drugs policy fails because it does not address the real reasons why peasants grow coca. In Bolivia and Peru coca has been grown for centuries by indigenous communities. Coca leaf is a traditional remedy chewed by much of the population to relieve fatigue, hunger and altitude sickness. It is legal and piles of coca leaves are sold openly on the street. Today 70 per cent of the world's coca is grown in Colombia, where it is not grown by indigenous people (who make up just 2 per cent of the

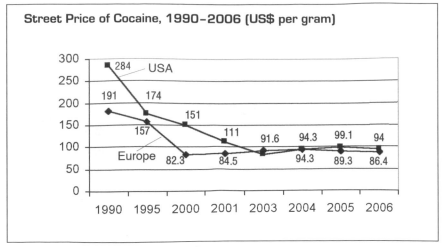

Source: United Nations World Drug Report 2008

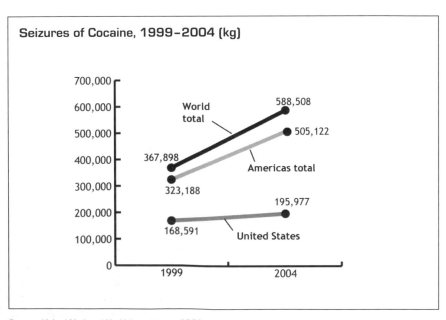

Source: United Nations World Drug Report 2006

Colombian population), but by desperately poor farmers who find that coca is the only viable cash crop. Civilians in rural areas have borne the brunt of Colombia's forty-year-long civil war, and since 1985 over two million people have fled their homes. Land concentration has led to rising rural poverty and the growth of a land-hungry underclass.

Most coca is grown in the remote southeastern plains and the Amazon region in southern Colombia. Thousands of people have migrated to these regions having been displaced by violence or squeezed out by large landowners. Each new wave of settlers (*colonos* or colonizers) travels deeper into the Amazon, cutting down rainforest to obtain farmland. During the first migratory wave of 1973–85, the population of Amazonia rose by 90 per cent. The original indigenous population is now a minority in all Amazonian states except Vaupés. Coca booms have accelerated migration trends. One straightforward way to reduce coca cultivation would be to carry out land reform in the fertile, more central regions of Colombia.

Today Colombian farmers are finding it difficult to compete in the globalized economy; agricultural output fell 6.7 per cent per capita in the 1990s and by the end of the decade 80 per cent of people in the countryside lived below the poverty line, according to government figures. The collapse of the international coffee pricing agreement in 1989 had a devastating impact on the Colombian coffee industry (coffee is the country's second-largest export after oil). Between 1990 and 2000, coffee output fell 25 per cent and export earnings halved. A direct relationship between the agrarian crisis and illicit cultivation can be seen: after 1989, thousands of small coffee farmers switched to growing opium poppies which, like coffee bushes, grow at high altitudes. Poppy cultivation soared from 13,244 hectares in 1991 to 20,000 hectares the following year.[1]

The Economic Advantages of Coca

Unlike indigenous communities, the Colombian settlers in the south are not subsistence farmers. They aim to buy a small plot of land and sell their produce for a small profit so that they can buy household necessities and, in theory at least, reinvest the surplus in the farm. All the settlers hope to bequeath land to their children. The goal for many Colombian small farmers is to become cattle ranchers, although few make enough money to achieve their dream. Life in this region is hard; there are few roads and outside the towns many households are without electricity. The countryside is controlled by left-wing guerrillas and the government's presence is weak. There is virtually no state health or education provision in the countryside.

In these isolated areas there are many advantages to growing coca, the most obvious being that there is always a high demand for the product. Peasants harvest the leaves and turn them into a paste, which is then sold to an intermediary. The coca paste is then taken to makeshift laboratories and refined into cocaine. The intermediary will normally come to the farm to buy the coca paste, which is a light compact product. In contrast a peasant who is growing yucca, maize or fruit will have to transport a very bulky cheap product to the nearest market, which may take

Meeting Coca Growers in the Amazon

Making the journey to meet coca growers gives one a clear sense of just how isolated they are from nearby towns and markets. First I took a 32-seater plane from Bogotá to San Vicente del Caguán, a small town on the edge of the Amazon. This is a town of settlers and it looks like a frontier town. The buildings are made of brightly painted wood with verandas. Country music blares from the bars. The men wear cowboy boots, and many ride horses.

I went to the small harbour to catch the one boat that travels up the river each day. After a two-hour journey, during which the boat got stuck in the mud three times because the water was shallow, I arrived at a small hamlet. My guide now had to borrow another boat from an acquaintance because the ferry service stopped here. We travelled along minor branches of the river, waving away the creepers that hung down into the water, for another two hours. After mooring the boat, we walked for another four hours across scrubland and through forest. Who on earth would make this journey for a few pounds of yucca or bananas? Only coca is worth transporting this far.

The families we meet are friendly, straightforward country people. They offer us food and drink. Their houses are built of wood and have chickens clucking on the veranda. Clara Gutiérrez moved here with her husband when she was sixteen. They had no land and longed to have their own farm. As well as coca, they cultivate various tropical fruits, sugar and fish.

Lydia Buendía is forty-six and has three children. She is a second-generation migrant. Lydia's parents were originally from Valle del Cauca, but fled their homes during La Violencia, a brutally violent civil war which racked the country between 1948 and 1953. Lydia and her husband have a small farm which contains one hectare of coca, as well as three cows, chickens, some recently planted macaco and caimacho trees and a large fish pond. Their aim is eventually to replace the coca altogether, but they cannot afford to do so yet.

Ana is eighteen. She is a *raspuchín,* a day labourer who picks coca. Her parents do not have enough land on their small farm to keep her at home. Wearing wellington boots and very short shorts, she describes how she travels from farm to farm at harvest time. She is unanimated, morose even, clearly unhappy at her lot. At weekends, she hangs out with her friends, and perhaps has a beer. Like most people here she has never taken cocaine. When asked what she thinks of young people in the West taking drugs, she shrugs, having no concept of what their lives are like. She simply hopes that she will earn enough money to educate her one-year-old son so he will have a better life than hers.

I visited the families during a time of relative peace. The government had set up a demilitarized zone in the south in order to hold talks with left-wing FARC guerrillas. The coca growers I met lived a few hours outside the zone, but still benefited from the reduced level of conflict. However, talks collapsed in 2002 and the Uribe government launched a military offensive in this region. Life for the coca growers is now even harder, with three constant dangers: war, aerial pesticide spraying and hunger.   Author's trip to Colombia, 2000.

Making Cocaine

To make coca paste, coca leaves are sprinkled with cement, then squeezed through a wooden press. They are then soaked in a barrel with kerosene and water. This liquid is then put in a bucket with sulphuric acid. By the slow addition of sodium bicarbonate, a hard paste separates from the solution; it is filtered, and then dried in the sun. The paste will then be sold to a middleman who takes it to a more advanced 'jungle laboratory' to be refined into cocaine.

The Environmental Cost of Cocaine
The chemicals used in the production of coca paste and cocaine, as well the fertilizers used in intensive coca cultivation, damage the environment. The waste from processing coca paste and cocaine is rarely disposed of safely; it is usually dumped on land or in rivers. Growers cannot ask for official help with disposal because coca paste manufacturing is illegal.

Seventy-two million kilos of cement, 72 million gallons of gasoline and 1.7 million litres of sulphuric acid were used in the rural production of coca paste in Colombia in 2005. 900,000 tonnes of precursor chemicals (including potassium permanganate, hydrochloric acid and acetone) were used in the production of cocaine between 1984 and 1998, the Colombian environment ministry estimates.

several hours or even days given there are virtually no paved roads. The cost of transport is high and the price of the product so low that the farmer is likely to lose money. A study carried out by Cifisam, a Catholic charity helping families grow alternatives to coca, found that for farmers provided with technical assistance (training, the loan of equipment, technical advice), the net profit margin of traditional products such as vegetables, tropical fruit, fish and poultry was 4.52 per cent.[2] For each dollar invested, the farmer would get back an additional 4.5 cents, barely enough to buy essentials for the family, let alone reinvest in the farm. Even worse, the study found that without the charity's assistance, legal products made a loss of 49.2 per cent. In contrast coca had a net profit margin of 49.1 per cent. That is not to say that a coca grower is rich; studies carried out in the 1990s found that a farmer who cultivates one hectare of coca will earn between US$1,060 and US$1,792 a year, compared with the Colombian minimum wage of US$1,419.[3] A coca grower earns just 0.1 per cent to 0.3 per cent of the final street price of cocaine.

Who are the Drugs Traffickers?

The structure of the drugs trafficking business has changed in recent years. Two large cartels, the Medellín and the Cali, dominated the trade in the 1980s and 1990s. When their leaders were caught and the cartels were dismantled, the drugs trafficking business decentralized. A larger number of small, amorphous and more anonymous syndicates took over. Mexican cartels play a larger role and are now mainly responsible for the later stages of the process: smuggling the product into the United States and finding US buyers. Although for political reasons, the US has targeted so-called 'narco-guerrillas' with measures such as Plan Colombia, the truth is that right-wing paramilitaries have had a greater involvement in the trade. According to Klaus Nyholm, the representative of the United Nations Drugs Control Programme (UNDCP) in Colombia, 'The paramilitaries are involved [in drugs trafficking] even more than the FARC, to the extent that in some regions it is difficult to distinguish between the drugs traffickers and the paramilitaries.'[4]

The link is unsurprising, given that many paramilitary groups were founded as protection forces by the drugs traffickers themselves. Carlos Castaño, the former leader of the Auto Defensas Unidas de Colombia (AUC), once Colombia's largest paramilitary group, estimated that 70 per cent of their money came from drugs. The United States requested the extradition of Castaño and another AUC leader, Salvatore Mancuso, on drugs charges in 2002. (Castaño has since been murdered and Mancuso has been exempted from extradition as part of a paramilitary demobilization plan.)

Drugs trafficking corrupted the highest echelons of Colombian society, as a number of scandals in the 1990s showed. President Ernesto Samper's entire term in office (1994–98) was dogged by claims that his campaign was funded by the Cali cartel. Although Samper was acquitted by congress, his defence minister, his campaign manager and the attorney general were all convicted of accepting money from the cartel. The armed forces have been particularly susceptible to the lure of drugs money – the brother of another defence minister, Luis Camacho Leiva, was found with cocaine on a government plane. When an elite anti-narcotics force was established in 1989, it was created within the police force because the military was so tainted by drugs money. Even so, the commander of this force, Colonel Hugo Martínez, and the head of the national police force, General Vargas, were later accused of taking money from the Cali cartel. There have also been many examples of lower-ranking officers involved in drugs trafficking. Drug-related corruption in all branches of government undermined the counter-narcotics struggle in Colombia, the US State Department reported in 1999.[5] High-ranking politicians still maintain links with the paramilitaries who are heavily embroiled in the drugs trade. A third of the politicians sitting in the Colombian congress, most of whom were allies of President Uribe, were accused by the Colombian public prosecutor of having links to paramilitaries in 2006–08.

Narco-guerrillas?

US politicians often claim that left-wing guerrillas control the drugs trade. The concept of the 'narco-guerrilla' was useful to the United States after the Cold War because it gave the Pentagon a justification for intervening in Colombia even though there was no longer a threat from the Communist bloc. Today the more common term is 'narco-terrorist'. But no serious observer believes that the FARC guerrillas control the drug trade in Colombia, although in recent years they have stepped up their involvement. When the first wave of migrants came to settle in the southeast, an area controlled by the FARC, the guerrillas – moralistic Marxists – were opposed to the growing of coca. But they soon realized they could do little to stop it and began to tax the trade in coca paste (not finished cocaine). The peasants often welcomed their intervention because the guerrillas ensured they got a fair price from the paste traders. The FARC maintained this parasitical and lucrative practice of taxing the trade throughout the 1990s. Some units then decided to cut out the middleman and take over the trade in coca paste, rather than merely taxing the exchange. Politically, this gave the FARC a more antagonistic relationship with local peasants because the guerrillas now had an interest in securing the lowest possible price from the seller. It also gave them a closer relationship with the drugs traffickers to whom they now sold the paste directly.

The head of the US Drug Enforcement Administration testified to the US Congress in 2001 that, while the FARC had a peripheral role in the drugs trade, they were not themselves international traffickers:

> The most recent DEA reporting indicates that some FARC units in southern Colombia are indeed involved in drug trafficking activities such as controlling local cocaine base markets. Some insurgent units have assisted drug trafficking groups in transporting and storing cocaine and marijuana within Colombia … however … there is no evidence that any FARC or ELN units have established international transportation, wholesale distribution or drug money laundering networks in the United States or Europe.[6]

The UNDCP representative Klaus Nyholm held a similar opinion. In 2001 he remarked: 'We don't consider the FARC to be drugs traffickers … However, they finance their war via the drug trade. They have their system of *gramaje* (tax on coca paste) and in some areas they also control the trade in coca paste.'[7] Nyholm updated his remarks in 2002: 'Since then we have seen several cases of international drug trafficking on the part of the FARC. Not very sophisticated, though, mainly bartering drugs for arms in neighbouring countries.'[8]

In 2006 the US attorney general claimed that the FARC controlled at least half of the international trade in cocaine from Colombia and indicted 50 rebels. It seems unlikely that in just four years the FARC's role could have changed so dramatically, that it could have wrested control of the multi-billion-dollar trade from entrenched traffickers, many with links deep in the establishment. It is more probable that the US exaggerates the FARC's involvement for political reasons.

Fumigation

The US anti-narcotics strategy targets the poverty-stricken peasant, rather than the people higher up the drugs trafficking chain. The US promotes aerial spraying of herbicides on coca farms. This 'fumigation' is carried out only in Colombia because the governments of Bolivia and Peru have refused to allow it in their countries for environmental and health reasons. The Colombian anti-narcotics police, trained, funded and sometimes accompanied by US forces, have been spraying coca plantations in Colombia since 1978. A variety of chemicals have been used including Paraquat, Triclopyr and Tebuthiuron, but since 1986 glyphosate has been the most commonly used herbicide. Chemical spraying was an integral part of Plan Colombia, the US-funded, heavily militarized anti-drugs strategy launched in 2000. Intensive spraying of herbicides in the Colombian countryside, including national parks, has been going on ever since.

The Herbicide

Glyphosate (N-phosphonomethyl) is a 'non-selective herbicide'. Its biggest-selling commercial formulation is Roundup, made by the US company Monsanto. According to the manufacturer's label, it causes eye and skin irritation and handlers are advised to wear protective clothing and goggles. Rural workers exposed to glyphosate have reported nausea, dizziness, respiratory problems, stomach ailments and increased blood pressure. Laboratory tests suggest glyphosate may cause lung dysfunction, infertility and cancer.[9] The US Environmental Protection Agency, however, claims it is 'less toxic than common salt, aspirin, caffeine, nicotine and even vitamin A'.[10]

What official studies fail to take into account is that Roundup does not only contain glyphosate. Monsanto's Roundup Ultra formula, for example, contains a surfactant, which spreads the mixture evenly on the surface of the plants. Monsanto has refused to confirm what the surfactant is, but researchers believe it to be polyoxyethylamine (POEA). Mixing Roundup with POEA increases its toxicity. Although the State Department refused to accept publicly that the herbicide was dangerous, in 2004 it switched to an alternative glyphosate formulation on the advice of the Environmental Protection Agency.[11] The new formulation has not been named but it is likely to be one of the weaker versions of Roundup – Roundup Pro or Roundup Weathermax.

In Colombia, two other chemicals are added to the spray mixture, Cosmo-Flux 411F and Cosmo-In-D. This is done against the advice given on the manufacturer's label which states 'this is an end use product. Monsanto does not intend and has not registered it for reformulation.' Cosmo-Flux has a particularly pernicious effect; it ensures that the corrosive mixtures sticks to the surface – leaf or skin – on which it is sprayed. This has resulted in humans and animals suffering skin burns. To make matters worse, the herbicide is being used in Colombia at far higher concentrations than recommended by the manufacturer and US regulatory bodies (23.66 litres per hectare, rather than 2.5 litres) and it is being sprayed from above the recommended height of ten metres. In the United States, when herbicides are sprayed, farm workers are advised to keep clear; in Colombia, however, aerial spraying takes place without warning and consequently humans and animals have been doused in the poisonous chemicals.

Effects on Health of Glyphosate-containing Herbicides

'Roundup is one of the most common of the herbicides that cause human poisoning incidents ... Cases of accidental poisoning or intentional ingestion as well as occupational exposure of Roundup were studied by Japanese doctors and the following symptoms of acute poisoning were reported: gastrointestinal pain, massive loss of gastrointestinal liquid, vomiting, excessive fluid in the lungs, congestion and lung dysfunction, pneumonia, loss of consciousness, destruction of red blood cells, abnormal electrocardiograms, low blood pressure, and damaged or reduced hepatic function ...

The surfactant in Roundup is considered to be the principal cause of the toxicity of this formulation. POEA has an acute toxicity three times greater than that of glyphosate, and causes gastrointestinal and central nervous system damage, respiratory problems, and the destruction of red blood cells in humans ...

Reproductive Effects: In rat and rabbit feeding studies, glyphosate affected semen quality and sperm counts (Cox 1995, Dinham 1998). According to the US Environmental Protection Agency (EPA), continual exposure to residue in water in concentrations higher than 0.7 mg/L can cause reproductive problems in humans.

Carcinogenicity. ... Concerns regarding the potential carcinogenicity of glyphosate persist, because of the contaminant N-nitroso-glyphosate (NNG) ... It is known that the majority of N-nitroso compounds are carcinogenic. And there is no safe dose for carcinogens. Additionally, in the case of Roundup, the surfactant POEA is contaminated with 1-4 dioxane, which has caused cancer in animals, and liver and kidney damage in humans. Formaldehyde, another known carcinogen, is also a breakdown compound of glyphosate.'

Source: 'Effects on Health and the Environment of Herbicides which Contain Glyphosate' Extracts of a speech by Dr Elsa Nivia, Pesticide Action Network – November 2000, www.usfumigation.org/NovPressconfspeakers/ElsaNivia/ElsaNivia.htm

Poisoning the Population?

From December 2000, after the launch of Plan Colombia, the remote Amazonian state of Putumayo was subjected to intensive aerial spraying. Putumayo is one of the poorest areas of Colombia; 19 per cent of children under five suffer from chronic malnutrition and only half of households have access to clean water and electricity.[12] After the spraying began, residents began to complain of feeling ill. The Putumayo public health department received 4,833 complaints about the effects of fumigation.[13] These were: respiratory problems (946 complaints); gastrointestinal complaints (876); skin problems, including rashes, burns, welts and boils (524); fever (516); dizzy spells (137); eye problems (32) and others (including hair loss and vaginal haemorrhage).

The authorities also received complaints that the pesticides had caused illness in or killed a total of 373,944 animals. Most were fish, but the figures also included cows, horses, pigs, dogs, cats, rabbits, turkeys, ducks and doves.[14] As well as spraying coca plants, the pesticides were doused over plantations of maize, yucca, bananas, tropical fruit and pasture. Colombia's national ombudsman, who carried out a study in Putumayo, concluded: 'The aerial spraying of chemicals … threatens food security, health and the population's right to a healthy environment.'[15] Even families who had signed manual eradication pacts with the government and switched to producing alternative crops had their farms sprayed. Ironically, this encouraged them to revert to coca, a robust plant, which was easier to re-establish in the polluted soil than food crops. The ombudsman lamented:

> It is hard to understand how the authorities can continue releasing resources from the national budget to carry out various alternative development and coca substitution projects, only for them to be damaged by indiscriminate chemical fumigation.[16]

He warned that the chemical spraying and the intensification of the armed conflict had caused a 'humanitarian crisis' in Putumayo.

Contaminating Neighbouring Countries

Putumayo lies on the border with Ecuador, and Ecuadorian farmers have also complained of illnesses after chemicals drifted across into their territory. A study commissioned by the Ecuadorian ombudsman apparently showed that people subjected to the fumigation chemicals suffered genetic damage.[17] The findings were incorporated into a larger report, drawing together the results of various studies and sponsored by various NGOs. It concluded:

> After the fumigations, illnesses previously unknown to the population have arisen and it has been possible to note systemic damage in people, such as respiratory, skin and digestive infections and nervous complaints. The local inhabitants say that the intensity of some of these illnesses is uncommon for the region … The results found in the blood analyses indicate that the population living near the frontier are exposed as a result of the level of chromosome damage to a greater risk of developing cancer, mutations and congenital malformations. The fumigations may be the cause of the chromosome aberrations.[18]

These local studies are not conclusive and there is an urgent need for an independent study of the effects of chemical spraying over a wider area. Ignoring widespread calls for a UN inquiry, Colombia instead commissioned an environmental and human health assessment from the Inter-American Drug Abuse Control Commission, an arm of the OAS. Their report concluded 'that the risks for people and for human health in the use of glyphosate and Cosmo-Flux in the eradication of coca and poppies in Colombia were minimal'.[19] Numerous organizations condemned the report as a whitewash. The Environmental Studies Institute of the National University of Colombia noted that the study was not based on an analysis of the herbicide mixture actually being used in Colombia, but on the effects of glyphosate used elsewhere. It also pointed out that half of the data used in the report were taken from Monsanto sources.

Opposition to the Poison

Herbicide spraying continues across Colombia, even in areas supposedly protected by environmental legislation, such as national parks. Nationally, fumigation has drawn criticism from Colombian governors, senators, the comptroller's office, the national ombudsman, scientists, the media and numerous environmental organizations.

Biological Warfare?

The US Congress approved the use of a fungus, *fusarium oxysporum*, as a biological agent for eradicating coca crops in Colombia. Biological agents were originally part of Plan Colombia, but an international outcry prompted the Colombian government and the UN to withdraw their support. Critics had warned that unleashing biological agents on the Colombian environment could have devastating and unpredictable results.

Yet US-funded research into the fusarium continued and since 2001 US scientists have also been carrying out tests on a 'Colombian creole fungus' which they argue could be safer because it is of local origin.

In October 2003, the US asked the Colombian government to resume research into the use of mycoherbicides on poppy and coca crops. President Alvaro Uribe expressed interest and requested training for experts from the Colombian Agricultural Institute. Talks between the two governments continue.

The prospect of unleashing biological agents into the delicate biosphere of the Colombian Amazon is frightening. One US environmental official warned:

> Fusarium species are capable of evolving rapidly ... Mutagenicity is by far the most disturbing factor in attempting to use a fusarium species as a bio-herbicide. It is difficult, if not impossible, to control the spread of fusarium species. The mutated fungi can cause disease in a large number of crops, including tomatoes, peppers, flowers, corn and vines and are normally considered a threat to farmers as a pest, rather than as a pesticide. Fusarium species are more active in warm soils and can stay resident in soils for years.

Although the UN withdrew its support for the fusarium trials, it continued to support research into another fungus (*Pleospora papaveracea*) for use against opium poppies in Afghanistan. Experiments with this fungus were carried out in Uzbekistan, funded by the UK.

Source: The Re-emergence of the Biological War on Drugs ,Transnational Institute (TNI) Drug Policy Briefing 7, May 2004. The warning quoted was contained in a letter from David Struh, head of Florida's Environmental Protection Department, to the Florida 'drug czar', Jim McDonough, 6 April 1999. As a result, Florida decided against using the fungus against marijuana plantations in the state.

Internationally, both the European Parliament and the Andean Parliament have called for a suspension of the fumigations. The Ecuadorian government has requested an end to spraying in the border area, while the German government persuaded the Colombian government temporarily to stop spraying in two Colombian states where European-funded alternative development projects were under way. Many NGOs have expressed their concern, including the World Wildlife Fund, Greenpeace, Oxfam, Cafod, Christian Aid, Save the Children, Caritas International and Survival International.

Why Fumigation Doesn't Work: the Balloon Effect

For all the misery it causes, fumigation does not even achieve its aim. Anti-narcotics police have been spraying glyphosate in Colombia since 1986, yet since that date coca cultivation has grown by over 500 per cent. Neither Bolivia nor Peru permit fumigation in their territory and in both those countries coca cultivation has fallen significantly in the same period (see graph). Coca cultivation did fall for two years after Plan Colombia was launched, but then began to rise again; by 2006 it was higher than when the plan was launched in 2000 and had almost reached its 2001 peak. Overall in the Andean region, coca cultivation has risen by 25 per cent since 1986. Clearly, the herbicide strategy does not work.

The strategy fails because it doesn't address why peasants in Colombia grow coca: they are poor and have no alternative. When their farms are sprayed, most families simply move to another area and start replanting coca there. This is called the 'balloon effect' – you squeeze the balloon at one end and it expands at the other. The balloon effect can be seen clearly in the southern states of Colombia. During the 1990s, most coca was grown in the southeastern state of Guaviare, and an intensive

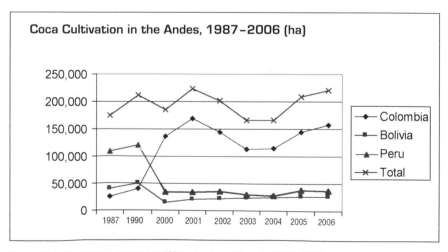

Source: State Department, International Narcotics Control Reports 1996–2008.

The Balloon Effect in the South and Southeastern States of Colombia, 1991-2000

State	Coca cultivation (% of national cultivation)		
	1991	1999	2000
Meta	na	7	7
Guaviare	57	18	11
Putumayo	6	36	41
Caquetá	23	15	16
Total of the four states	86	76	75

Sources: Figures for 1999-2000 from UN International Drug Program (UNDCP) 'Colombia: Annual Coca Cultivation Survey 2001', March 2002. Figures for 1991 from Colombian Environment Ministry, cited in *Los Cultivos Ilícitos: Política Mundial y Realidad en Colombia*, Defensoría del Pueblo, Bogotá, August 2000, p. 40.

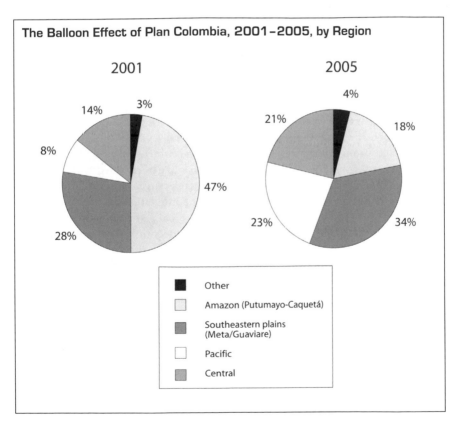

The Balloon Effect of Plan Colombia, 2001-2005, by Region

2001

2005

Legend:
- Other
- Amazon (Putumayo-Caquetá)
- Southeastern plains (Meta/Guaviare)
- Pacific
- Central

Source: United Nations Office on Drugs and Crime (UNODC), World Drug Report 2006

spraying campaign was launched. This led peasants to migrate deeper into the Amazon, often cutting down forest as they went, to set up new farms. By the year 2000, the Amazonian states of Caquetá and Putumayo accounted for 57 per cent of all coca growing in the country. Plan Colombia therefore targeted this area, and Putumayo in particular was sprayed intensively in 2000–01. Although this led to a reduction of coca planting in Putumayo, it was simply displaced to other parts of the country (see pie charts). Coca farms used to be concentrated in the southeastern plains and the Amazon; now they are more widely dispersed across the country.

Why Coca Production Moved to Colombia

All of the world's coca is grown in three Andean countries. During the 1980s and early 1990s, most of it was grown in Peru and Bolivia, but in the late 1990s production was largely displaced to Colombia. There were a number of reasons for this development. First, the structure of the drugs cartels changed; the Cali cartel, for example, used to buy coca leaf in Peru (and to a lesser extent Bolivia), then export it to Colombia for processing. Once this cartel was disbanded, the newer, smaller drugs trafficking organizations thought it made more sense to bring together all stages of drug processing into one country and began to encourage cultivation of coca in Colombia – the so-called 'verticalization' of drugs production. The increasingly effective US-funded cross-border interdiction efforts also encouraged the drugs cartels to switch production to Colombia. When the traffickers stopped buying coca leaf in Peru, the price fell sharply, leading to a further drop in production there. By 2004, according to the US State Department's *Narcotics Control Report 2006*, Colombia accounted for 69 per cent of the world's coca production; Peru (18 per cent) and Bolivia (13 per cent) produced the remainder.

Coca cultivation in Peru was also hit by a fungus which caused several thousand coca plants to wilt and die. The fungus was probably naturally occurring, although there were rumours that it had been deliberately released into the environment by anti-narcotics forces. The Peruvian fungus was the inspiration for the research into the possible use of biological agents in Colombia. Finally, the intensification of the war in Colombia, which left large swathes of land uncontrolled by the government and led to the displacement of two million poverty-stricken and land-hungry peasants, made Colombia the perfect place for illicit cultivation. In Peru the relationship between insurgents and coca growing differed in that the Peruvian guerrilla group, Shining Path, never developed such a strong relationship with the coca growers as did the FARC. Shining Path controlled just one of ten coca-growing regions in Peru and although they co-existed with local coca-growing peasantry, they did not attempt to take over the trade.

Coca in Bolivia and Peru

The majority of the population in Bolivia and Peru is indigenous. Coca leaf is a traditional product used at weddings and other ceremonies. It is also chewed to alleviate hunger and fatigue and is used in the manufacture of products such as tea and soap. The planting, sale and consumption of coca leaf are legal activities in Bolivia and Peru, unlike Colombia. Both the Bolivian and Peruvian governments make a clear legal distinction between coca leaf and cocaine.

In Bolivia, indigenous migrants from the Andean mountains settled in the subtropical valleys of the Yungas in pre-Hispanic times; they began to plant coca leaf in the colonial era, and the Yungas became known as Bolivia's traditional coca-producing area. In the twentieth century, the government encouraged migration to the tropical Chapare region in eastern Bolivia to relieve land pressure on the densely populated *altiplano*. Thousands of migrants moved to the Chapare in 1970s, as the rise in drugs trafficking led to a sharp rise in the price of coca leaf. US-sponsored anti-narcotics strategies have typically distinguished between the traditional zone of the Yungas and the non-traditional Chapare region. Most alternative development projects and forced eradication efforts have taken place in the Chapare. Many of the Chapare coca growers, however, are now second-generation settlers and believe they have a right to cultivate a product which is, after all, legal in Bolivia. Forced eradication, carried out by the Bolivian army, funded and trained by the United States, led to many bloody clashes in which dozens of peasants were killed. Chapare peasant coca growers established militant coca-grower unions to oppose forced eradication and to demand realistic alternatives. It was as a leader of this movement that Evo Morales rose to prominence.

Evo Morales was elected President in 2005 and a year later unveiled his strategy for coca leaf: 'Strategy for the Struggle Against Drug Trafficking and the Re-evaluation of Coca Leaf, 2007–2010'. The key points were:

- coca is a question of sovereignty
- coca leaf is not cocaine
- the launch of a campaign to make coca leaf a legal export. International trade in coca leaf is currently outlawed by the United Nations
- raising the legal limit of total domestic cultivation of coca leaf from 12,000 hectares to 20,000 hectares
- no forced eradication
- voluntary and consensual eradication programmes
- alternative development projects
- the industrialization and development of coca products, such as coca tea
- a crackdown on the production and smuggling of cocaine, including monitoring the sale of chemicals used in the production of cocaine; investigation of money laundering and seizure of drugs traffickers' assets
- cooperation with international efforts to intercept cocaine traffickers
- investment in treatment and the prevention of drug use
- drug policy should not be imposed from abroad, but should be a shared international responsibility.

It is unclear what the real size of the market for coca leaf is in Bolivia. The figure of 12,000 hectares was established in the late 1970s. The Bolivian government is

Evo Morales Takes a Coca Leaf to the United Nations

The Bolivian president addressed the UN General Assembly in September 2006 with a coca leaf in his hand. He brought the coca leaf, he said, to demonstrate it was not a drug.

'… I would like to take advantage of this opportunity, Ms President, to say that there are … historical injustices, such as the criminalization of the coca leaf. I want to say, this is a green coca leaf, it is not the white of cocaine, this coca leaf represents Andean culture, it is a coca leaf that represents the environment and the hope of our peoples …

We want to say that it is important that the United Nations recognize that with the help of North American universities, with European universities, we have scientifically demonstrated that the coca leaf does not damage human health.

It is very lamentable that due to customs, to bad customs, the coca leaf is derailed into an illegal problem; we are conscious of that, that is why we say as producers of the coca leaf that there will not be free coca cultivation, but nor will there be zero coca.

The previously implemented policies, that had conditions imposed, talked of zero coca; zero coca is like talking of zero Quechuas, Aymaras, Mojenos, Chiquitanos …

I want to say with great respect to the government of the United States, we are not going to change anything, we don't need blackmail and threats, the so-called certification or decertification in the fight against narco-trafficking is simply an instrument of recolonialization or colonialization of the Andean countries, that is unacceptable, that can not be permitted.

I want to say to you that we have, and we need, an alliance to fight against narco-trafficking, but one that is real and effective, so that the war on drugs can not be used as an instrument, a pretext, for them to subjugate the countries of the Andean region, just like they invented preventative wars to intervene into some countries of the Middle East.

We need a real fight against narco-trafficking, and I call on the United Nations, I invite the government of the United States to make an agreement, an effective alliance to fight against narco-trafficking, so that the war on drugs is not used as a pretext to dominate us, or to humiliate us, or to try to establish military bases. In our country they use the pretext of the fight against narco-trafficking …'

Evo Morales, United Nations, New York, 22 September 2006

under pressure from international donors to carry out a new study and, in theory, the official Institute of National Statistics is due to undertake one, but is waiting for sufficient international aid. The findings may not please the government because many experts believe that 20,000 hectares of coca is far higher than the domestic market can support (although there is a sizeable informal export trade to northern Argentina, where coca leaf is consumed). The Morales government argues that if the ban on exporting the leaf is lifted and if a number of coca products are developed, the market will be able to sustain the 20,000-hectare figure.

Another problem the government will face is whether alternative development plans can prosper where so many previous plans have failed. Many of these were badly designed, failing to take into account the wishes of local people or market conditions; for example, a dairy plant built in the Chapare went bankrupt due to insufficient demand for milk. Meanwhile peasants who, on government advice, switched to growing palm hearts found that prices never reached their promised level. Previous governments have been unwilling to subsidize the price of alternative crops or to finance export promotion. The new government promises to make alternative crops a part of an overall development strategy, which will include subsidizing the price of alternative crops if necessary. As in Colombia, the root problem is economic: peasants want to grow a crop they know they can they sell.

Peru, Coca and the Government of Alan García

The Peruvian president Alan García was elected to office in 2006 on a promise to 'de-narcotize' relations with the United States. García said he would end forced eradication of coca, which as in Bolivia had been a source of bloody conflict between peasants and security forces. Since García has taken office, however, forced eradication has continued, under pressure from the United States. Coca growing in Peru is dispersed in ten different regions, and the coca growers' unions are bitterly divided. They are therefore a much weaker force than in Bolivia and it has been easier for the Peruvian government to withstand their demands. Nevertheless García, like Morales, agrees that coca leaf should be a legal export. On an international stage García has argued that coca leaf is not a drug, that it has many uses – medicinal and culinary – and that new markets for the leaf should be found.[20]

The US Response

The United States is highly suspicious of the *cocalero* (coca growers) movements in Bolivia and Peru and has little sympathy for arguments based on sovereignty and tradition. US ambassador Manual Rocha described Evo Morales as a 'narco *cocalero*' during the 2002 presidential election campaign. Since Morales's election as president in 2005, there has been considerable trepidation in Washington. A month after his inauguration Secretary of State Condoleezza Rice warned:

We have reached out to Mr Morales [but] ... Statements about coca and coca production are problematic because we believe trying to wipe out the drug trade in the Andean region has been one of the strongest and most important elements of our policy for a long time, dating back a couple of Administrations now, and we want to see that continue ... [W]e are going to have problems with the Morales Government if that remains their policy. But we are reaching out to them to see if we can get them to adopt more responsible policies in that regard.[21]

Not long after, the State Department's Bureau for International Narcotics and Law Enforcement Affairs spelt out its worries in its annual drug control report:

Bolivia and Peru, which had drastically reduced their coca cultivation in the past five years, now face campaigns to roll back these achievements. The challenge comes from increasingly active *cocalero* (coca grower) associations that link coca cultivation to issues of cultural identity and national pride. These farmer unions, often exploited by trafficking interests, glorify coca cultivation and consumption as ancient and sacred indigenous traditions that must be protected against international efforts to destroy them. They portray coca reduction programs as a means for a mainly white, urban governing minority to limit the economic advancement of a rural indigenous majority.

Cocalero influence has been greatest in Bolivia, where the Bolivian *cocaleros'* founder and leader, Evo Morales, won the country's presidency in the December 2005 Bolivian Election. ... the trend is disquieting, as it shows no signs of being reversible in the short run.[22]

The United States responded negatively to Evo Morales's 2006 coca strategy. It opposes raising the legal limit of coca cultivation from 12,000 to 20,000 hectares, a move which it says breaks international conventions. 'The US seeks policies that reduce, not increase, coca in Bolivia,' said US ambassador Philip Goldberg.[23] Industrializing coca would make it easier for drugs traffickers to get hold of coca leaf, he added. The US is also against Bolivia's campaign to legalize the export of coca leaf. Just days after Bolivia's coca strategy was announced, the United States cut its anti-narcotics aid budget to Bolivia by 25 per cent.[24]

Alternatives

Persuading coca growers to grow different crops is an obvious way to reduce the supply of coca but, as the examples from Bolivia show, alternative development can be difficult to sustain. Coca is a hardy plant that can be harvested four to six times a year in tropical regions. It is easy to transport and there is always a high demand for it. To make alternative crops viable, peasants need credit and investment in local infrastructure. It therefore seems counterproductive of the United States to cut Bolivia's aid budget by 25 per cent just as it is about to embark on alternative development with renewed vigour. On the edges of the Colombian Amazon, local communities have experimented with a variety of products including tropical fruits (guava, palm chestnuts, copazu, minche), vegetables, herbs, fish and poultry. These projects try to choose goods that are suitable for extra local processing – like jam or herbal remedies – which allow local farmers to add value to their products and secure a higher price. These projects too will only have success if the government is prepared to invest in road building and other forms of transport. In the most isolated Amazonian regions, however, market-orientated farming may never be cost-effective or necessarily desirable. The Amazon is not suited to farming or ranching and its soil is quickly exhausted. One of the most effective measures in Colombia therefore would be to carry out land reform in the more fertile central and northern regions of the country.

Finding markets for alternative products is the most difficult problem and it is here that the coca growers come up against the unfair global trading system. The United States has introduced the Andean Trade Preference Act (APTA) which allows Bolivia, Colombia and Peru to export many products duty-free to the US market. But some products are exempted from the agreement and the Act is used as a political tool to force governments to conform to US wishes. APTA is reviewed regularly and the threat of its suspension remains a stick with which to threaten the Andean countries. International trade is not a game played on a balanced playing field, as the next chapter shows. Even with tariff-free access, poor countries remain at a disadvantage because both the United States and Europe heavily subsidize their agricultural industries, making it hard for Third World countries to compete on price. If poor countries do start to make a competitive product, the rich countries suddenly slap on tariffs, as Brazil has found to its cost with, for example, steel. Meanwhile, processed goods, which are far more profitable than raw materials, are rarely given duty-free access to the rich countries.

Reducing Demand

The majority of cocaine is consumed in North America and Europe. An estimated 60 per cent of the world's cocaine is destined for the US market.[25] After seizures by police, more than 300 metric tonnes of cocaine enter the US every year. Together, the US and Europe are home to 67 per cent of the world's cocaine users, according to the UNDCP World Drug Report 2000.

Latin American governments argue that instead of making poor farmers bear the brunt of anti-narcotics strategy, a greater emphasis should be placed by the US on reducing demand at home. For the past decade, approximately 70 per cent of the US federal drugs control budget has been spent on supply reduction (including domestic law enforcement) and just 30 per cent on reducing demand and prevention. Studies show that treatment and preventative education are far more effective ways of reducing consumption. Rand, a think-tank established by the US military, analysed how much the government would have to spend on each method – treatment, domestic law enforcement, interdiction and 'source control' (that is, eradication of crops) – to decrease cocaine consumption in the US by 1 per cent. It found that treatment was overwhelmingly the most cost-effective way of reducing cocaine consumption and its resulting social costs – 7 times more cost-effective than domestic law enforcement, 10 times more effective than interdiction and 23 times more effective than 'source control'.[26] An alternative would be to legalize and regulate the trade in drugs, a move that would stop the criminalization of some of the poorest people in the hemisphere. Few politicians in either Latin America or the United States, though, are willing publicly to advocate legalization.

Latin American politicians are united, however, in their opposition to the high-handed manner in which the US pursues its drugs policy. Every year the US considers whether each country has been cooperative enough in the drugs war to be 'certified' and therefore receive aid. This unilateral practice of certification causes indignation and resentment throughout the hemisphere. (Bolivia has suggested that Western countries be certified for their efforts to reduce drug consumption.) Most countries are critical of the US emphasis on chemical spraying, and countries bordering Colombia – Brazil, Peru, Venezuela and Ecuador – have expressed concern about the effects the herbicides may have on their environment. The militarized approach to the drugs problem also causes concern. Many countries suspect that the US uses drugs as a pretext for intervening in Latin America in the post-Cold War world, given that it has

---

Marijuana Cultivation

Marijuana cultivation is widely dispersed throughout the world. It is grown in more than 120 countries, and Colombia accounts for just 1 per cent of the world's crop. The US regards Mexico, Colombia and Jamaica as the most important cannabis producers in the Americas, but some experts say the largest producer in the region is the US itself. Although the US government has calculated the exact amount of marijuana produced in Latin American countries, it has no idea how much is grown in the US. According to the Netherlands-based Transnational Institute, half of all cannabis consumed in the US is produced domestically. Marijuana is an important cash crop in Kentucky, California, Alabama, Connecticut, Hawaii, Tennessee, West Virginia, Virginia, Maine and Rhode Island.

The US began to spray domestic cannabis plants with the herbicide Paraquat in the late 1970s, but stopped after the government accepted that smoking Paraquat-tainted cannabis could cause permanent lung scarring. The US then was accused of hypocrisy when it encouraged fumigation abroad, so in the 1990s it restarted domestic spraying. Only Hawaii, however, has been sprayed on a large scale. Here too, people complained of headaches, nausea and diarrhoea following the fumigations.

Sources: Ricardo Vargas, *Fumigación y Conflicto*, Executive Summary, Transnacional Institute, www.tni.org. 'We have no accurate estimate of the extent of domestic marijuana cultivation, much of the marijuana smoked in the US is cultivated domestically – commercially, privately, outdoors and indoors.' 12 March 1997, statement by Barry McCaffrey, Director, ONDCP, testimony to Senate SubCommittee on Western Hemisphere and Peace Corps. M. Jelsma, *Vicious Circle: The Chemical and Biological War on Drugs*, Transnational Institute, 2001, p. 15. J. Gettman and P. Armentano, NORML Report on US Domestic Marijuana Production,1998 Marijuana Crop Report, An Evaluation of Marijuana Production, Value, and Eradication Efforts in the United States, NORML, October 1998.

built a network of air bases and radar sites across the continent in the name of fighting drugs. Latin American countries do not want drugs policies imposed from abroad, they want international cooperation carried out with mutual respect. Such an approach is long overdue and may well come up with more effective remedies. The US counter-narcotics strategy has not only caused misery, health problems and environmental damage, it has also failed to reduce the supply of drugs.

10

Money, Multinationals and Misery

An ordinary bus journey in a Latin American city is a lesson in the human cost of neoliberal economics. School-aged children will board the bus and offer to sell you freshly fried plantain crisps, rebottled tap water, plastic trinkets or homemade sweets. A woman with a sun-creased face will give you a demonstration of magic stain-removing powder or a prematurely ageing man will give a speech explaining how he once had a proper job but redundancy has forced him to humble himself in front of you in order to feed his family. There is no greater indictment of the International Monetary Fund (IMF) and the World Bank than the fact that after twenty years of 'stabilization plans' and 'structural adjustment', the percentage of Latin Americans living in poverty has risen. After decades of falling poverty rates since the Second World War, the trend was abruptly reversed. In 1980, 40.5 per cent of the people of Latin America lived below the poverty line; by 2002, this figure had risen to 44 per cent. In absolute terms, the picture is even starker: the number of people living in poverty during the same period has risen from 136 million to 221 million.

In the smaller, less-developed countries, the proportion of people living in poverty rises to even greater levels: Guatemala (60 per cent); Paraguay (61 per cent); Bolivia (62 per cent); Nicaragua (69 per cent); Honduras (77 per cent). Poverty is worst in the countryside; 62 per cent of the rural population in Latin America live in poverty – 74.8 million people.[1]

In the cities, hundreds of thousands of people have been thrown out of regular work and are now forced to scrape a living selling trinkets on the street or collecting and reselling rubbish, to name just two of the most common jobs in what economists benignly call the 'informal sector'. These workers pay no tax and receive no social security benefits, pensions or health insurance. They have been abandoned by employers and the state. They are left to fend for themselves in the most brutal and competitive market of all, the city street. For millions of Latin Americans, this is the reality of the neoliberal dream.

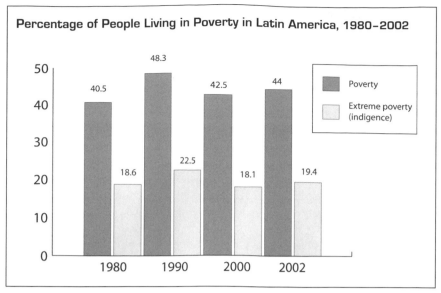

Source: *Social Panorama of Latin America 2005*, United Nations Economic Commission for Latin America and the Caribbean (ECLAC), Santiago, 2006.

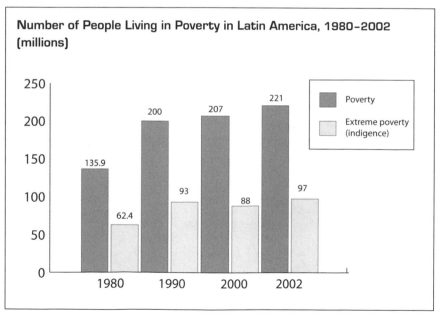

Source: *Social Panorama of Latin America 2005*, United Nations Economic Commission for Latin America and the Caribbean (ECLAC), Santiago, 2006.

Latin America's Development Dilemma

The IMF and international financial institutions must shoulder some of the blame for the current economic malaise, but the failure to transform Latin America into a continent of advanced and equitable economies has a far longer history. Latin American policy makers were receptive to the neoliberal message precisely because the previous development model had failed. Economic problems are fundamentally political. Although Latin America is not the poorest region in the world, it is one of the most unequal. Small elites own the vast majority of the wealth, while the mass of the population live in poverty. This inequality has had long-term economic consequences. Historically Latin America has suffered from small domestic markets, making it hard for companies to grow. High levels of poverty have resulted in a very low savings rate, leaving businesses reliant on foreign investment. And since the majority are so poor, tax revenues are low. Governments face constant budget crises, which in turn means they require loans and have little money to invest in national infrastructure or social programmes. Political instability is also a recurring problem because Latin America is home to large numbers of people with no land or jobs to sustain themselves. Long before the IMF appeared on the scene, the US played a part in maintaining this unequal status quo by propping up dictators, sustaining greedy elites and undermining reform movements that tried to redistribute wealth.

Inequality Rates, 1997–2001

	Share of the wealthiest top 10% of population in total income [%]	Share of the bottom 20% of population in total income [%]
Brazil	47.2	2.6
Guatemala	46.8	2.4
Colombia	46.5	2.7
Chile	47.0	3.4
Mexico	43.1	3.1
Argentina	38.9	3.1
Costa Rica	34.8	4.2
Uruguay	33.5	4.8
United States	30.5	5.2

Source: D. Ferranti et al., *Inequality in Latin America: Breaking with History*, Washington, World Bank, 2004, p. 2.

Since independence, Latin America has traditionally exported foodstuffs and raw materials such as coffee, bananas, sugar and copper, while importing manufactured goods. Relying on one or two commodities made Latin American economies vulnerable to swings in world prices and demand. After the Second World War, Latin American governments attempted to address these weaknesses. They raised high tariff barriers and gave subsidies to industrialists to encourage domestic industry to make the goods that had previously been imported – the so-called import-substitution industrialization (ISI). By the 1960s, the first stage of ISI was complete with Argentina, Mexico and Brazil producing many consumer goods. But these countries found they were still reliant on the First World for capital goods, such as machinery and factory equipment. Embarking on the second stage of ISI, the authoritarian governments of this period borrowed huge sums of money to invest in mega-projects such as dams and steelworks, while inviting multinational companies to build car plants and other high-tech factories. US investment in the region soared from US$8.3 billion in 1960 to US$14.7 billion in 1970.[2] Foreign companies had the best of both worlds, because they were protected from competition by high tariff barriers and so could inflate their prices in the Latin American market. Car makers Ford, General Motors and Chrysler, along with Germany's Volkswagen, built plants in Mexico, Argentina and Brazil, and by the end of the 1970s multinationals controlled 85 per cent of car production in these countries. Manufacturers of pharmaceuticals, consumer goods and processed foods rushed to take advantage of the protected market. In Brazil, for example, Alcoa, Atlantic Richfield, GM, General Electric and Johnson & Johnson set up operations.[3] Domestic companies too were protected from international competition, and were able to charge inflated prices for their goods.

The oil price rises of 1973 and 1979, which hit oil importers like Brazil particularly hard, showed that Latin America was still vulnerable to external shocks. And when the US Federal Reserve raised interest rates in the early 1980s, the debt bubble burst. Mexico defaulted on its US$80 billion debt in 1982, and Argentina and Brazil soon followed suit. These three countries owed foreign creditors US$200bn, a debt of such magnitude that it posed a threat to the international financial system. Latin Americans – who had not elected the military governments that had amassed these huge debts – were nevertheless forced to pay the price of economic crisis in the 1980s.

The IMF and the World Bank

The IMF and the International Bank of Reconstruction and Development (World Bank) were conceived at a conference in Bretton Woods, New Hampshire, in 1944. Their aim was to avert international economic crises such as the Great Depression of the 1930s. In the early post-war years, the IMF and World Bank gave loans to European countries to fund reconstruction. The IMF continued to lend to rich countries during the 1970s, but after 1982 it did not make a loan to a developed country for 25 years until the global financial crisis forced it to bail out Iceland in 2008. In contrast, its influence in the developing world has expanded enormously. By the mid-1980s, three quarters of Latin American countries and two thirds of African countries were under some kind of IMF–World Bank supervision.[4] As it became an exclusively Third World lender, the IMF expanded its operations from providing short-term loans to offering longer-term 'structural adjustment' packages. In doing so, it assumed far greater control over each recipient's long-term economic policy and imposed wide-ranging conditions that no First World government would tolerate.[5]

The dominance of the US, the world's largest economy, was clear at the IMF's founding conference, when the US dollar was chosen as the international unit of exchange. The voting system also gave the US preponderant influence with 17 per cent of the vote, enough to veto policy decisions, which requires 15 per cent of the vote. The influence of the rich countries has in fact increased over the years. Today, the industrialized countries have a total of 62 per cent of the votes, while the developing countries have just 38 per cent. The influence of an individual developing country is miniscule. What chance does poverty-stricken Bolivia have of influencing IMF policy when its share of the vote is just 0.1 per cent? Even bigger countries like Argentina and Brazil can have little influence when their voting power is just 0.9 per cent and 1.4 per cent respectively.

In practice, most countries do not get a voice at all because decisions are taken by the IMF's Board of 24 directors. The five richest countries (US, Japan, Germany, France, UK) each have a seat on the board and wield powerful voting shares. Other directors' seats are taken by China (2.9 per cent) Russia (2.7 per cent) and Saudi Arabia (3.2 per cent).[6] Developing countries do not have a seat each but are herded into groups. For example, South America has two directors representing fifteen countries. Together they have a voting power of 2.8 per cent. Central American countries are represented by a director from Spain, who alternates with a Mexican director. Their voting share is 4.2 per cent, with Spain wielding by far the most power. The IMF announced reforms to its voting system in 2006, when China, Korea, Mexico and Turkey were given a greater voting share (in return for larger contributions to IMF funds) and other emerging countries will have their shares re-evaluated in subsequent years. Although the IMF heralded this change as its most important structural reform in six decades, the increases were small – Mexico's voting share, for example, rises from approximately 1.2 per cent to 1.4 per cent of the total votes – leaving the balance of power clearly in favour of the rich countries.

Neoliberalism and the IMF

Neoliberals believe the free market is the essence of a free society. Neoliberalism is a selective revival of nineteenth-century classical liberalism, a revival that arose in opposition to both Keynesian social democracy and Soviet state control. Neoliberals are fundamentally antipathetic to government intervention in the economy and instead advocate free markets, free trade, liberalized capital markets and privatization. The father of neoliberalism is Friedrich von Hayek, author of *The Road to Serfdom*, who was trained at the Austrian School of Economics in Vienna in the early twentieth century and went on to become a professor at the London School of Economics in the 1930s and the University of Chicago in the 1950s. The University of Chicago became the nexus of neoliberal thought. Founded by Fred Knight, an opponent of Roosevelt's New Deal, it produced a generation of neoliberal thinkers, the most famous of whom was Milton Friedman. Neoliberalism remained a minority current in academia and government circles in the decades after the Second World War, but gained currency in the 1970s as the European social democratic model appeared to be sinking into a morass of unemployment, inflation and stagnation. The elections of Ronald Reagan and Margaret Thatcher heralded the political victory of neoliberalism, and the personnel who now staffed the world's largest financial institutions, such as the IMF and World Bank, reflected the change.

The new men controlling the world's purse strings had supreme confidence in their own judgement and the infallibility of neoliberal ideas. This is particularly serious because some of the IMF's underlying precepts are deeply questionable. It argues, for example, that economic development is best achieved with a free market and free trade. However, the United States, most of Western Europe and the emerging Asian economies industrialized behind protective barriers. The only successful industrialized countries that did not use protective tariffs were the UK and the Netherlands, which at the time were the most economically advanced powers in the world with no serious competitors.

Another questionable neoliberal idea is that there is no such thing as involuntary unemployment because demand always equals supply. Dole queues must therefore be the fault of lazy workers, greedy trade unions or meddling governments. In contrast, if the market is left unfettered, unemployment will evaporate. Armed with these supposedly unassailable theories, the IMF metes out directives not only on fiscal policy (balancing the budget), but on trade tariffs, industrial policy, labour relations, pension law and privatization. If a poor country shuns IMF advice, it will not simply miss out on IMF funds; most international lenders, including the World Bank, the InterAmerican Development Bank and foreign private banks, will not lend to a developing country unless the IMF has given it the stamp of approval.

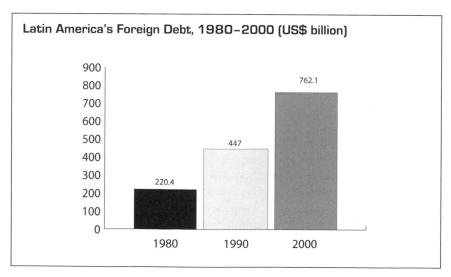

Latin America's Foreign Debt, 1980–2000 (US$ billion)

Source: *Economic Survey of Latin America 1996–1997*, United Nations Economic Commission for Latin America and the Caribbean, 1997.

The IMF and Latin America

The IMF and the World Bank first became significant players in Latin America during the 1980s debt crisis. The IMF worked closely with foreign banks to ensure that their debts would be repaid. Together with foreign governments, they presented the debtor nations with a united front, using divide-and-rule tactics to ensure that Latin American governments would not call a joint moratorium and default on their debts – an event that would have had serious consequences for the banks of the lender countries. When the Peruvian government declared a partial moratorium no Latin American government followed suit and Peru paid a heavy price, as capital flight soared and the economy plunged into an inflationary crisis. Meanwhile, those governments that did service the debt found that, despite making regular payments, the overall debt continued to rise as interest mounted. Latin America's foreign debt grew from US$220 billion in 1980 to US$447 billion in 1990.[7] This decade also saw a huge transfer of wealth from Latin America to the rich countries: a net capital outflow of US$218 billion between 1980 and 1991.[8]

The Lost Decade

The 1980s are known in Latin America as the 'lost decade'; Latin American economies sank into recession. Businesses went bankrupt, unemployment soared and poverty rose. Unusually for economies in recession, inflation did not abate and Latin America was instead inflicted with a new – at least, to Latin America – disease: stagflation (a shrinking economy coupled with rising prices). The IMF signed more than 100 loan agreements with Latin American and Caribbean countries in the 1980s, 1990s and 2000s, deals that came with an increasing number of conditions. The IMF's early advice was to cut public spending in order to balance the budget. It suggested sacking public sector workers, reducing wages and cutting subsidies aimed at the poor and at domestic industries. (The IMF always focuses on the so-called 'primary budget' – which includes all government finances except debt repayments. It recommends cutting social spending to achieve a primary surplus, but never proposes reducing debt repayments, which are by far the largest part of the overall budget deficit.) The IMF and World Bank went on to propose the lifting of trade barriers, which led to the collapse of several thousand Latin American businesses, and the liberalization of the banking system and stock markets, which made Latin America more vulnerable to market panics. The neoliberal programme in the 1990s was extended to the privatization of state assets and public services.

Some Latin American governments (notably Peru, Brazil and Argentina) were resistant to IMF advice in the 1980s and tried other ways to stabilize their economies. But these so-called heterodox (as opposed to the IMF's 'orthodox') plans failed and gradually Latin American elites came to the conclusion that there was no alternative to neoliberalism. In any case, for the richest Latin Americans there was much to gain from the free market. Such policies remained highly unpopular with the poor, and many cities were shaken by 'IMF riots' as thousands of angry citizens took to the streets to protest against cuts. Politicians often campaigned on an anti-IMF platform, but did a *volte face* on achieving office. This was the case with Argentina's Carlos Menem, an apparent nationalist who, on becoming president, privatized every sellable asset the state owned. In other instances, the voters were so exhausted with hyperinflation and uncertainty that any effective stabilization plan, however, painful, was preferable: so, for example, Brazil's Fernando Henrique Cardoso, whose new currency had defeated inflation, was elected on an openly neoliberal manifesto.

The Impact of Two Decades of IMF 'Medicine'

As we have seen, after two decades of IMF medicine, poverty was higher in Latin America in 2008 than it was in 1980. Economic growth slumped to an annual per capita average of 0.5 per cent between 1980 and 2001, compared with a world average of 1.4 per cent and a Latin American average of 2.8 per cent in the previous two decades (1960–80). Meanwhile foreign debt tripled from US$220 billion in 1980 to US$762 billion in 2000. Perhaps most telling, the gap between rich and poor has widened significantly. The Gini index, the world standard for measuring inequality, rose from an average of 48.4 in the 1970s to 52.2 in the 1990s, in a region that was already one of the most unequal in the world.

It may be a fairer test of neoliberal policies to consider Latin America's fortunes in the 1990s separately from the 1980s, which after all was the lost decade of the debt crisis. Per capita economic growth in Latin America between 1990 and 2001 was 1.1 per cent, lower than the world average of 1.4%. Furthermore the decade was punctuated by a series of economic crises, caused or exacerbated by panics on the world market (to which Latin America is now much more vulnerable), such as the Mexican devaluation, 1994, fallout from the Asian Crisis of 1996–98, Brazil's election panic of 2002, and the Argentine default of 2000–01. Inequality worsened in the 1990s: the Gini index rose throughout the decade from 50.8 to 52.2.

Poverty, Unemployment and Falling Wages in the 1990s

Poverty rates show a more mixed picture. During the 1990s, poverty fell in Brazil, Chile, Ecuador, Mexico and Uruguay, but rose in Argentina, Bolivia, Colombia, Paraguay, Peru and Venezuela.[9] Poverty was measured from a very low base in the first place, because the 1980s were a decade of severe crisis, and an improvement from this period ought to be expected. The most shocking case is that of Argentina, a country that once had the highest standard of living in Latin America and aspired to become a First World country. The proportion of Argentinians living in poverty more than doubled in the 1990s, from 21 per cent to 45 per cent. Poverty fell in Central America during the 1990s, although the main factor was the ending of the wars in that region. Nevertheless Central America remains the poorest part of Latin America, with over 60 per cent of people living below the poverty line.

The impact of free market policies on unemployment and wages has been stark. Official urban unemployment in Latin America rose from 7.3 per cent in 1990 to

The Informal Economy: Working on the Street

Coffee and flavoured-water seller, single mother, thirty-five years old, one son (aged sixteen)

'I wake up at 4am and prepare the coffee and cool drinks for the first shift, I make breakfast and lunch and clean up the house. I say goodbye to my son as he goes to school. I get my thermos flask and my cart and I start selling to shops, to businesses and to other street traders. I walk all morning and then I go home about 1pm and have lunch. I fill up the flask for the second shift and then I do the same thing again in the afternoon. I get home about 7 pm, prepare supper and eat with my son, I ask him about school and his homework. Thank God he's turned out to be a good lad. My job is hard work, it's very tiring, and dragging the cart along hurts my back. I once did a course in beauty treatments and if I had the choice I would like to start my own beauty business so I could work from home and take care of my son.'

Mobile phone-call seller, single mother, twenty-three years old, two children (aged two and four)

'I used to work in an office as a cleaner but when the contract ended they didn't renew it. Every day I wake up at 4am, wash and get the breakfast and lunch ready for my children. One of my sisters comes to look after them. I tidy up and then I go out. I have a pitch in Parque Santander. I like to get there early because there are lots of offices around there and while the people are queuing to get into work, I offer them phone calls. I stay there all day. Then I go home about 7.30pm, prepare the meal, put my children to bed and go to sleep myself. I don't like this work because I hardly ever see my children. I don't like it because it hurts my throat a lot (imagine saying '*minuto celular, minuto celular, minuto celular*' all day). It also hurts my feet and my face gets sore. But I like the money and watching shows in the square. I also see lots of people. When I was a cleaner it was hard work, but at least I got to see my children and earned more. It was in an office and they treated me well. I wish I could have my old job back.'

Bogotá, 2006

10% in 2004. [10] Average income has fallen in eleven out of sixteen Latin American countries.[11] Meanwhile, the proportion of people working in the informal sector, with no tax or social security benefits, has risen in twelve out of sixteen countries. In Venezuela, for example, the number of informal sector workers more than doubled from 18 per cent to 40 per cent between 1980 and 2002. In the same period, Colombia too has a seen a catastrophic rise in the number of people working in the streets with no welfare to protect them, from 26 per cent to 41 per cent.

Foreign Investment and Capital Outflows

The privatization of state companies and services in Latin America led to a bonanza of foreign direct investment in the late 1990s, which reached a peak of US$79.3 billion in 1999.[12] But this level of foreign direct investment was not sustained once the largest state companies were sold off, and by 2003 foreign direct investment had fallen to less than half that level, US$31.7 billion. Despite the surge in foreign investment, Latin America has become once again an exporter of capital to the rich countries. The net resource transfer turned negative in 1999, meaning that more money was sent abroad in profits and debt repayments than was received in investment and new loans. In 2004, a net total of US$63.7 billion was sent out of the region.

The IMF Ties Lula's Hands

Left-wing governments often get a cool reception from foreign investors. In Brazil, a crisis occurred before a left-winger was even elected. When the Workers' Party presidential candidate, Luiz Inácio Lula da Silva, started to top the opinion polls, the Brazilian currency started to depreciate. Between January and October 2002, the Brazilian *real* fell by 36 per cent against the dollar. The main reason given by currency traders was Lula's impending victory.

To reassure the markets, the IMF granted Brazil a U$30 billion loan in August 2002. Crucially, all presidential candidates agreed that they would abide by the IMF's austerity conditions. The deal may have stopped investors pushing Brazil towards debt default and hyperinflation, but Lula, who was duly elected as Brazil's first left-wing president in October 2002, had his hands tied before he even took office.

The Strategies of US Corporations in the 1990s

US corporations had a two-pronged strategy in Latin America in the 1990s and early 2000.[13] In the globalized world economy, US corporations had to compete with foreign companies – from China and other parts of Asia in particular – selling cheap goods in the US market. US companies therefore sought to lower production costs for products they sold in the US. Thus we saw the boom in the maquiladora industry in Latin America, where products were assembled by low-waged labour, then exported back to North America. The push for free trade in the Americas came primarily from large US corporations who wanted to be able to search the globe for low-waged workers in order to sell their products back to the US without paying import tariffs. As the UN noted, this strategy led to a 'race to the bottom' with respect to production costs (wages, exchange rates and benefits) and crowded out local Latin American firms while failing to stimulate local development.[14] US manufacturers also established themselves in Brazil in order to sell within the regional South American trade bloc, Mercosur.

'Water is a human right'

If privatization meant that you had to pay a fifth of your family's income just for water ... if you had built an alternative water system in your area, dug a well, built a network of pipes because no government or company had done it ... then one day a private company comes along and says this system belongs to us and we're not going to give you one *peso* compensation ... If you had lived in a peasant community, where for centuries they took water from lakes, lagoons, rivers, wells and along comes privatization and they say, from now on, these water sources can be bought by any investor ... if they say it's prohibited even to collect rainwater! ... you are not going to sit there with your arms crossed and do nothing ... We want the transnational Bechtel to leave and we want a law that guarantees water is recognized as a common good, a human right, our common heritage.

Oscar Olivera, *La Coordinadora* [Coalition in Defence of Water and Life], Bolivia, interviewed by the author, London July 2006.

The IMF's Role in Argentina's Downfall

Argentina was the IMF's model pupil during the 1990s. It liberalized trade, undertook a rapid and extensive privatization programme, laid off thousands of public sector employees and privatized pensions. At the heart of the programme was the Convertibility Plan which pegged the peso to the US dollar at a rate of 1:1. Although unemployment soared, the IMF and World Bank judged the experiment to be a success because the economy began to grow and inflation was low, in contrast to the years of hyperinflation in the 1980s.

However, the peso became overvalued, particularly when Brazil devalued its currency in 1999. Argentina's exports slumped, while the strong peso sucked in cheap foreign imports. The trade deficit ballooned. Investors began to fear that a devaluation was imminent and began to withdraw. As the pressure on the peso intensified, interest rates rose dramatically and the economy dipped into recession. To reassure investors that the Argentine government had the funds to defend its currency, the IMF granted a series of large loans, culminating in a US$40 billion emergency loan in 2001. The Bush administration was intimately involved in the negotiations with Argentina. According to the *New York Times*:

> It is not unusual for the United States, the largest single shareholder in the fund, to play an important role in shaping an emergency aid package to a large developing country. But several people involved in the talks said the administration's role was especially intricate in this case, with many late-night sessions held in [US] Treasury offices rather than at the IMF headquarters nearby.

→ As recession gripped Argentina, the IMF demanded that the government slash spending to achieve a 'zero deficit'. Cutting spending during a recession is like turning off a life support machine to a patient in a coma, and the economy, which had shrunk in per capita terms by 5.7 per cent in 2001, contracted by an incredible 11.7 per cent in 2002. As the economy plunged into crisis in late 2001, the government defaulted on its US$90 billion debt and froze bank accounts so Argentinians could not get access to their money.

Argentina, a relatively prosperous country, was transformed. The proportion of people living in poverty doubled from 21 per cent to 45 per cent between 1990 and 2002. Open unemployment tripled from 6 per cent to 19 per cent between 1990 and 2003.

By December 2001, the desperate population could take it no more. Thousands took to the streets. Shops were looted for food. The finance ministry and two banks were set on fire. After days of running battles between police and protestors in the streets of Buenos Aires, President Fernando de la Rúa resigned. He left the presidential palace by helicopter, as crowds cheered his departure.

The new nationalist governments of Eduardo Duhalde (2002–03), Néstor Kirchner (2003–07) and Cristina Fernández de Kirchner (2007–) have been much firmer in their dealings with the IMF and have carried out a more independent economic policy.

Sources: R. Peet, *Unholy Trinity*, 2003, p. 84. *Social Panorama of Latin America, 2005*, ECLAC, 2006, Table 22.

The transnationals' other major preoccupation in the globalized economy was the aggressive search for new markets for services such as banking, energy and utilities. This contributed to the wave of deregulation and privatization in Latin America in the 1990s. US energy giants AES and Southern Electric, for example, were particularly active, spending more than US$5 billion on privatized electricity companies in Latin America between 1994 and 1997. Southern Electric bought assets in Trinidad and Tobago, Brazil and Argentina. Enron invested heavily in natural gas in Latin America, acquiring assets in Argentina, Colombia, Bolivia and Brazil. Mobil and CM Energy also competed energetically in the Latin American gas market. Bell South became a major player in the Latin American telecoms industry, investing a total of US$2.8 billion in the 1990s, particularly in mobile phone technology, acquiring assets in Venezuela, Guatemala, Peru, Brazil, Argentina and Bolivia. Overall, the United States accounted for just under a third of all direct foreign investment in Latin America in 1996–2002. Spanish multinationals also invested heavily in Latin American service sector companies, particularly in banking, telecoms and energy. Spain has now overtaken the US as the largest investor in Chile and Argentina. Among the Spanish giants are Telefonica, Banco Santander, Endesa, Iberdola and Repsol.

Privatization of Basic Services

The IMF and World Bank often made it a condition of loans that governments privatize basic services such as water and electricity. The privatization of water, in particular, has been a highly contentious issue across Latin America. It is not surprising that the improved services promised by private water companies never came because it requires heavy investment to connect the poorest areas, such as shantytowns, to the water supply and the residents were often too poor to pay the charges. In Colombia, for example, 73 per cent of the people who were cut off came from the five poorest deciles of income distribution.[15] In Buenos Aires, the water consortium run by Suez raised prices by 88 per cent between 1993 and 2002, while failing to carry out 57 per cent of its promised investment in sewerage expansion.[16] The water companies' demands caused particular anger in Bolivia because many rural indigenous communities had previously had their own free water supplies from wells and streams, and were now being asked to pay for what they saw as a basic human right.

The World Trade Organization

The WTO, formed in 1995, is the newest of the international financial bodies but is rapidly becoming one of the most powerful, with the power to challenge a sovereign country's domestic laws. Its remit is broad; it not only regulates trade in physical goods, but also services (banking, tourism, consultancy), intellectual property rights (TRIPs) and investments (TRIMs). Rich countries are also pushing to expand its powers to cover water provision and other basic services.

The WTO is highly secretive and undemocratic. Although in theory it is fairer than the IMF because the voting system is 'one member, one vote', in practice decisions are taken by consensus of those present at meetings. This penalizes poorer countries which have small delegations to the WTO or have no permanent representative at all. Furthermore most of the bargaining is done in closed, private meetings which are by invitation only. After the WTO meeting in Seattle, both the African delegation and a group of Latin American and Caribbean countries issued statements complaining of the lack of transparency and, in the words of the African group, of 'being marginalized and generally excluded on issues of vital importance for our peoples and their future'.[17] The public are barred from all of the WTO's meetings, heightening the secretive nature of the deals. Business groups, in contrast, play a powerful role in shaping WTO policy. They are invited to informal meetings and take direct part in negotiations as technical advisers. For example, the US Coalition of Services Industries and British Invisibles, an organization that promotes UK business interests abroad, played an important role in the negotiation of the General Agreement on Trade Services (GATS) rules, while pharmaceutical companies helped to shape the rules on patents (TRIPs).[18]

The WTO vigorously promotes free trade and free markets. As already noted, most rich countries protected their industries in the early stages, a path that is now

Trade Facts

- The United States exports cotton at 35 per cent below the cost of production.
- The United States exports wheat at 47 per cent below the cost of production.
- The United States pays subsidies to rice growers which account for 92 per cent of the cost of production.
- The United States grows wheat at a loss of 50 per cent.
- The European Union exports sugar at 44 per cent below the cost of production.
- The EU exports beef at 47 per cent below the cost of production.

Source: 'A Round for Free: How rich countries are getting a free ride on agricultural subsidies at the WTO', Oxfam International, briefing paper, June 2005.

closed to poor countries if they want to remain members of the world trading club. Despite the fact that they are disadvantaged, many developing countries are willing to play by the rules of the game, but merely ask that rich countries do the same. The biggest problem poor countries face is that while they are urged to lift trade barriers, deregulate and welcome foreign takeovers of their public services, wealthy countries are unwilling to stop subsidizing their own farmers. The poorest countries, which predominantly trade agricultural goods and textiles, cannot compete because the West gives its farmers exorbitant subsidies. Not only does this mean that poor countries find it hard to export their produce, but the rich countries also dump cheap, subsidized goods on those same poorer countries, destroying the livelihoods of local farmers.

The impact of these subsidies is devastating. Guatemala is a case in point. As a diligent member of the WTO, Guatemala lowered import tariffs on maize from 35 per cent to 5 per cent in 1996. Over the next four years the volume of US maize imports doubled. By the year 2001, US maize imports totalled 600,000 tonnes – more than half of Guatemala's entire maize output. The US had given its maize growers subsidies totalling US$38 billion in 1995–2003, making it impossible for Guatemalan farmers to compete on price.[19] Thousands of families who relied on maize crops were forced into even greater hardship, in a country that was already one of the poorest in Latin America.

Although the wealthy countries demand that the poor abide by WTO rules, they do not follow suit. Brazil brought a case against the US in 2003, claiming its subsidies had depressed world cotton prices by 4 per cent. Although the WTO ruled in Brazil's favour and ordered the US to eliminate the cotton subsidies, to date the US has not done so. Cotton dumping affects the poorest countries in the world; African nations, for example, have lost US$441 million a year because of the catastrophic fall in cotton prices. In total, US agricultural subsidies were US$40 billion in 2003.[20] Although George Bush espoused neoliberalism, he raised import tariffs on steel to protect US industry – a move which sparked another dispute with Brazil. Third World textile makers also find it hard to get access to the US tariff-protected markets. The US rule appears to be: free trade is fine while we can beat your prices, but if you start producing more cheaply than us, the barriers will come up.

The poor countries agreed to join the WTO (or its predecessor, the GATT) on the promise that they would be given market access for their agriculture and textiles. However in the past twenty years, the annual total subsidy for farming in the wealthy Organisation for Economic Co-operation and Development (OECD) countries has actually increased in real terms, from US$241 billion in 1986 to US$257 billion, according to the OECD.[21] This figure is larger than the GDP of all Latin American countries, apart from Brazil, Mexico, Argentina and Colombia. The European Union is the worst offender. The cost of the Common Agricultural Policy (CAP) to the taxpayer is US$138 billion a year. One of the biggest recipients of CAP subsidies in the UK is the Duke of Marlborough, the fourteenth-richest man in the world.[22] Another CAP beneficiary is sugar giant Tate & Lyle, which in the year 2003–2004 received US$120 million of taxpayers' money.[23]

Bilateral Free Trade Agreements with the United States	
Chile	2004
Central America and Dominican Republic	2006 (Came into force in 2006 in the Dominican Republic, Guatemala, Nicaragua and El Salvador. Pending ratification in Costa Rica)
Peru	Signed 2005 (pending ratification by Peruvian and US congresses)
Colombia	Signed 2005 (pending ratification by Colombian and US congresses)
Ecuador	Talks suspended 2006
Panama	Talks ongoing 2006

Free Trade Deals

The ambition of the United States during the Clinton and Bush years was to turn the whole of the Americas into a free trading block. It had hoped to sign the Free Trade Area of the Americas (FTAA) by 2005, but talks stalled and a deal was not signed. Free trade is a highly controversial issue in Latin America. The titles of two books by left-wing authors, *The FTAA: The Path to Annexation* and *The Road to Recolonization: the FTAA*,[24] give a flavour of the debate. As one might expect, radical presidents such as Venezuela's Hugo Chávez and Bolivia's Evo Morales are firmly against a free trade deal, viewing it as a new form of colonialism, but there is also opposition from politicians of all stripes in Brazil and Argentina, who fear that their native industries and agriculture could be swamped by cheap US imports and that basic state services could be taken over by US companies.

The United States is now trying a different approach; instead of signing a universal agreement it is negotiating bilateral trade deals. Bilateral deals are even worse for Latin America because individual countries have less leverage and cannot force the US to negotiate on broader issues such as agricultural subsidies. However, free trade deals with Chile came into force in 2004 and with Central America (the Central America Free Trade Agreement, CAFTA) in 2006.

NAFTA

For insight into how free trade deals work in practice, it is instructive to look at Mexico, which joined a free trade area with the United States and Canada on 1 January 1994. The date was marked by the Zapatista uprising, a revolt by poverty-stricken indigenous peoples in southern Mexico, who claimed that free trade would simply make them poorer. The North American Free Trade Agreement (NAFTA) has remained contentious ever since.

NAFTA covers not only trade but foreign investment and patent rights. Its main objectives and governing principles are as follows:

- trade barriers to be reduced over fifteen years
- investment in all sectors to be permitted, with certain restrictions in the Mexican oil industry, Canadian culture, and US airlines and radio communications
- government procurement opened up to private investment
- immigration to be excluded from the agreement
- any country to be able to leave with six months' notice
- any new country to be able to join.

Although NAFTA allows for the free trade of goods and services, it does not allow for the free movement of labour such as exists in the original multi-national trading bloc, the European Union. Mexican migrants seeking higher living standards across the border face deportation and criminalization. More than 1,600 Mexicans died trying to cross the border between 1998 and 2004, according to the US advocacy group Public Citizen.

NAFTA's advocates say it has been a singular success. The Mexican export industry has boomed; total exports have tripled from US$61 billion to US$214 billion and Mexico has had a trade surplus with the United States every year since NAFTA came into force. Foreign investment in Mexico has risen fivefold. Per capita GDP grew 1.8 per cent a year between 1990 and 2001, not a particularly impressive rate but faster than the Latin American average of 1.6 per cent. Yet despite this, unemployment rose and average incomes fell, just as they did in most of the region.

Agriculture under NAFTA

NAFTA benefits the large farming conglomerates at the expense of the smallholder on both sides of the border. In Mexico, 1.3 million small farmers and agricultural workers have been driven off the land.[25] In the US, 38,000 small farmers have gone bankrupt; 11 per cent of Canadian family farms have gone under.[26] Under NAFTA, the US exports about US$1 billion more agricultural goods a year to Mexico than it imports, but both countries have tripled the value of their agricultural exports to each other. But it is the conglomerates that have pocketed the profits. Some 80 per cent of US corn, for example, is produced by three firms: Cargil, ADM and Zen Noh.[27] Four US beef-packing firms control 80 per cent of the market and the four largest chicken companies own half of US processing and production. For some economists, it is natural that the number of people employed in agriculture should fall as an economy develops. But the problem in Mexico, at least, is that there are not enough jobs in the cities to employ those leaving the countryside. The Mexican small farmer's dream of expanding the farm so that his or her children can inherit it is effectively dead. There is no hope of emulating the model that served the US so well: a nation of prosperous family farms.

Maquiladoras

Growth in the export industry has not translated into broader economic development in Mexico and if we look more closely at the impact of NAFTA it is easy to see why. The most obvious result has been the growth of the maquiladoras. Maquiladoras are factories whose inputs are imported from abroad and assembled by low-paid Mexican workers. The number of maquiladora firms rose from 1,703 in 1990 to 2,860 in 2003.[28] But their growth has had only a limited impact on the wider economy because Mexican companies are not required to supply the machinery for the factories or the materials for the finished products, except in a few cases of very low-value inputs. The machinery and materials are all shipped in and shipped out by foreign companies. One Mexican study found that although a network of small Mexican firms has grown up to provide services such as food and shops in maquiladora areas, the larger supply contracts still go to foreign firms.[29]

In fact, the rest of Mexico has suffered a deindustrialization, as small- and medium-sized manufacturing firms find they cannot compete with US imports. The share of small and medium-sized companies in total manufacturing fell from 50 per cent to 43 per cent between 1988 and 1998. This trend can be seen in all NAFTA countries; large companies, usually transnationals, have been putting the small players out of business. Although the maquila sector has provided jobs, it has hurt the living standards of Mexico's skilled workers, because the jobs in the maquila industry require fewer skills and are lower paid than those in the rest of manufacturing industry. Wages in both sectors have fallen since 1994, by 5 per cent in the non-maquila manufacturing sector and by 4.5 per cent in the maquiladoras, as big union-busting foreign companies gain in strength.[30] NAFTA has not been good for workers in the US either. There, trade unions have been weakened because during labour disputes employers frequently threaten to move production abroad. Three million manufacturing jobs have been lost, and the government itself admits that at least 500,000 of those losses are as a result of NAFTA.[31] Manufacturing jobs have been replaced by employment in the low-skilled service sector where wages are 35 per cent to 77 per cent lower.

The maquiladora industry produces everything imaginable: clothes, electronics equipment, cars, toys, furniture and food. Not only North American companies are based in Mexico but European and Asian companies as well, attracted by the low wages and access to the vast US market. Among the companies that run maquiladoras in Mexico are: Acer, Bayer Corp, BMW, Chrysler, Canon, Eastman Kodak , Ericsson, Fisher Price, Ford, General Electric Company, Hewlett Packard, Honda, Honeywell, IBM, Mattel, Mercedes Benz, Motorola, Nissan, Toshiba, VW, Xerox and Zenith.

The TV manufacturing industry gives one a sense of the scope of maquiladora use by big companies.[32] Some 90 per cent of the televisions sold in North America are made in Mexico. The TV assembly industry there employs 90,000 people and produces 25 million sets a year. Hitachi, Daewoo, LG Electronics, JVC, Mitsubishi,

---

Made in Mexico

Made in Mexico is a 'maquiladora management services' company. Published below is an extract from its website which sets out the advantages to US firms of switching to maquiladora

'Your Connection to Mexico's Low-Cost Labor Force

At *Made in Mexico* we would be delighted to walk you through the A to Zs of *Maquiladoras* and the Mexico manufacturing industry and explain how it can net big gains for your organization's bottom line. And by that we mean savings up to 75 per cent or more of your labor costs!

...

- The entry-level wage for low level jobs in Mexico is approximately 25 per cent of the hourly wage paid to workers in the US, which nets you enormous cost savings
- Mexico's standard work-week of 48 hours yields unbeatable speed of production without the financial drain of overtime pay ...

... When it comes to increasing your company's bottom line through Mexico's lower labor costs, there's no need to reinvent the wheel. Simply draw on *Made in Mexico Inc.*'s wealth of knowledge and years of experience in the maquiladora industry.

Contact *Made in Mexico Inc.* today, and we'll analyze your company's individual needs and determine the best-case scenario for maximizing your profits.'

www.madeinmexicoinc.com

Philips, Samsung, Sanyo and Thomson all run plants in northern Mexico. Sony has five television manufacturing factories there.

The population in the Mexican border area has grown rapidly as migrants arrived to seek work, and the infrastructure cannot cope with the sanitation needs of the new population or with the disposal of industrial waste. Millions of tonnes of raw sewage and hazardous chemicals are flowing into rivers and into the water supply on both sides of the border.[33]

Goods Made in Mexico's Maquiladoras, 2005 (%)

Transport equipment	22
Other manufactured goods	14
Clothing and textiles	12
Machinery, electronic and electrical equipment	12
Electrical and electronic parts/accessories	22
Furniture, metal and wood products	7
Services	4
Chemicals	3
Tools	2
Processed foods	2

Source: National Mexican Statistics Institute (INEGI)

More than a million people are employed in the Mexican maquiladoras. The average employee is a woman between the ages of 16 and 29. A maquiladora worker earns between 90 cents and US$1.50 per hour, far less than their equivalent would earn in the US (US$18 per hour). But the rate is higher than the Mexican minimum wage and is attractive to unskilled workers in a country with high unemployment. Working conditions are worse than in the US. A survey of maquiladora workers in the Mexican state of Sonora found that 61 per cent of the workers complained of back pain, 52 per cent of bruised hands and fingers, 37 per cent of eye problems and 31 per cent of frequent respiratory illnesses.[34] Some 37 per cent said they had been exposed to dangerous chemicals. One of the most common discriminatory practices is the mandatory pregnancy test. Many women have to undergo pregnancy tests when they start employment; women are even required to show used sanitary towels to company representatives for up to three months, according to a study by Human Rights Watch:

> Manuela Barca Zapata, 36 years old, worked at Río Bravo Eléctricos [owned by General Motors] in Ciudad Juárez from August 1996 to January 1997. She was informed when she was hired that she would have to return to the company in a month to show her sanitary napkin. The nurse waited outside the door, and then Barca Zapata opened the door to show her sanitary napkin. Barca Zapata described this experience as very shameful.[35]

Trade unions are present in some Mexican maquila factories but in many cases

Maquiladoras in Central America – an Overview

Country	No. of Maquiladoras	No. of Employees	Companies	Women
El Salvador	213 (1998)	60,000	GAP, Liz Claiborne, Bugle Boy, JC Penney, Fruit of the Loom, Macy's Osh-Kosh, Eddie Bauer	78% of maquila workers are women. Average age 16 to 30.
Honduras	250 (1999)	111,000	Osh-Kosh, Philips, Van-Heusen, JC Penney, Sara Lee, Maidenform, Jansport	80% are women. Average age 14 to 24.
Nicaragua*	30 (1999)	30,000	JC Penney, Sears & Roebuck, Kmart, Wal-Mart, Montgomery Ward, Target, Kohl's, Bugle Boy, Tommy Hilfiger	80% are women. Average age 16 to 30.
Guatemala	700 (c.2002)	80,000	Sears, JC Penney, Van Heusen, Fruit of the Loom, Target, Wal-Mart, Liz Claiborne	80% are women. Average age 16 to 25.

Source: R. Armbruster-Sandoval, *Globalization and Cross-Border Labor Solidarity in the Americas*, Routledge, London, 2005, p. 117.
*The Nicaragua figures refer only to the state-run Las Mercedes free trade zone.

they are company-approved unions. Some employees have demanded the right to be represented by independent trade unions and have managed to win improved conditions in their factories. As the maquiladora industry becomes more complex, the types of jobs on offer also become more varied and there are more skilled posts available. Although as many as half the workers can be employed on short-term contracts, once a worker gains a permanent job she is entitled to social security, holiday pay and maternity leave. Companies, however, have already started to look to China where labour is cheaper. Now that Central America has joined the North America free trade bloc (see below), there is a danger that manufacturers will move south, where they will benefit from far lower labour costs but still have tariff-free access to the United States.

Maquiladoras in Central America

In the early 1990s, Central American governments established free trade zones, areas on domestic soil where foreign companies could set up factories exempt from taxes and duties. Under trade agreements with the US, many products from Central America could enter the US duty-free. Maquiladora production, mainly of textiles and clothes, boomed. The Central American Free Trade Area came into force in 2006 and a greater growth of the maquila industry is expected. Conditions in Central American maquiladoras are even worse than in Mexican ones. Wages are much lower – 15 to 30 cents an hour in Nicaragua for example.[36] The women employed tend to be younger. Employment rights and health and safety conditions are worse. One investigation in the Nicaraguan Las Mercedes free trade zone found complaints of long hours; workers being forced to do overtime with no additional pay; verbal and physical abuse of workers; an overwhelming sense of fear and pressure to work faster; sexual harassment; body searches; exposure to dangerous chemicals (used for dying jeans); workers being fired for being sick; workers living in overcrowded stick-and-tin-roof homes, with cardboard walls, dirt floors, no running water and outdoor latrines; workers being fired for union organizing.[37]

Maquiladoras in El Salvador, Honduras, Guatemala and Nicaragua are isolated from outsiders and protected by armed guards. In most cases, independent trade unions are not tolerated and if activists are discovered they are summarily sacked. Sometimes the companies simply close down or relocate the factory.

US Trade with Latin America

Latin America has always been a valuable market for US exporters. In 1910, Latin America bought 18 per cent of US exports, the percentage rising to a historic high of 28 per cent in 1950.[38] When Latin American governments raised protective tariffs in the 1960s and 1970s, the share of US exports sold in Latin America fell to about 15 per cent. With the neoliberal opening of the 1990s, US exports to Latin America rose again to 20 per cent of the total, although Mexico accounts for more than half of that amount. The US and Latin America are by no means equal partners. The US has great economic leverage over Latin American countries because, with the exception of Mexico, each nation only accounts for a miniscule amount of total US trade. For example, US exports to Colombia only account for 0.5 per cent of total US exports. Even giant Brazil buys only 1.4 per cent of the US's total exports. However, the US is a vital market for most Latin American countries. Colombia and Venezuela, for example, buy a third of their imports from the US and sell more than 40 per cent of their exports to the US.

Targeting Gap in El Salvador

There have been some impressive examples of cross-border solidarity in which Latin American trade unionists have allied with activists in the US. The most well-known case is the campaign against Gap.

'Mandarin International was a factory in a free trade zone in El Salvador whose largest supplier was Gap. Workers at the Mandarin plant set up a trade union in 1993. Among their complaints were low wages, verbal and physical abuse (Mandarin's manager used to hit workers on the head with his fists for 'poor quality work'); forced overtime, lack of drinking water, poor ventilation, regulated bathroom breaks, and the mistreatment of pregnant women. After the company responded by firing union members, the union organized two strikes in 1995 that shut down the whole free trade zone. Mandarin responded by firing all the union members, effectively destroying the union.

The National Labor Committee, a US-based labour rights organization, began a campaign targeting Gap, which claimed to be a 'socially responsible' company. Two workers from the *maquiladora* were flown to the US where they went on a twenty-five-city speaking tour. Students, trade unions, women's groups and religious organizations took up the campaign and began to picket Gap stores. Students in one women's college held an 'alternative fashion show, wearing clothes with price tags stating 'teenage girls get 38 cents an hour to sew this garment.' Hundreds of students cut the labels off their Gap clothes and sent them to the company's chief executive.

A year after the NLC campaign was launched, Gap agreed to accept independent monitoring at the factory, the first such monitoring agreement in any *maquiladora*. Working conditions greatly improved after the independent monitoring started: workers were no longer physically or verbally abused, they have unrestricted bathroom use and access to safe drinking water. They also have health insurance. However, most of the fired trade unionists were not re-employed and wages remain low.'

Source: R. Armbruster-Sandoval, *Globalization and Cross-Border Labor Solidarity in the Americas*, London, Routledge, 2005, pp. 61–84.

The Economic Interests of the US State in Latin America

US governments seek to foster private enterprise, encourage pro-capitalist governments and promote the interests of US companies. Corporate strategies in Latin America have changed over the decades from simple resource extraction, to high-tech manufacturing in protected markets, to maquiladora assemblage and investments in services. When making economic policy, the government has to mediate between conflicting corporate interests, as well as other stakeholders (US trade unions, smallholders, etc.). For the past two decades US corporations have

US Exports and Imports, 2003

Region/Country	Export destination (as % share of total US exports)	Import supplier (as % share of total US imports)
Industrial Countries	55	48
Canada	23	17
Japan	7	9
European Union	20.8	19.3
France	2	2
Germany	4	5
UK	5	3
Developing Countries	45	52
Africa	1	3
Asia	19	27
China & Hong Kong	6	14
India	1	1
Korea	3	3
Malaysia	2	2
Thailand	1	1
Singapore	2	1
Middle East	3	3
Latin America	20.6	17.1
Argentina	0.3	0.3
Bolivia	0.03	0.01
Brazil	1.5	1.5
Chile	0.4	0.3
Colombia	0.5	0.5
Costa Rica	0.5	0.3
Dominican Republic	0.6	0.3
Ecuador	0.2	0.2
El Salvador	0.3	0.2
Guatemala	0.3	0.2
Haiti	0.1	0.0
Honduras	0.4	0.3
Mexico	13.5	10.7
Nicaragua	0.1	0.1
Panama	0.3	0.02
Paraguay	0.1	0.0
Peru	0.2	0.2
Trinidad and Tobago	0.1	0.4
Uruguay	0.05	0.02
Venezuela	0.4	1.4
Cuba	0.0	0.0

Source: IMF, Direction of Trade Statistics, 2003

Importance of the US for Latin American Trade, 2002–03

Country	Exports to US as % of total exports	Imports from US as % of total imports
Mexico	88	62
Honduras	69	53
El Salvador	63	38
Guatemala	59	34
Panama	48	34
Colombia	47	30
Venezuela	45	32
Ecuador	40	27
Nicaragua	36	25
Paraguay	34	22
Costa Rica	29	35
Peru	26	27
Brazil	23	20
Chile	16	13
Bolivia	14	16
Argentina	11	16
Uruguay	8	9

Source: IMF, Direction of Trade Statistics

been promoting free trade in Latin America, but since the global economic crisis of 2008–2009 there have been powerful voices in the US calling for protectionist measures and US policy may shift as a result. US corporations have also directly influenced US policy in Latin America; for example, United Fruit's support for the coup in Guatemala or the manoeuvring of ITT and Pepsi against Allende in Chile. More recently, the vice-president of the US oil company Occidental Petroleum testified to US Congress that the guerrilla war in Colombia was hindering oil exploration in southern Colombia; meanwhile the Bush administration was sympathetic to ExxonMobil's complaints about Chávez's nationalist oil policies in Venezuela.

Energy security is certainly a concern of the US government, so important that it is sometimes classed as a defence issue. The US already imports 55 per cent of its oil from the Americas, including Canada, compared with 24 per cent from the Persian Gulf. Latin America has proven oil reserves of 103 billion barrels.[39] Although this is just 8.6 per cent of the world's total, Latin America is consuming its oil at a far slower rate than the US is consuming its own oil. At current production and consumption levels, Latin America's oil will last for 41 years, whereas the US's own supply will run out in less than 12 years. Furthermore large tracts of Latin America remain unexplored – southern Colombia for example, the Amazon, and the waters round Cuba. Latin America also contains 248 trillion cubic feet of natural gas, an important energy source. This accounts for 3.9 per cent of the world total, but once again it is being consumed at a far slower rate than elsewhere. Latin America's reserves are forecast to last 52 years, while US gas is expected to run dry in 10 years' time. Looking further to the future, Latin America is home to the world's most biodiverse region, the Amazon, which is already of great interest to pharmaceutical and biochemical companies. And as global warming looms, water is likely to become one of the world's most important commodities. Latin America is home to 30 per cent of the world's freshwater reserves: in the Amazon, Orinoco, Sao Francisco, Paraná, Paraguay and Magdalena rivers. As the globe's natural resources become more scarce, the US will do its utmost to keep resource-rich Latin America within its sphere of influence.

Top US Oil Suppliers, 2004 (thousand barrels/day)

Country	US imports of oil	% of total US oil imports
Canada	1616	16
Mexico	1598	16
Saudi Arabia	1495	15
Venezuela	1297	13
Nigeria	1078	11

Source: US Energy Information Administration

The Threat from China

China is still a minor player in Latin America, but Chinese trade and investment is growing very fast. China's imports from Latin America grew 600 per cent between 1999 and 2004, from almost US$3 billion to US$21.7 billion. The top Latin American exporters to China in 2004 were Brazil (US$8.7 billion), Chile (U$3.7 billion), Argentina (US$3.3 billion), Mexico (US$2.1 billion), and Peru (US$1.5 billion). China's exports to Latin America rose by 245 per cent between 1999 and 2004, from US$5.3 billion to US$18.3 billion. Although Chinese overseas foreign investment is relatively low (making up just 0.48 per cent of global foreign direct investment stock in 2003), more than a third of China's foreign direct investment went to Latin America in 2003 (US$1.04 billion of US$2.85 billion). China's rapidly expanding economy needs Latin America's natural resources, in particular oil, copper and iron, as well as food. China also sees Latin America as a potentially large export market. In both of these areas, China is competing with US companies. Chinese investment so far has concentrated on the extraction and production of natural resources, but it has also built manufacturing assembly plants and invested in more high-tech areas such as telecoms. While China is clearly a threat to US interests in Latin America, it also represents a challenge to governments in Mexico, Central America and the Caribbean who base their economic model on supplying cheaply made imports to the US. Chinese manufacturers produce the very goods that Mexico and Central America specializes in, and are undercutting the already low costs of the maquiladoras. Central American policy makers need to consider whether basing a strategy on low wages and tariff-free access to the US is sustainable.

Alternatives to Neoliberalism in Latin America

At the ballot box in recent years, the tide turned against neoliberalism as left-wingers took power in Argentina, Brazil, Bolivia, Chile, Nicaragua, Uruguay, Venezuela and Paraguay. Some may not regard the Socialist-Christian Democratic alliance in Chile as left-wing, but the coalition governments that have been in power there since 1990 have transformed Pinochet's exclusionary economic model into one that shares more fairly the benefits of export growth. Uruguay and Brazil have followed the Chilean model, combining orthodox economic policies with targeted anti-poverty programmes. Eleven million Brazilian families, a quarter of the population, receive a minimum income from the government in exchange for educating and vaccinating their children. The gap between rich and poor, in this most unequal of countries in an unequal region, is closing.[40] Nevertheless in a country with such deep-rooted structural inequalities as Brazil, such policies have had a limited impact, and many people have been disappointed by President Lula's lack of progress. President Kirchner of Argentina was more interventionist – albeit because his country had already touched the abyss. He forced foreign creditors to write off large amounts of debt, renationalized some industries and created new state companies.

The clearest break with the neoliberal model has come from Venezuela's Hugo Chávez. The Venezuelan state has become much more powerful, although it is important to separate the reality from the rhetoric. The country's most important company, PDVSA, the oil-producing giant, was already state-owned. Steel, cement and telecoms giants have been nationalized. Large uncultivated tracts of land have been expropriated and leased to peasants, while workers have been given a greater say in the running of companies. The state has started to produce or import basic foodstuffs such as rice and beans, which are sold cheaply at state-run shops (although by 2008 all shops were suffering food shortages). But Venezuela has not, so far, copied the Cuban model of central state control. Most banks and businesses remain in private hands and Venezuela is still a mixed economy. Nevertheless it is possible that Venezuelan businesses will refuse to invest in a country where state intervention is unpredictable and access to capital is tightly controlled.

Perhaps the greatest challenges to US economic dominance have been the moves towards regional integration and alternative trade alliances. At global trade talks and economic summits, Brazil joins an informal alliance as one of the so-called BRIC economies – Brazil, Russia, India and China – to extract concessions from the United States. Meanwhile Venezuela, Bolivia and Ecuador have joined Brazil, Argentina, Uruguay and Paraguay in the South American trade block Mercosur. They have plans to build snaking oil and gas pipelines across the Southern Cone, directly challenging US energy giants. Yet while South America tries to create a regional power bloc, many smaller Latin American nations have signed free trade deals with the US, enticed by the promise of access to the US market. The battle for Latin American markets and natural resources is by no means over.

Appendix

The United States accounted for just under a third of all foreign direct investment (FDI) in Latin America in 1996–2002. Spain is the second largest investor, with an 18% share, followed by the Netherlands (8%) and France (4.5%). (Source: Foreign Investment in Latin America and the Caribbean 2003, ECLAC, UN, 2004)

US Investment Shares by Country, 1996–2002

Country	US share of total investment in each country [%]	Largest investor
Mexico	64	US
Costa Rica	63	US
Honduras	45	US
Bolivia	34.6	US
El Salvador	34.5	US
Paraguay	34.5	US
Ecuador	28.2	US
Colombia	23	US
Venezuela	22	US
Brazil	22	US
Chile	22	Spain 30%
Argentina	18	Spain 43%
Peru	14	UK 30%

Source: Foreign Investment in Latin America and the Caribbean 2004, ECLAC, UN, 2005

11

Coca-Cola, Cartoons and Caricature

Were it not for the proximity of the civilizing influence of the United States, this country would by degrees revert to the aboriginal state in which Alvarado the Spaniard found it.[1]

So wrote the US consul to the Nicaraguan city of León in 1848. Writing half a century later, in 1927, the author of a popular US magazine explained to his readers:

The feelings, emotions and mental processes of the Mexican Indian are much the same today as they were 400 years ago ... Mexican Christianity is a surface veneer of Mexican primalism ... [the Mexicans] are at bottom Amerind pagans who cling with all the red man's tenacity to race ideals grounded in primitivism.[2]

A sense of overwhelming racial and cultural superiority has shaped US policy towards Latin America, indeed it is hardly possible to understand its actions in the region without considering the cultural assumptions of the US governing class. It was commonplace in eighteenth- and nineteenth-century United States to believe in a racial hierarchy with the white race at the top. Black and indigenous peoples were viewed as primitive, ignorant, venal and destined to historical insignificance. The assumption of cultural superiority rationalized the westward expansion and the annihilation of the American Indian in the nineteenth century, as well as the enslavement of the black population. The evangelical citing of 'Manifest Destiny', of a God-given mission to spread the civilizing values of the United States, accompanied the troops into Mexico in 1846. But the annexation of half of Mexico met with dissenting voices at home who warned that the uncivilized Indian was not fit for the US political system. One senator declared:

A degraded population, far inferior to the Aztec race in civility and personage, accustomed only to obey ... to incorporate such a disjointed and degraded mass into even a limited participation with our social and political rights, would be

215

fatally destructive to the institutions of our country. There is a moral pestilence attached to such a people which is contagious – a leprosy that will destroy.[3]

The terror of diluting the purity of Anglo-Saxon blood and draining vigour from the thrusting white nation was one reason why the United States did not expand its territory further into Central America.

Democracy is 'an ideal for which only the very highest races are fit'.
Theodore Roosevelt (1901–09)

'The whole hemisphere will be ours in fact as, by the superiority of our race, it already is ours morally.'
President William Howard Taft (1909–13)

'The racial destiny of Mexico and of the islands and coasts of the Spanish Main is clear. The white man is being rapidly bred out by the negroes on the islands and by Indians on the mainland ... with an ever-thinning veneer of white culture of the "Latin" type.'
Madison Grant, 1916

'Latin-Indians ... in the final analysis recognize no argument but force.'
James R. Sheffield, US ambassador to Mexico, 1925

Sources: Roosevelt cited in D. Healy, *US Expansionism: The Imperialist Urge in the 1890s*, Wisconsin, University of Wisconsin Press, 1970. Taft cited in J. Pearce, *Under the Eagle: US Intervention in Central America and the Caribbean*, London, Latin America Bureau, 1981, p. 17. Grant, *The Passing of the Great Race or the Racial Basis of European History*, and Sheffield, cited in S. Sharbach, *Stereotypes of Latin America and US Foreign Policy 1920–1933*, New York, Garland, 1993.

By the early twentieth century, social Darwinism and other pseudo-scientific theories gave a veneer of academic respectability to this prejudice. Learned journals and the press parroted the claims that the intelligence and temperament of the non-white races were inferior. In an insightful study of stereotypes and press images of Latin Americans in the 1920s and 1930s, Sarah Sharbach has shown how racism was popularized in magazines and newspapers. The author of one 1928 article entitled 'What's Wrong with Mexico' wrote: 'It has been fairly well demonstrated ... that it takes a considerable proportion of white blood to change the characteristics of the Indian,' while another author wrote that the Mexicans 'are people but little affected by the veneer of civilization under which they have lived for four hundred years'.[4] A piece in the *North American Review* entitled 'The Mexican As He Is' pontificated that the Mexican 'has inherited most of the evil traits of two races' [Indian and Spanish] and is 'a child in thought and action, a savage in civilization'.[5] It was not only the press that promoted these stereotypes: a Foreign Service School set up by the US State Department in 1925 advised students that many Latin American

Source: King, 'Attending to his Correspondence', *Chicago Tribune*, 1915, reprinted in J. Johnson, *Latin America in Caricature*, Austin, University of Texas Press, 1980.

governments looked to US diplomats as 'guides for the proper conduct of their own affairs'; political progress was often impeded by the 'Latin temperament and climate' while in Central America specifically the 'low racial quality' had contributed to backward conditions. The lecturer told the diplomats-in-training that Latins were 'very easy people to deal with if properly managed'.[6]

Cartoons of the time clearly illustrate the prejudices of US society. John Johnson's *Latin America in Caricature*, a collection of cartoons from the nineteenth and twentieth centuries, shows how negative views of the peninsular Spanish as decadent, backward, authoritarian, venal, workshy and cruel were mixed with racist assumptions about Native Americans and black people to create new stereotypes.[7] Latin American elites were depicted as 'ideologically immature' and 'economically improvident ... disinclined to defer immediate pleasures of the moment in favour of the greater good of the morrow.' Such condemnation was juxtaposed to a vision of the Anglo-American's rationality, pragmatism, temperance, honesty, industry and frugality. Cartoonists frequently depicted Latin American nations as children or as grossly drawn 'negros', very often mixing the two images. In one cartoon, entitled 'More Trouble in the Nursery', four little boys named Honduras, Nicaragua, Mexico and Guatemala are tucked up in bed, the latter two punching each other, while father-figure Uncle Sam administers 'Mediation soothing syrup'. In another, two ragged children depicting Haiti and Mexico fight on the floor, while Uncle Sam sits at a desk saying 'Hush that rumpus, you kids!' Infantilizing Latin Americans remains a common form of denigration. The minutes of a US National Security Council meeting in 1959, shortly after the Cuban revolution, tell us that 'Mr Allen Dulles [the CIA director] pointed out the new Cuban officials had to be treated more or less like children. They had to be led rather than rebuffed. If they were rebuffed, like children, they were capable of doing almost anything.'[8] More recently US Defense Secretary Donald Rumsfeld gave his thoughts on the appeal of populism in Latin America:

> You know, it's not unique to Latin America. We've seen populism in many countries, many parts of the world. And it can have a certain attraction …
>
> I guess I'm not surprised that we see it from time to time in different places, but … over time, they're going to reject what seems to be an attractive whim of the moment, in favor of behaving in a more mature way, which is to be willing to defer an immediate appetite or pleasure in favor of a longer-term benefit, which is what people do at that point where they begin to reach the age of reason – 12, 13, 14, 15, whatever it is.[9]

In a more subtle way, today's constant chiding of Latin American leaders by US secretaries of state, urging them to act 'responsibly' and implement 'responsible policies', has echoes of the parent–child relationship assumed in previous centuries.

Palestinian intellectual Edward Said described in his book *Orientalism* how a dominating power denigrates the culture, history and supposed racial characteristics of a people in order to dominate it. The imperial power creates the image of 'the Other' in order to subordinate it. Painting 'latin indians' as a primordial, threatening, savage, unknowable people justified US expansionism in the nineteenth century, and updated but related attributes of ignorance, laziness, inefficiency, irrationalism and emotionalism provided cultural justification for US intervention in Latin

---

Negative Stereotypes of Latin Americans

Respondents in a nationwide poll conducted in the US in 1940 were given 19 words and asked to indicate those words that best described the people of Latin America.

Dark-skinned	80%	Imaginative	23%
Quick-tempered	49%	Shrewd	16%
Emotional	47%	Intelligent	15%
Religious	45%	Honest	13%
Backward	44%	Brave	12%
Lazy	41%	Generous	12%
Ignorant	34%	Progressive	11%
Suspicious	32%	Efficient	5%
Friendly	30%	No Answer	4%
Dirty	28%	No Opinion	0%
Proud	26%		

Sources: J. Johnson, *Latin America in Caricature*, Austin, Texas University Press, 1980; A.H. Cantril, *Public Opinion 1935–1946*, Princeton, Princeton University Press, 1951

America in the twentieth century. Of course, within the United States there are plenty of people who do not espouse simplistic and condescending stereotypes. The greats of Latin American literature, from Octavio Paz to Gabriel García Márquez, have plenty of admirers, Bill Clinton among them. Che Guevara was an icon to some on the Left (although stereotypes cling to Che too – the dashing, romantic bandit figure). Still, the dominant attitude of the US to its southern neighbours over the past two centuries has been a negative one – one that emphasizes Latin America's difference, its 'otherness' and, crucially, one that provided a rationalization for its subordination. As academic Lars Schoults has put it:

> A belief in Latin American inferiority is the essential core of United States policy toward Latin America ... a hegemonic attitude developed gradually, so slowly that it went unnoticed. [B]y the end of the nineteenth century, the notion of controlling the behaviour of Latin Americans seemed as natural to US officials as it did to Thucydides ['Large nations do what they wish, while small nations do what they must'].[10]

Film and television exert powerful influences on US opinion.[11] Perhaps the most common Hollywood stereotype has been that of the Mexican bandit, either vicious, violent and corrupt, or a dim-witted buffoon. Mexico – which, for Hollywood, remains a shorthand for all of Latin America – has been for decades painted in cinema as a sleepy backwater with dusty villages, sombrero-wearing peasants slumbering under trees, and alluring senoritas. *Viva Villa!* (1934), *Bandido* (1956), *The Magnificent Seven* (1960), *A Fistful of Dollars* (1964) and *Bandolero!* (1968) are examples of the well-trodden genre. Common to these films is the view that one gringo can defeat many bandits, perpetuating, as Rubie and Reyes note, 'the long-held myth of US Manifest Destiny in foreign policy ... that it takes many Mexicans to equal or best a Yankee'.[12] A variation on the theme of the bandit was the Mexican greaser – a low-life, violent no-hoper, seen in *Bronco Billy and the Greaser* (1914) and *The Greaser's Revenge* (1914). The violent bandit/greaser has translated into modern-day films portraying Latin American gangsters, criminals and sadistic drugs lords – *Scarface* (1983); *Carlito's Way* (1993); *Clear and Present Danger* (1994) – or violent street-gang members – *Falling Down* (1993). The other main male stereotype of Latin Americans, dating from the silent-movie era, was the Latin lover – smouldering, handsome, dark, with more than a hint of danger about him – typified by Mexican heart-throb Gilberto Roland and the urbane polo-playing Argentinian Ricardo Montalban.

There was a brief break in the negative stereotyping during the Second World War, when the Roosevelt administration made a concerted effort to win the hearts and minds of Latin Americans. In 1940, the Office of the Coordinator of Inter-American Affairs (OCIAA) was set up to counter Nazi propaganda and promote the American way of life. The negative male *bandido*/greaser stereotype was taken off the screens and did not reappear until the Cold War. Instead Hollywood produced *Juarez* (1939), an epic biopic of Mexico's legendary liberal president, and lavish musicals, such as *They Met in Argentina* (1941), *That Night in Rio* (1941) and *Holiday in Mexico* (1946), that aimed to show Latin America in a positive light. The 'Brazilian bombshell' Carmen Miranda, complete with fruit-topped headdresses and singing a one-size-fits-all 'Latin' rhythm, made her name in this period. One early attempt to make a light-hearted musical with a Latin theme misfired spectacularly. *Argentine Nights* (1940), which featured the Andrews Sisters singing 'Rumboogie' and 'Brooklyn-nonga', songs that derived not from Argentinian music but from Cuba's Afro-Caribbean rumba and conga, provoked indignation and even riots in Buenos Aires.

The musicals perpetuated another common image: Latin America as an exotic holiday destination for gringos. This began with early classics like *Flying down to Rio* (1936) and continued after the war with Elvis's *Fun in Acapulco* (1963) and the teen flick *Losin' It* (1983) or the much darker portrayal of Mexico as exotica in *Born on the Fourth of July* (1989) in which disabled Vietnam veterans try to slay their demons on Mexican beaches with the help of mescal and prostitutes.[13] Latin America as an untamable wilderness is another recurring theme which can be seen in *Treasure of the Sierra Madre* (1948) and *Raiders of the Lost Ark* (1981), in which Harrison Ford is chased by half-naked Indians after stealing a golden idol from a temple in a South American forest; *Jurassic Park* (1993) has Isla del Coco, off the coast of Costa Rica, as the setting for the re-emergence of dinosaurs, and *Romancing the Stone* (1984) has Michael Douglas and Kathleen Turner brave South American jungles to free a kidnap victim. A similar kidnap drama is played out in the fictional South American country of Tecala, by Meg Ryan and Russell Crowe in *Proof of Life* (2000).

There are two enduring Latin American female stereotypes in Hollywood films: the virginal *señorita*, alluring but unobtainable, and the exotic, lustful, sexually available harlot. The two stereotypes often merged, suggesting that in Hollywood's eyes 'at heart every Latina is a Jezebel.'[14] In the western genre, both the virgin and the jezebel tend to fall in love with the *gringo*, often betraying the cruel, unshaven Latin man, but the *gringo* usually rides into the sunset alone. Although attractive, the Latin harlot is flawed – promiscuous, devious – so does not win her man. A common depiction of *latina* women in the 1980s and 1990s was that of a maid/cleaner/waitress, reflecting society's dominant view that Hispanics in the US were uneducated and lower class. Examples include Elizabeth Peña's maid in *Down and Out in Beverly Hills* (1986), Rosie Pérez in *Untamed Heart* (1993) and Jennifer López in *Maid in Manhattan* (2002). More than any other, Puerto Rican actress Rosie Pérez, star of *Do the Right Thing* (1989) and *White Men Can't Jump* (1992), has typified the Hollywood version of the streetwise, sassy, working-class *latina*.

But the images of Latinos in film and television are changing, thanks mainly to the growing Latino community within the US, a vocal presence and a valuable market that cannot be ignored. In some senses stars of the Latin Boom, such as Jennifer Lopez, Salma Hayek, Ricky Martin, Andy Garcia and Shakira, fit the familiar 'sexy and exotic' stereotype: witness Salma Hayek's famous snake dance in *From Dusk till Dawn* or Ricky Martin's gyrations. But Hayek and Lopez in particular have taken on increasingly varied roles. Of Puerto Rican descent, Lopez has played a US marshal, a child psychologist and an investigative reporter. When she does play a love interest, as in *The Wedding Planner* and *Monster in Law*, she gets to marry her

(Anglo-American) man. These latter films might be dismissed as middle-of-the-road fodder, but it's noteworthy that Lopez, the highest-paid *latina* actress in Hollywood, is playing roles that are not ethnically defined and that could equally be played by an Anglo-American actress.

Mexican-born actress Salma Hayek set up her own production company in 2000, making a number of films, including a biopic of the artist Frida Kahlo (2002), in which she played the title role. She went on to coproduce the award-winning TV show *Ugly Betty*, a remake of a Colombian *telenovela*. *Ugly Betty* has challenged stereotypical views of latinos in a number of ways. The title role is played by the Honduran-American America Ferrera, wearing teeth braces and thick glasses: she is not the slim, exotic, sexually defined 'other'. She makes the audience laugh, but the jokes do not stem from her ethnicity. She is intelligent but shy, and the audience identifies with her. Her brother gives a stereotype-busting performance of a young man exploring his sexuality, while her father's storyline provided mainstream audiences with a sympathetic take on immigration issues. Betty's sister is a stereotypical *latina*, played in an overexaggerated way that only serves to emphasize Betty's 'normality'.

The Changing Face of Cartoon Latin Americans

Dora The Explorer

Dora The Explorer, a US-made cartoon television series first broadcast in 1999, is an example of the changing image of *latinas*. She's a resourceful girl, with a mainstream US accent, who solves a problem in every episode and teaches the audience Spanish. The cartoon is popular in the US and Latin America.

Speedy Gonzalez

Speedy Gonzalez, launched by Warner Brothers in 1955, is a heavily accented sombrero-wearing Mexican mouse with a red necktie. The Cartoon Network axed the eponymous cartoon in 1999, but reinstated it after protests led by the League of United Latin American Citizens, which argued that Speedy was a quick-witted hero who always outwitted his foe, Greengo Pussygato.

How Latin America Sees the US

Spanish America had little contact with North America in the eighteenth century, but as news filtered through, often via Spain and France, of the English colonies' declaration of independence, intellectuals and freethinkers began to wonder if the United States was a model they could emulate. George Washington and Benjamin Franklin were venerated by those Latin American intellectuals who knew of them. The independence leader José de Miranda travelled through the United States in

1783–84 and wrote glowing accounts of the new country's dynamism, prosperity and democracy, noting with surprise that notables ate and drank with common folk, 'passing the plate around and drinking out of the same glass'. 'A more democratic assembly could not be imagined. America incarnates all that our poets and historians imagined about the mores of the free people of Ancient Greece.'[15]

Domingo Saramiento, Argentina's second president and the author of a seminal text on national identity, was a great admirer of the US. His *Facundo: Civilization and Barbarism* (1845), which paints an epic battle between the town (civilization) and the wild half-Indian gaucho (barbarism), illustrated that the Latin American elite often shared the disdain of the early leaders of the United States for the Indian and their belief in racial determinism.

In the early nineteenth century, only a minority feared the imperialist ambitions of the United States. Foreshadowing what would soon become a dominant current of thought, the Cuban Francisco Aragno y Parreno wrote thus:

> In the North, there is growing a colossus composed of all castes and languages that threatens to swallow, if not all of our Americas, at least the northern part of it … The only escape is to grow along with that giant, sharing with him his very breath of life[16]

When US President James Monroe declared the Monroe Doctrine in 1823, most Latin America thinkers did not view it as a statement of imperial ambition. Simon Bolívar, although an admirer of Washington and US political institutions, was unique among the early leaders of Latin America in warning of the expansionist ambitions of their northern neighbour. In 1829, he wrote: 'The United States appears destined by Providence to plague our America with misery in the name of Liberty.'

It was only after the US annexation of Mexico and the filibusterer William Walker's invasion of Nicaragua that fears of US imperial ambitions became more

---

'The Haughtiness of the United States'

The arrogance of the United States has been perhaps the most enduring complaint of Latin Americans throughout the centuries. Below are two early examples of that sentiment.

'The haughtiness of these republicans will not allow them to look upon us as equals but merely as inferiors, and in my judgement their vanity goes so far as to believe that their capital will be that of all the Americas.'
Manuel Zozaya, Mexican minister to the United States, 1822.

'The contempt with which … the United States have viewed us; they send their merchant ships to our ports as they would send them to an uninhabited coast, threatening it with their warships as they would the blacks of Senegal.'
Antonio José de Irisarri, Chilean minister to London, 1818.

Sources: J. Reid, *Spanish American Images of the United States, 1790–1960*, Gainsville, University of Florida, 1977, p. 25. A. McPherson (ed.), *Anti-Americanism in Latin America and the Caribbean*, New York, Berghahn Books, 2006, p. 11.

widespread; as John Reid writes: 'seemingly peripheral incidents in the national life of the United States were powerful determinants of the attitudes taken by Spanish Americans toward their northern neighbours.'[17] This apprehension was mixed with admiration for the amazing technological progress of the United States, which was building cities, railways, canals, steamships and machinery at a phenomenal pace. The disparity between the material progress of the US and the stasis of Latin America, which was mired in factional fighting and revolts, was stark. By the Roosevelt era, the US had indeed become an economic colossus and was now unabashedly espousing its imperial ambitions. José Martí, Cuban independence leader and opponent of US hemispherical domination, voiced the concern of many when he wrote in 1891: 'The scorn of our formidable neighbor, who does not know us, is the greatest danger for our America.'[18]

Writing in 1900 using characters from *The Tempest*, José Enrique Rodó cast the United States as the avaricious and monstrous Caliban and Latin America as the spiritual Ariel. The poet Rubén Darío echoed the same theme in 'The Triumph of Caliban'. Rodó's juxtaposition of a philistine, money-driven society with a more humane, spiritual, intellectual one became a recurring motif of Latin American thought. Meanwhile Martí condemned those 'born in America who are ashamed of the mother who reared them because she wears an Indian apron'.[19] His call for racial unity provided a new basis for Latin American nationalism, which took pride in America's cultural heritage, and acted as a counterweight to the early racial

---

Mr Danger

Hugo Chávez caused amusement and bemusement in the English-speaking world when he started describing George W. Bush as 'Mr Danger'. It was a literary allusion to one of Venezuela's most famous novels, Doña Barbara.

'He was a great mass of muscles under a ruddy skin, with a pair of very blue eyes and flaxen hair. He had arrived some years before with a rifle on his shoulder ... The country pleased him because it was as savage as his own soul, a good land to conquer, inhabited by people he considered inferior because they did not have his light hair and blue eyes. Despite the rifle, it was generally believed that he had come to establish a ranch and bring in new ideas; so many hopes were placed in him and he was cordially received. But he had contented himself with placing four corner posts in land belonging to someone else, without asking permission to do so, and throwing over them a palm thatch roof; and once this cabin was built, he hung up his hammock and rifle, lay down, lighted his pipe, stretched his arms, swelling the powerful muscles and exclaimed:

"All right! Now I'm at home".'

Source: Rómulo Gallegos, *Doña Barbara*, 1929. Translation taken from F. Toscano, and J. Hiester, *Anti-Yankee Feelings in Latin America*, New York, University Press of America, 1982, p. 129.

pessimism of the elites. As the era of 'dollar diplomacy' began, US actions in Central America and the Caribbean – including, as we have seen, the repeated dispatching of marines, the appropriation of customs houses, the befriending of dictators, the exploitation by the fruit companies and the scornful disdain of US oil executives – all served to cement the image of the imperialist Yankee exploiter, ignorant and uninterested in Latin American life, personified in the figure of Rómulo Gallegos's Mr Danger.

Even if the arrogant imperialist Yankee became an enduring and potent image in twentieth-century Latin America, it did not of course reflect the kaleidoscope of changing views felt by the populations of thirty-two countries – from Brazil, which regards itself as a great power to rival the United States, to Nicaragua, whose entire history has been shaped by US interference; from Colombia, where internal problems have generated more despair than an external foe, except when the US's high-handed handling of the drugs issue causes national indignation, to Venezuela, where the American way of life seemed accepted only for Hugo Chávez to tap into a rich stream of resentment dating back to the US oil barons of the 1920s. A balanced study of views of the US in Latin America is also hampered by the lack of material. John Reid's *Spanish American Images of the United States*, one of the few books on the subject, notes that despite the dominant stereotype of the arrogant *gringo*, public opinion polls taken between 1940 and 1960 often revealed positive attitudes towards the US. An international survey taken in 1940 illustrates the mixture of feelings: out of all the nationalities questioned, the Mexican respondents were the only ones to describe the US as an 'unfriendly' nation, but nevertheless more Mexicans categorized the US as friendly than as unfriendly. (No other Latin American nationalities took part in the survey.) Recent surveys show similar contradictory responses (see box).

The attacks of 11 September 2001 prompted soul-searching and a renewed interest in what the world thought of the US. A new academic field of 'anti-Americanism studies' opened up in Latin America and elsewhere.[20] The problem with this literature, however, is that, as the name implies, it focuses solely on negative images of the US. A plethora of international opinion polls were carried out, but the surveys were taken at a time when, thanks to George W. Bush's aggressive unilateralism, the standing of the United States had reached an historic low. In a 2003 poll, 40 per cent of Brazilians said they had a negative image of the US. Yet when the same question was asked just three years earlier, before Bush was in office, only 18 per cent held the same view. So-called 'anti-Americanism' is likely to diminish when a president with a less aggressive foreign policy takes office. Indeed one of the fairly obvious conclusions of the anti-Americanism school is that anti-Americanism is 'not an *a priori* ideology but a response to US policy'.[21]

A number of other observations can be made. Although iconic figures such as Fidel Castro, Che Guevara or Hugo Chávez attract international attention, most Latin American governments have been allies of the US, begrudgingly or otherwise. Yet it remains a feature of Latin American life that even the elites, who often live US-style lifestyles and implement US-friendly policies, do not openly eulogize the

United States – which would seem unpatriotic – but frame their policies in terms of the national good. While voluble sections of the intelligentsia, including university students from Brasilia to Tegucigalpa, espouse anti-imperialism, an equal number go on to study at Harvard and US business schools and come home to staff banks and ministries. More generally the Latin American population has had a greater opportunity to consume a positive image of the US (or at least the image that the US wants to portray) than their North American counterparts have had in relation to them because they see so many US-made films and programmes on their television screens, often showing idealized versions of the US way of life. In communities where poverty is rife, El Norte can appear an El Dorado: a place worth risking family separation and tough border controls to reach.

Latin American opinions on US culture

Do you like American movies, music and TV?

Country	Like [%]	Dislike [%]
Argentina	52	38
Bolivia	39	54
Brazil	69	29
Guatemala	70	26
Honduras	71	25
Mexico	60	30
Pakistan	4	79
Peru	46	43
Venezuela	78	20
UK	76	19

Do you like the spread of American ideals and customs?

Country	Like [%]	Dislike [%]
Argentina	16	73
Bolivia	22	73
Brazil	30	62
Guatemala	40	53
Honduras	44	53
Mexico	22	65
Peru	37	50
Venezuela	44	52
UK	39	50
Pakistan	2	81

Source: 2002 Pew Global Attitudes Project, based on 38,000 interviews in 44 countries
http://pewresearch.org

What Impact Has US Culture Had on Latin America?

In Latin America, US culture is ubiquitous: Coca-Cola is on sale in the remotest village, US-style shopping malls have sprung up in all major cities and are quickly stocked with shoppers who prize US brand names such as Levi's, Nike, McDonald's and Pizza Hut. Every street sports US-made cars – even in Cuba, where after fifty years of isolation glorious 1950s gas guzzlers still bump along the roads. But for all its commercial and cultural influence, when you cross the border into Latin America it has not become an extension of the United States, but still looks, feels and tastes unmistakably different.

Is it possible to measure the impact of US culture on Latin America? Cultural studies, social theory and 'identity politics' are now among the most popular fields of research.[22] Many scholars have moved away from the framework of 'cultural imperialism' popular in the 1960s and 1970s. This envisaged the dominant power imposing its culture on the dominated population in order to justify and facilitate its exploitation and in so doing destroying the existing indigenous culture. One of the best examples of this genre is Ariel Dorfman's *How to Read Donald Duck: Imperialist Ideology in the Disney Comic* (1972), which examines the subtext of Disney comic strips. Today many academics, schooled in the post-modernist, post-structuralist and post-colonialist schools of thought, reject a linear view or 'top-down' approach to history, emphasizing instead multiple identities, two-way processes, varying points of view and a layered approach in which various different cultures can coexist or create new hybrids.

There are a number of conceptual difficulties to consider when examining the impact of US culture on Latin America. The first is the problem of identifying what Latin American culture is or was. Culture evolves, and it is naïve to imagine a hermetically sealed 'pure' culture that existed before foreign intrusions. The Mexican Academy of Language was fighting a losing battle, for example, when it tried to persuade the population to use the terms *neblumo* instead of smog and *balompié* instead of fútbol.[23] But they needn't have worried, there is little danger of the Spanish language being swamped by English words; instead we find alien words being Spanishified. Would English speakers understand *jonron* ('home run') or *blecaute* ('blackout' in Brazilian Portuguese)? Another problem is identifying what US culture is – is the individualist, consumerist, brand culture so identified with the United States not simply the culture of global capitalism? And what about minority US cultures? The African-American music genres of hip-hop and rap have a great impact on Latin American music. Crowded buses in Caracas or Bogotá are just as likely to boom out the bass of reggaetón, a Panamanian-based fusion of Jamaican dancehall, rap, hip-hop and Latin sounds, as a traditional salsa song. Salsa, of course, is itself the perfect example of two-way cultural influences, created by Cubans and Puerto Ricans in New York, then exported back to the Americas where each country reinvented it in its own particular style. Or take the example of rebellious Mexican youth who listened to Elvis, Chuck Berry and Little Richard in the 1950s to rebel against the staid orthodoxies of the Mexican state.[24] A decade later Mexican counter-culture moved on to Hendrix, Led Zeppelin and Dylan. Anti-authoritarians in South America rarely invoked the *political* freedoms of the United States (a banner raised so effectively in the Soviet bloc), because here the dictatorships were associated with Washington, but they were quick to assimilate the music of US counter-culture.

In a larger sense, culture encompasses not only art, music and literature, but can be more broadly defined as what we eat, drink, wear and so on. The everyday life of a Latin American is not yet overwhelmed by US brands, despite the image of the economic colossus. Latin America has a large food industry and supplies fresh meat, fish, fruit, vegetables, biscuits, cakes and most of its staples like rice, bread and maize.[25] Foreign companies dominate the market in frozen foods, ready meals, highly processed dairy products, including powdered baby milk. But these are relatively expensive and it tends to be the upper and middle classes that buy highly processed foods and shop in supermarkets. The biggest foreign food company in the region is not in fact US but the Swiss giant Nestlé which, as well as selling yoghurts, baby food, confectionery, and frozen foods, controls 90 per cent of Brazil's instant coffee market. The US company that has the largest presence in the region is Procter & Gamble, followed by Coca-Cola, CPC and Pepsi Co. The sale of branded, highly processed foods may increase if free trade deals bring prices down; as incomes rise, more women go out to work and lifestyles change. Kellogg's, for example, has launched a drive to persuade Latin Americans to eat cereals for breakfast instead of the typical tortilla, arepa or bread-based meal. The clothes industry shows a similar pattern. US brands such as Levi's, Benetton, Wranglers, Nike are only within the reach of higher-income groups. But the dazzling displays in shopping malls and the ubiquity of these styles on imported television progammes have made these aspirational products for those seeking to emulate US lifestyles.

US Influence on Latin American Media

The United States has had an influence on the Latin America media since the early days of radio in the 1930s, when US-based corporations CBS and NBC operated radio networks in Latin America, and some private US companies ran radio stations there in order to advertise their products. US involvement rose sharply during the Second World War, as Rockefeller's Office of the Coordinator of Inter-American Affairs (OCIAA) tried to win the Latin American audience to the Allied cause. The OCIAA wrote and distributed articles to over 1,200 newspapers and magazines, and sent a daily news service to over 200 radio stations.[26] By the end of the war, 75 per cent of international news in Latin American newspapers came from the State Department and the OICAA. The OICAA also sponsored art exhibitions, concerts and carefully vetted translations of US novels. According to the State Department, 'It was the greatest outpouring of propagandistic material by a state ever.'[27]

Television broadcasting began in the 1950s in Latin America and quickly became reliant on US investment, programming and advertising. The major US players, NBC, CBS and ABC, had investments in Latin American television stations. By the

1970s, according to one study, US films and programmes made up half of the content of Latin American television and cinemas' screenings, and US news wires supplied 60 to 80 per cent of the international news in Latin American newspapers.[28] It was in this context that fears about 'cultural imperialism' began to resonate. Latin American governments began to introduce greater regulation and to invest in public broadcasting. The military dictatorships of the 1970s heavily censored the media, but also invested in broadcasting technology. Large homegrown television networks emerged, such as Brazil's Globo and Mexico's Televisa, and most countries started to make their own programmes, particularly dramas, quiz shows and news programmes. Most popular were the *telenovela* soap operas, which were exported not only throughout Latin America but as far afield as Russia. By the 1980s, Latin American television had come of age and homegrown Latin programmes dominated the prime-time slots, although US imports were still used as fillers.

But the rapid development of media communications in the past two decades has once again led to an influx of US programming and prompted Latin American stations to make alliances with global corporations. Viewers can still watch locally made programmes on terrestrial TV, but there is a proliferation of new channels available on cable and satellite, and 90 per cent of cable and satellite signals come from the United States.[29] Among the US companies providing Spanish- or Portuguese-language programming in Latin America are: CBS, MTV, Ted Turner's CNN, Time-Warner Sony's HBO Olé; Rupert Murdoch's Fox Latin America, Spelling Entertainment's TeleUNO, and the Discovery Channel. US media companies are becoming increasingly sophisticated at tailoring their output for specific audiences; so, for example, MTV provides not only Spanish and Portuguese services, but broadcasts separate feeds for Mexican and Argentinian audiences, with specially made programmes of local interest. Such specialized targeting provides a real challenge to local programme-makers. Meanwhile Latin American networks are increasingly internationalized; Mexico's Televisa has not only formed an association with Murdoch's Sky, but most of Televisa's revenue comes from its programming to Hispanics in the United States. A US-based audience is, therefore, determining what programmes Mexico's main broadcaster should produce. Miami is now a real powerhouse of Latin American communications and has even taken over from Mexico City and Rio de Janeiro as the centre for dubbing programmes into Spanish and Portuguese.

Globalization has led to the emergence of media behemoths. There are two main regional satellite services run by an alliance of large US and Latin companies: Galaxy (Hughes Electronics, Venezuela's Cisneros Group, Brazil's Grupo Abril, Mexico's Multivision and Argentina's Grupo Clarín) and Sky Latin America (News Corporation, TCI, Televisa and Grupo Globo).[30] Media conglomerates have stakes in Internet portals and a wide range of other businesses. Venezuela's Cisneros group, for example, which owns the Venezuelan TV station Venevisión and the largest Spanish-speaking network in the US, Univisión, has a joint venture with AOL-Time Warner. It also has joint ventures with Coca-Cola, Pizza Hut, Hicks & Muse and Tate & Furst. As in the rest of the world, the media revolution potentially gives the

---

The Media Revolution

Digital TV is currently only available by subscription in Latin America (via digital cable, satellite and DSL) and reaches just 12 per cent of homes. Free multi-channel digital signals are due to be launched; digital TV will then reach much more of the population.

Subscription TV (cable, satellite, DSL) reaches 22 per cent of homes in Latin America, rising to 26 per cent in Chile and 43 per cent in Argentina.

Source: *Latin American TV*, Informa Media Group, London, 2007

---

consumer more choice, but the stranglehold of a small number of global corporations is serving up a homogenous diet of middle-of-the-road fodder. US companies may be dominant, but the big Latin American players have not been obliterated; they have joined the ranks of a globalized media elite, broadcasting sanitized, corporate-friendly entertainment.

Latinizing the United States

Latinos are now the largest ethnic minority group in the United States and are making a significant impact on its culture and politics. The number of Latinos is rising rapidly: from 36 million people (12.6 per cent of the US population) in 2000 to a projected 48 million (15.5 per cent) in 2010. This makes US Latinos the third-largest Spanish-speaking population in the world and the third-largest Latin American economy (after Mexico and Brazil). By 2050, Latinos are expected to make up 24 per cent of the total US population, according to the US Bureau of Census. Most Latinos have legal immigration status. (There were an estimated 11.5 million illegal immigrants living in the US in 2005, of which 8.6 million, or 75 per cent, were thought to be Hispanic, according to the Pew Hispanic Center.)

Latinos are still poorer than the average US citizen and more likely to have lower-skilled jobs. Yet they have a higher average income than the average black American and are less likely to be unemployed. Although 20.6 per cent of the Latino population lives below the poverty line, the average household income in 2006 was almost US$38,000, large enough to put them in the mainstream of society and for businesses to view them as a lucrative market. They are increasingly seen by business analysts as an entrepreneurial, upwardly mobile group keen to own their own businesses and homes.[31] New car and truck registrations by Hispanics grew by 20 per cent a year in the 1990s, twice the rate of the overall vehicle market.

This thriving Latino population is having an impact on US society in a number of ways. The US consumer's palate is changing and developing a taste for Mexican flavour, according to a market analysis by Becker.[32] The consumption of chili doubled and the consumption of red peppers tripled between 1980 and 2000. Tequila sales in the US outstrip those in Mexico, and salsa sales in the US have overtaken sales of

Poverty, Income and Employment of US Population by Ethnicity, 2006

	Overall US population	White	Black	Hispanic
Poverty [%]	12	10	24	21
Average household Income [$]	48,000	51,000	32,000	38,000
Unemployment [%]		4	9	5.5

Source: US Department of Labor and Bureau of Census. Numbers rounded up

Occupation by Ethnicity, 2006

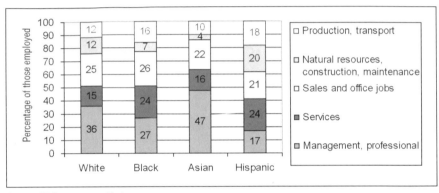

Source: US Department of Labor

ketchup. Imported beers, led by Mexican brands, doubled their market share in the 1990s. Tacos, tortilla chips and fajitas are all snacks familiar to the English-speaking consumer. The Latin influence is evident in other sectors: sales of Latin music rose 25 per cent in 2000, even though the music industry saw total revenues fall. Football (soccer) is increasingly popular, and Latin stars thrive in the baseball league. Latino-themed shows from *Ugly Betty* to *Dora the Explorer* are popular with mainstream audiences. Spanish is the most widely taught language in schools after English and is by far the most popular language course in colleges and universities.

But perhaps the most significant impact is in the area of politics. No political candidate can ignore the Latino vote any more: witness the scramble by presidential hopefuls Hillary Clinton and Barack Obama in 2008 to secure the crucial Latino vote in the Democratic primaries. All major candidates produce their manifestos and electioneering literature and television commercials in English and Spanish, and many, including George W. Bush, John Kerry, Hillary Clinton, Barack Obama and Rudy Giuliani, have addressed the audience in Spanish with varying degrees of fluency. The White House began recording George W. Bush's weekly address in

The Language and Identity of Latinos

The Spanish spoken by Latinos in the United States is gradually evolving. It has its own accent (Mexican-Americans, for example, say *lao* instead of *lado*, *cuete* instead of *cohete*), it adopts anglicisms (known as *pochismos*) and turns English verbs into Spanish verbs (*rentar*, to rent; *watchar*, to watch, *cookiar*, to cook; *parkiar*, to park). It is very common to mix English and Spanish in the same sentence, so-called Spanglish or TexMex. Latino children have traditionally spoken English in schools, and there is debate over whether bilingual teaching would help or hinder them.

The blending of languages and cultures, added to a sense of not belonging to mainstream American society or to Latin America, has given rise to a rich stream of poetry and prose examining the Latino identity.

Not Neither
Being Puertorriqueña-Dominicana
Borinqueña-Quisqueyana
Taina-Africana,
born in the Bronx, not really jíbara,
not really hablando bien,
but yet, not gringa either...

We defy translation.
Ni tengo nombre. Nameless,
we are a whole culture once removed.
Lolita alive for twenty-five years,
ni soy, pero soy, Puertorriqueña cómo ella,
giving blood to the independent star.
Daily transfusions into the river
of la sangre viva.
Sandra María Esteves

Asimilao
assimilated? que assimilated,
brother, yo soy asimilao
asi mi la o sí es verdad
tengo un lado asimilao
Tato Laviera

Source: S. M. Esteves, *Tropical Rain: A Bilingual Downpour*, New York, African Caribbean Poetry Theater, 1984. T. Laviera, *AmeRican*, Houston, Arte Público Press, 1985.

Spanish in 2001, and in the same year it celebrated Mexico's Independence Day for the first time. The congressional Democrats also produce a Spanish version of their weekly broadcast.

But how do Latinos vote? The older Cuban exile community were staunch Republicans but the younger generation of Cubans and the more recent arrivals have less strong allegiances. Economic migrants from Latin America are thought to be liberal on economic issues, so sympathetic towards the Democratic Party, but can be swayed by conservative policies on social issues (such as abortion and criminal justice). Yet these generalizations are harder to maintain as the Latino population grows and becomes more heterogeneous. George W. Bush secured a record 44 per cent of the Latino vote in the 2004 presidential elections, according to exit polls. But the Latino vote for Republicans slumped to 29 per cent in the 2006 congressional elections, a fall attributed to the Republicans' hard line on immigration. Barack Obama won an estimated 67 per cent of the Latino vote in the 2008 presidential elections.[33] Latinos cannot only swing the vote in key states like Florida and New Jersey, but are a force to be reckoned with nationwide. They have already won the attention of politicians, and they now have the potential to help shape the electoral agenda and future policies of the United States.

Postscript

With the election of Barack Obama as President in 2008, the United States has an opportunity to shape a new relationship with Latin America, after the blundering conspiracies and scaremongering of the Bush era. A new beginning should mean an end to the double standards on trade, an end to the destructive and environmentally damaging drugs war, an end to the imposition of neoliberal economic policy and, above all, an end to the constant interference in the domestic affairs of sovereign nations.

Wishful thinking? Perhaps. There are powerful global forces at play. Multinational corporations continue to scour the globe for the cheapest labour and new markets, driving down wages and tearing down borders to compete with the low-wage economies of Asia. Stock markets still shudder whenever a left-wing candidate rises in the opinion polls. But the US relationship with Latin America is changing. With the exception of Cuba, all governments in the region are now democratically elected. Latin Americans have a new confidence in their countries and are building regional alliances which will counterbalance the power of the United States. The region is now politically nuanced; several nations have elected left-wing or centre-left governments that are challenging neoliberalism, and trying to reverse decades of poverty, unemployment and inequality.

The US economic grip on the hemisphere is loosening. If we exclude Mexico from the picture, the US accounts for less than a third of investment in Latin America and less than half of its trade. The Southern Cone countries, in particular, have diversified trade and sought investment from Europe and, increasingly, from the rising star China. Brazil is pursuing alliances with China, India and other Third World countries to challenge the US's stranglehold on global diplomacy, and is increasingly preventing it from dictating the terms at international forums such as the World Trade Organization. US hegemony, once a durable certainty, is being chipped away; it is unlikely that the United States will ever again enjoy the unrivalled economic and cultural dominance it had in the past.

Since the global economic crisis broke in 2008–09, the United States has abandoned free-market dogma at home and approved a multi-billion dollar bailout of the financial system and grants to the motor industry. The Obama administration plans to invest large sums of money in upgrading public infrastructure. Meanwhile, the IMF's managing director, Dominique Strauss-Kahn, called in late 2008 for 'a fiscal stimulus … everywhere, everywhere, where it is possible'. So are we witnessing the death of neoliberalism? Or more precisely, the end of the imposition of neoliberalism on poor countries? Early indications suggest caution. The first IMF agreements signed with developing countries such as Belarus and the Seychelles in the wake of the crisis contained the same old demands for wage cuts, public sector job losses, pension cuts and privatization (although there was no call for fiscal tightening in the agreement with Iceland). But while they would welcome an end to blanket imposition of free-market policies and the mantra of free trade, Latin American governments would not favour a new era of US protectionism; what they want is all countries to play by the same rules, put simply: an end to one law for the rich and another for the poor.

US double standards are evident in other areas of policy. The government vehemently criticizes human rights violations in Venezuela, yet remains silent about abuses in neighbouring Colombia, its favoured ally, when all international bodies agree that the situation is far worse in the latter. It demanded that political prisoners in Cuba should be released while it maintained a prison camp of dubious legality on that very island. The United States' moral sheen was gravely tarnished in the Americas, and indeed the rest of the world, by the Bush administration's aggressive unilateral foreign policy – the illegal invasion of Iraq, the refusal to respect the jurisdiction of the International Criminal Court, and the secret torture rendition flights. President Obama's decision to close the Guantánamo Bay prison camp in Cuba is welcome and needs to be the first of many steps towards a more enlightened foreign policy.

A change from the Cold War mentality towards Cuba is long overdue. Almost all Latin American governments (Costa Rica and El Salvador are notable exceptions) have normal diplomatic relations with Cuba and regard the US stance as an anachronism. Lifting the embargo would not only ease hardship; it would give the population in Cuba greater contact with the outside world and help achieve the US's professed aim of encouraging democracy on the island. For many years, Cuba policy has been disproportionately influenced by a small number of Cuban-Americans resident in Miami, but the Latino population in the United States is now far more heterogeneous, comprising people of all ages and political persuasions, and most of them favour a more constructive, less confrontational approach to Cuba.

Colombia is another area where a more considered and less belligerent policy would pay dividends. US drugs policy has demonstrably failed: the aerial spraying of pesticides has harmed human health, killed animals and food crops and threatened to cause lasting damage to the environment, yet it has failed to reduce the supply of drugs. US policy makers, first, need to acknowledge that the drugs trade is created by demand in the drugs-consuming countries of the North. In Colombia, it is a social and economic issue; peasants grow the crop from which they can make a living. Land reform, market access, job creation, and alternative development projects, rather than fumigation, are the types of policy most likely to reduce illicit crop cultivation. The Colombian civil war, too, has social and economic causes – land hunger, poverty and unemployment – yet the United States has insisted on seeing it purely as a military or 'terrorist' problem. US forces are embroiled in the counter-insurgency war, working alongside a government army that regularly abuses human rights. The FARC, as a peasant army fortified by drugs money, probably have the ability to maintain a low-level guerrilla war in their rural strongholds. Yet the FARC are now in a weaker position, militarily and politically, than they have been for two decades, and they have been universally condemned for their abhorrent practice of kidnapping civilians. With no hope of taking power and with very little support domestically or internationally, the FARC, or parts of it, may now be willing to lay down their arms and seriously commit to peace negotiations. This is a historic opportunity, but rather than use its influence to reach a negotiated settlement and end forty years of civil strife, the US has been urging the Colombian elite to hold out until total victory, however elusive that might be, however much more bloodshed and hardship this stance causes.

As this book has shown, US military policy and US economic policy have been inextricably intertwined since the annexation of Mexican territory in 1846. The US's economic dominance was entrenched in the early twentieth century with the aid of gunboats and decade-long military occupations of Central American and Caribbean countries. The US has always been willing to defend its hegemony by force, even if in recent years Roosevelt's canon has more often been replaced by a signature on an IMF agreement. The US has become a waning superpower, overstretched and under fire in the Middle East and Afghanistan. The cost of the Iraq war has drained an economy already suffering a home-grown crisis. Will fighting on so many fronts compromise the US's ability to maintain hegemony over its own backyard? The military imbalance between the US and Latin America will remain for the foreseeable future, but full-scale invasions of Latin America have been rare since the 1930s. Indirect intervention has been the most typical form of interference – backing coups and propping up dictators, training repressive armies or paramilitaries, dispatching private contractors or small numbers of US special forces. These types of interventions are far less costly both in military resources and US lives, yet whether they remain politically tenable is another matter.

In most cases, these repressive interventions have been carried out in alliance with the elites of Latin America. As democracy spreads in the region, the political will of elected governments and the strength of civil society will determine whether the US, in alliance with the Latin American upper classes or military, has the capacity to distort public life or to undermine democracy in the way it has in the past. Bringing the armed forces, once a powerful autonomous force, under democratic control is a crucial task. The recent prosecutions of military officials in Argentina and

Chile, including Augusto Pinochet, the lifting of amnesty laws in some countries, and the decision by Argentina, Uruguay, Venezuela and Bolivia to remove their armed forces from the School of the Americas are steps of historical significance.

The policies of the United States, of course, also depend on the willingness of the US electorate to call their own leaders to account. These issues have a direct relevance to voters. It is not simply a question of funding a small guerrilla war or backing a tinpot dictator in a distant country. Political violence, dictatorship and repression cause millions to flee their homes, as does IMF-sponsored poverty and unemployment. Too often, the response from US politicians has been to stoke fear and loathing of migrants. But if the US sows destitution and despair in the Americas, people are bound to seek a better life across the border, however many walls are built. In the globalized world, the consequences of foreign policy are felt at home.

Appendix A
US Military Interventions in Latin America in the Twentieth Century

1823–1900	US intervenes militarily 39 times in Latin America and the Caribbean
1898–1902	US troops occupy Cuba
1901	US acquires Puerto Rico
1901	US troops are sent to Colombia (state of Panama)
1902	US marines are sent to Colombia (state of Panama)
1903–14	US marines are stationed in Panama
1903, 1905, 1907	US troops are sent to Honduras
1903, 1904	US troops are sent to Dominican Republic
1906–09	US troops occupy Cuba
1908	US troops are sent to Panama
1909–10	US troops land at Bluefields, providing a rear guard for conservative rebels overthrowing Nicaraguan president Zelaya
1911, 1912	US troops are sent to Honduras
1912	US troops are sent to Panama
1912	US troops are sent to Cuba
1913	US marines are sent to Mexico to evacuate US citizens (after Mexican revolution)
1912–25	US marines occupy Nicaragua
1914	US naval force is sent to Dominican Republic to quell revolutionary disturbance
1914–17	US army expeditions in Mexico include the capture of Vera Cruz and Pershing's expedition into northern Mexico
1915–34	US marines occupy Haiti to maintain order during period of chronic and threatened insurrection
1916–24	US marines occupy Dominican Republic
1917–22	US marines occupy Cuba
1918–19	US troops enter Mexico to pursue bandits: three times in 1918 and six times in 1919
1918	US and Mexican troops fight at Nogales
1918	US troops are sent to Panama
1919	US troops are sent to Honduras to maintain order during an attempted revolution

1920	US troops are sent to Guatemala
1921	US naval squadrons demonstrate off coast of Costa Rica and Panama to prevent war over boundary dispute.
1924, 1925	US marines land in Honduras
1925	US troops are sent to Panama to keep order during strikes and riots
1926–33	US marines occupy Nicaragua
1932	US warships stand by during El Salvador peasant massacre
1933	US naval forces stand by during overthrow of Cuban president Machado
1954	CIA organizes paramilitary invasion of Guatemala, CIA planes bomb Guatemala city, President Arbenz is overthrown
1961	Abortive CIA-organized Bay of Pigs invasion of Cuba
1965	US invades Dominican Republic to uphold military rule
1979–90	CIA trains Contra insurgents to fight against the elected Sandinista government. CIA mines Nicaraguan harbours (1984) and carries out sabotage attacks on other Nicaraguan infrastructure
1983	US invades Grenada
1989	US invades Panama
1994	US invades Haiti (to reinstate an elected president)

Main source: W. A. Williams, *Empire as a Way of Life*, New York, Oxford University Press, 1980.

Appendix B
Dictators Who Took Training Courses at the School of the Americas

Argentina	Gen Roberto Viola (1981) Gen Leopoldo Galtieri (1981-82)
Bolivia	Gen Hugo Banzer Suárez (1971-78) Gen Guido Vildoso Calderón (1982)
Ecuador	Gen Guillermo Rodríguez (1972-1976)
Guatemala	Gen Efraín Ríos Montt (1982-83)
Honduras	Gen Juan Melgar Castro (1975-78) Gen Policarpo Paz García (1980-82)
Peru	Gen Juan Velasco Alvarado (1968-1975)
Panama	Gen Omar Torrijos (1968-81) Gen Manuel Noriega (1981-89)

Source: School of Americas Watch, www.soaw.org

Notes

1 Introduction

1 The term 'pink tide' was used by commentators to describe the victories of left-wing candidates in Latin American presidential elections between 1998 and 2008: in Venezuela (1998, 2006), Chile (2000, 2006), Brazil (2002, 2006), Argentina (2003, 2007), Uruguay (2004), Bolivia (2006), Nicaragua (2006), Ecuador (2006) and Paraguay (2008). It was described as a pink, not a red, tide because the victors in many countries were moderate leftists, even if they had once had a more radical past: Luis Inácio Lula da Silva in Brazil, Ricardo Lagos and Michelle Bachelet in Chile and Tabaré Vázquez in Uruguay. See Chapter 8.

2 Donald Rumsfeld, Defense Secretary, Ministerial of the Americas, 17 November 2004.

3 General John Craddock, 'Governance and Security for the Americas in the 21st Century', speech to the First Annual Latin American Conference, University of Miami Center for Hemispheric Policy, 25 April 2006.

4 'The war on terror' was announced by President George W. Bush at a joint session of Congress on 20 September 2001, shortly after the attacks on New York and Washington. He declared: 'Our war on terror begins with al Qaeda, but it does not end there. It will not end until every terrorist group of global reach has been found, stopped and defeated.' This was the first use of the term 'war on terror' by a US president, although Ronald Reagan had previously spoken of a 'war on terrorism'.

5 Roger F. Noriega, Assistant Secretary of State for Western Hemisphere Affairs, Remarks to Council of the Americas, Washington, 3 May 2005.

6 Ronald Reagan, State of the Union Address, 1987.

7 US Department of State, Memorandum of Conversation, 7 October 1976, 'Subject: Secretary's Meeting with the Argentine Foreign Minister Guzzetti', National Security Archive.

8 Gunder Frank, A., *Capitalism and Underdevelopment in Latin America*, London, Monthly Review Press, 1967.

9 Harris, N., *The End of the Third World: Newly Industrializing Countries and the Decline of an Ideology*, London, Penguin, 1986.

10 Cardoso, F.H. and Faletto, E., *Dependency and Development in Latin America*, Berkeley, University of California Press, 1979.

11 See, for example, Petras, J. and Veltmeyer, H. with Vasapollo, L. and Casadio, M., *Empire with Imperialism: The Globalizing Dynamics of Neoliberal Capitalism*, London, Fernwood Publishing/Zed Books, 2005; Stoler, A.L., McGranahan, C. and Perdue, P., *Imperial Formations*, Santa Fe, NM, School For Advanced Research Press, 2007; and Grandin, G., *Empire's Workshop: Latin America, the United States and the Rise of the New Imperialism*, New York, Metropolitan Books, 2006.

12 See, for example, James O'Connor's definition of imperialism: 'formal or informal control over local economic resources in a manner advantageous to the metropolitan power and at the expense of the local economy', in O'Connor, J., 'The Meaning of Economic Imperialism' in Rhodes, R.I. (ed.), *Imperialism and Underdevelopment*, New York, Monthly Review Press, 1970.

13 Following the narrow definition of Peter Smith, hegemony is 'the capacity of an actor (or nation) to impose will over others without significant challenge'. See Smith, P., *Talons of the Eagle: Dynamics of US–Latin American Relations*, New York, Oxford University Press, 2000, p. 384, n. 9.

14 Secret report by George F. Kennan submitted to the US Secretary of State Dean Acheson, 1950. Kennan was the State Department's leading expert on the Soviet Union. Cited in Holden, R. and Zolov, E., *Latin America and the United States: A Documentary History*, New York, Oxford University Press, 2000, p. 195.

2 The Monroe Doctrine to the Second World War

1 See Smith, P., *Talons of the Eagle: Dynamics of US–Latin American Relations*, New York, Oxford University Press, 2000, p. 20. Estimates for the pre-conquest indigenous population in Latin America vary from 8.4 million to 112 million.

2 First used as early as the 1840s, and revived at the end of the nineteenth century, the term 'Manifest Destiny' expressed the belief that American expansion was not only for the good, but that it was obvious ('manifest') and certain ('destiny'). The term is no longer used, but the idea that America has been granted moral, and even divine, sanction to spread democracy throughout the world remains an influence on US foreign policy.

3 Senator Albert Brown, 1858, cited in Schoultz, L., *Beneath the United States: A History of US Policy toward Latin America*, Boston, Harvard University Press, 1998, p. 68.

4 Cited in Schoultz, *Beneath the United States*, p. 177.

5 The term 'dollar diplomacy' derives from a speech made in 1911 by Assistant Secretary of State Francis Huntington Wilson who said 'the substitution of dollars

for bullets' was the aim of US policy. He later gave a fuller explanation: 'Rotten little countries down there run heavily into debt to Europe. They won't pay. Europe comes along and demands payment. The United States must either let Europe land Marines and hold custom houses for security and so open the way for further penetration and for flagrant violation of the Monroe Doctrine, or else the United States must compel the little republics to be decent and to pay up ... If the United States lends a helping hand and helps Central America get on its feet and keeps the peace long enough for it to begin to develop, we shall soon have immediately at the doors of our southern states a great and valuable commerce. "Dollar diplomacy" simply means intelligent team work.' Cited in Schoultz, *Beneath the United States*, p. 209.

6   Excerpt from a State Department memorandum cited in Pearce, J., *Under the Eagle: US Intervention in Central America and the Caribbean*, London, Latin America Bureau, 1981, p. 19.

7   Bulmer-Thomas, V. and Dunkerley, J., *The United States and Latin America: The New Agenda*, London, Institute of Latin American Studies, University of London, 1999, p. 23.

8   Cardoso, E. and Helwege, A., *Latin America's Economy: Diversity, Trends and Conflicts*, Massachusetts, MIT Press, 1992, p. 49.

9   Cited in Smith, *Talons of the Eagle*, 2000, p. 71.

10   Smith, J., *The United States and Latin America: A History of American Diplomacy, 1776–2000*, London, Routledge, 2005, p. 110.

3 The Cold War: The Guatemalan Coup and the Cuban Revolution

1   Kennan, G., cited in Holden, R. and Zolov, E. (eds), *Latin America and the United States: A Documentary History*, New York, Oxford University Press, 2000, p. 195.

2   McClintock, M., *Instruments of Statecraft: US Guerrilla Warfare, Counter-insurgency and Counter-terrorism*, 1940–1990, New York, Pantheon Books, 1992, p. 138.

3   Smith, P., *Talons of the Eagle: Dynamics of US–Latin American Relations*, New York, Oxford University Press, 2000, p. 127.

4   Top Secret Memorandum for the Director of Central Intelligence, Subject: Guatemala General Plan of Action, September 11 1953, National Security Archive, GU00003.

5   'Program for PBSUCCESS', 12 November 1953, in Department of State, *Foreign Relations of the United States, 1952–54, 2003*, reprinted in Appendix D of CIA's official history: Cullather, N., *Secret History: The CIA's Classified Account of its Operations in Guatemala*, Palo Alto, CA, Stanford University Press, 2006, p. 152.

6   Cited in Schlesinger, S. and Kinzer, S., *Bitter Fruit: The Story of the American Coup in Guatemala*, London, Sinclair Browne, 1982, p. 170.

7   Matthews, Herbert L., 'With Castro in the Sierra Nevada', reprinted in Holden and Zolov, *Latin America and the United States*, p. 213.

8   Blight, G. and Kornbluh, P. (eds), *Politics of Illusion: The Bay of Pigs Invasion Reexamined*, Boulder, CO, Lynne Rienner, 1998, p. 159.

9   'Rough draft of summary of conversation between the vice president and Fidel Castro, 25 April 1959', reprinted in Jerry Safford, 'The Nixon-Castro Meeting of 19

April 1959', *Diplomatic History*, No. 4, Fall 1980, p. 423.

10   Gott, R., *Cuba: A New History*, London, Yale University Press, 2004, p. 180. Gott quotes Roy Rubottom, Assistant Secretary of State for Inter American Affairs, giving June 1959 as the month the NSC decided to remove Castro. Eisenhower's October decision is documented in Blight and Kornbluh, *Politics of Illusion*.

11   Chang, L. and Kornbluh, P. (eds), *The Cuban Missile Crisis, 1962: A National Security Archive Documents Reader*, New York, The New Press, 1992, p. 18.

12   Gott, *Cuba*, p. 199.

13   Ibid., p. 200, citing the Cuban government's official history.

14   Ibid., p. 208, citing official historian Tomás Diez Acosta.

15   Ramonet, I. (ed.), *Fidel Castro: My Life*, London, Allen Lane, 2007. Ramonet cites the figure and sources it to (former CIA agent) Philip Agee, 'Terrorism and Civil Society', *Counterpunch*, 9 August 2003, p. 5.

4 The Alliance for Progress

1   Cited in Klare, M., *War Without End: American Planning for the Next Vietnams*, New York, Alfred A. Knopf, 1972, p. 39.

2   Rabe, S., *The Most Dangerous Area in the World*, Chapel Hill, University of North Carolina Press, 1999, p. 131.

3   Cited in McClintock, M., *Instruments of Statecraft*, New York, Pantheon Books, 1992, p. 232, Manual no. FM 33-5.

4   Report of the US Senate Select Committee on Governmental Operations, 'Alleged Assassination Plots Involving Foreign Leaders', 1975.

5   Cited in Schlesinger Jr, A.M., *A Thousand Days: John F. Kennedy in the White House*, New York, Black Dog and Leventhal, 2005, p. 268.

6   Hartlyn, J., 'The Dominican Republic' in Lowenthal, A. (ed.), *Exporting Democracy: The United States and Latin America*, Baltimore, John Hopkins University Press, 1991, p. 198.

7   Pearce, J., *Under the Eagle: US Intervention in Central America and the Caribbean*, London, Latin America Bureau, 1981, p. 64.

8   Parker, P., *Brazil and the Quiet Intervention, 1964*, USA, University of Texas Press, 1979.

9   Skidmore, T. and Smith, P., *Modern Latin America*, New York, Oxford University Press, 2001, p. 51. More on Latin America's class structure and the exhaustion of the ISI strategy can be found in Skidmore and Smith, Chapter 2.

5 The Military Governments of the 1970s

1   The 'Rockefeller Report' in Holden, R. and Zolov, E. (eds), *Latin America and the United States: A Documentary History*, New York, Oxford University Press, 2000, p. 265.

2   The White House, Memorandum of Conversation, NSC Meeting – Chile (NSSM 97), 6 November 1970. The document is published in Kornbluh, P., *The Pinochet File: A Declassified Dossier on Atrocity and Accountability*, New York, New Press, 2003, p. 116.

3   'Covert Action in Chile 1963–1973', US Senate, Staff Report of the Select Committee to Study Governmental Operations with Respect to Intelligence Activities, 18 December 1975, 94th Congress, 1st Session.
4   Ibid.
5   Ibid.
6   Ibid.
7   Ibid.
8   CIA, Richard Helms, handwritten notes, 'Meeting with the President on Chile at 1525', 15 September 1970, in Kornbluh, *The Pinochet File*, Chapter 1, Document 1, p. 36.
9   CIA Secret Cable from Headquarters, 16 October 1970, in Kornbluh, *The Pinochet File*, p. 64.
10   See Kornbluh, *The Pinochet File*.
11   'CIA Activities in Chile', CIA report, 18 September 2000, https://www.cia.gov/library/reports/general-reports-1/chile/index.html
12   The White House, Secret Memorandum of Conversation, 'NSC Meeting – Chile (NSSM 97)', 6 November 1970, in Kornbluh, *The Pinochet File*, Chapter 2, Document 1.
13   'Covert Action in Chile', US Senate 1975.
14   Ibid. All the information in this paragraph is from the Senate report.
15   Ibid.
16   O'Shaughnessy, H., *Pinochet: The Politics of Torture*, London, Latin America Bureau, 2000, p. 38.
17   Ibid, p. 46.
18   Charges laid by the Crown Prosecution Service on behalf of the King of Spain, in the case of victim Pedro Hugo Arellano Carvajal, cited in O'Shaughnessy, *Pinochet*.
19   Department of State, Cable, 'USG Attitude Toward Junta', 13 September 1973, in Kornbluh, *The Pinochet File*, Chapter 4, Document 1, p. 234.
20   'Covert Action in Chile', US Senate, 1975.
21   Ibid.
22   Ibid.
23   Declassified memo sent by US Ambassador to Paraguay, Robert E. White, to Secretary of State Cyrus Vance, October 1978, National Security Archive.
24   Dinges, J., *The Condor Years*, New York, The New Press, 2004, pp. 121–3.
25   Loveman, B., *Chile: The Legacy of Hispanic Capitalism*, New York, Oxford University Press, 2001, p. 272.
26   'Secretary's Staff Meeting 1 October 1973', declassified memorandum, National Security Archive.
27   Declassified transcript of telephone call between Kissinger and the Assistant Secretary of State, 3 June 1976, National Security Archive.
28   Department of State, Secret Memorandum of Conversation between Henry Kissinger and Augusto Pinochet, 'US–Chilean Relations', 8 June 1976, National Security Archive, Kissinger Transcripts Collection, Item No. KT01964.
29   *Never Again: A Report by Argentina's National Commission on Disappeared People*, London, Faber and Faber, 1986, p. xiii.
30   A recently discovered report by the Chilean secret service, the DINA, gives a figure

of 22,000 between 1976 and 1978. See Dinges, *The Condor Years*, p. 139.

31 Memorandum of Conversation, Santiago Chile, 6 June 1976. Participants: the United States, the Secretary ... Argentina: Foreign Minister Guzzetti ...' National Security Archive.

32 National Security Archive Electronic Briefing Book No 133, edited by Osorio, C. and Costar, K., August 2004.

33 Department of State, Memorandum of Conversation, 7 October 1976, Subject: Secretary's Meeting with the Argentine Foreign Minister Guzzetti, National Security Archive.

34 Department of State, From Embassy Buenos Aires, To Secretary of State Washington, 19 October 1976, Subject: Foreign Minister Guzzetti Euphoric Over Visit to United States.

35 See Escudé, C., 'Argentina: The Cost of Contradiction', in Lowenthal, A. (ed.), *Exporting Democracy: The United States and Latin America*, Baltimore, Johns Hopkins University Press, 1991.

6 Reagan and the Central American Tragedy

1   Leiken, R. and Rubin, B. (eds), *The Central American Crisis Reader*, New York, Summit Books, 1987, p. 548.

2   For a fuller examination of the post-Vietnam splits in the establishment see Burbach, R., 'US Policy: Crisis and Conflict', in Burbach R. and Flynn P., *The Politics of Intervention*, USA, MR/CENSA Series on the Americas, 1984.

3   Kirkpatrick, J., 'Human Rights and Foreign Policy', in Baumann, F. (ed.), *Human Rights and American Foreign Policy*, Gambier, OH, Public Affairs Conference Center of Kenyon College, 1982.

4   Kirkpatrick, J. cited in Pearce, J., *Under the Eagle: US Intervention in Central America and the Caribbean*, London, Latin America Bureau, 1981, p. 173.

5   Ibid., p. 172.

6   Pentagon officials interviewed in Morley, M., *Washington, Somoza, and the Sandinistas*, New York, Cambridge University Press, 2004, p. 221.

7   John Pustay, cited in Morley, *Washington, Somoza, and the Sandinistas*, p. 222.

8   Department of State telegram from Secretary of State, July 30 1979, cited in Morley *Washington, Somoza, and the Sandinistas*, p. 229.

9   Pearce, *Under the Eagle*, p. 154.

10 Kornbluh, P. 'The Covert War', in Walker, T. (ed.), *Reagan Versus the Sandinistas*, Boulder, Westview Press, 1987, p. 24.

11 Cited in ibid. p. 27.

12 'Special Activities in Nicaragua', Memorandum 3/2/89 in Kornbluh, P. (ed.), *Nicaragua: The Making of US Policy, 1978–1990*, Washington, National Security Archive, 1991, p. 30.

13 Cited in ibid., p. 28.

14 Memorandum 2/27/85, in ibid., p. 30.

15 Smith, H., *Nicaragua: Self-determination and Survival*, London, Pluto Press, 1993, p. 150.

16 *The Challenge to Democracy in Central America*, a joint US State Department–Pentagon publication, 1986, cited in Linfield, M., 'Human Rights' in Walker, T. (ed.), *Revolution and Counter Revolution in Nicaragua*, Boulder, CO, Westview Press, 1991, p. 291, footnotes.

17 *Human Rights in Nicaragua: Reagan, Rhetoric and Reality*, Americas Watch Report, New York, 1985.

18 Linfield, 'Human Rights', p. 289.

19 Ibid., p. 286.

20 There were two major evacuations, one of 8,000 people in January/February 1982 and another evacuation of 6,000 Misquito and Sumo people in November 1982.

21 Walker, T., *Nicaragua: Living in the Shadow of the Eagle*, Boulder, CO, Westview Press, 2003, p. 48, citing a 1984 OAS Inter-American Commission on Human Rights report.

22 The number of hostages in Lebanon did not fall because although three were released, three more were taken.

23 Walsh, L., *Iran Contra: The Final Report*, New York, Times Books, 1994, p. xiv.

24 CIA agent Joseph Fernandez was also indicted for making false statements, but the prosecution was dropped after the Attorney General refused to declassify material needed for his defence.

25 Report of the Congressional Committees Investigating the Iran-Contra Affair, 100th Congress, 1 Session, 1987, p. 11.

26 Kenworthy, E., 'Selling the Policy', in Walker, *Reagan versus the Sandinistas*, p. 163.

27 Quoted in Dale Scott, P. and Marshall, J., *Cocaine Politics: Drugs, Armies and the CIA in Central America*, University of California Press, 1991, p. 23.

28 Channel, C. and Miller, R., 'Action Plan for 1986 Programs of the American Conservative Trust and the National Endowment for the Preservation of Liberty', in Iran Contra Report, Appendix A, p. 686, quoted in Dale Scott and Marshall, *Cocaine Politics*, p. 23.

29 'Drugs, Law Enforcement and Foreign Policy: A Report Prepared by the Sub-committee on Terrorism, Narcotics and International Operations of the Committee on Foreign Relations', United States Senate, December 1988 (hereafter Kerry Report), p. 36.

30 Ibid., p. 36.

31 Ibid., p. 2.

32 *El Salvador: The Potential for Violent Revolution: An Intelligence Assessment'*, National Foreign Assessment Center, Central Intelligence Agency, February 1980, Digital National Security Archive, El Salvador 1980–1994 Collection, EL00024.

33 Resolution 35/192 passed by the United Nations General Assembly, December 1980, in United Nations, *The United Nations and El Salvador 1990–1995*, New York, UN, 1995.

34 11,000 is the figure given by the UN Truth Commission for all politically motivated deaths from 1980 to 1983. The State Department figure for deaths on all sides is 18,000 for the same period. Contemporary human rights organizations put the figure as high as 30,000.

35 United Nations, *The United Nations and El Salvador 1990–1995*.

36 Archbishop Oscar Romero: Letter to President Carter, February 17 1980, in Leiken,

R. and Rubin, B. (eds), *The Central American Crisis Reader*, New York, Summit Books, 1987, p. 503.

37 State Department figures cited in *Comparison of US Administration Testimony and Reports with 1993 UN Truth Commission Report on El Salvador*, Report prepared for the Committee on Foreign Affairs, US House of Representatives by the Congressional Service, Library of Congress, 103rd Congress, 1st Session, July 1993, EL01383, p. 7.

38 *Comparison of US Administration Testimony and Reports*, p. 36.

39 Congressional hearing 1981, cited in Carothers, T., *In the Name of Democracy: US Policy Toward Latin America in the Reagan Years*, Berkeley and Los Angeles, University of California Press, 1991, p. 266.

40 Carothers, *In the Name of Democracy*, p. 155.

41 Briefing Paper on Right Wing Terrorism in El Salvador, CIA, October 27 1983, National Security Archive, EL00110.

42 Robert E. White, former US ambassador to El Salvador, Congressional Hearings, 9 April 1981, in *Comparison of US Administration Testimony and Reports*, p. 17.

43 'From Madness to Hope: Report of the Commission on the Truth for El Salvador, 1993', in United Nations, *The United Nations and El Salvador 1990–1995*, p. 360.

44 Cable from Ambassador William G. Walker, to Department of State, 'Roberto D'Aubuisson: The Opposition's perspective', 12 September 1990, National Security Archive, EL01194.

45 Cable from Ambassador Robert White, to US Embassy Guatemala, 'Activities of Robert D'Aubuisson', August 23 1980, National Security Archive, EL00676.

46 'Roberto D'Aubuisson: The Opposition's perspective', National Security Archive, EL01194.

47 Briefing Paper on Right Wing Terrorism in El Salvador, CIA, 27 October 1983.

48 Cable from Ambassador Deane Hinton, to Department of State, 'Conversation with Major Robert D'Aubuisson', 15 December 1991, National Security Archive, EL00730.

49 'Salvadoran Rightist Eludes Ban Against Entering US', *Washington Post*, 2 July 1980.

50 'D'Aubuisson Honored by Conservatives at Capitol Hill Dinner', *Washington Post*, 5 December 1984.

51 *Comparison of US Administration Testimony and Reports*, p. 34.

52 'From Madness to Hope', p. 348.

53 Congressional hearing 1 February 1982, cited in *Comparison of US Administration Testimony and Reports*, p. 40.

54 *Comparison of US Administration Testimony and Reports*.

55 Annual average of UN figures for 1984–1989 cited in 'From Madness to Hope'.

56 Carothers, *In the Name of Democracy*, p. 28.

57 Ibid., p. 49.

58 'Secret graves found in Honduras', BBC online, 28 April 2003.

59 Carothers, *In the Name of Democracy*, p. 61.

60 'Next Steps on Guatemala', Secret Cable, from Walter Stoessel, State Department, to United States Southern Command, 11 June 1981.

61 Carothers, *In the Name of Democracy*, p. 62.

62 Secret Memorandum from Constantine C. Menges and Oliver North, National

Security Council, to Robert McFarlane, NSC, 29 November 1983, National Security Archive, GU00987.

63 Report on the Guatemala Review, President's Intelligence Oversight Board, 28 June 1996, National Security Archive, GU0264, p. 3.

64 Ibid.

65 *Guatemala Memory of Silence*, Report of the Commission for Historical Clarification, Conclusions and Recommendations, 1999, CEH, National Security Archive, GU02070. The Commission for Historical Clarification was formed following the 1996 Peace Accords with the agreement of both sides, the Guatemalan government and the Guatemalan National Revolutionary Unity guerrilla group. The Guatemalan government provided funds, and its congress facilitated the adequate operation of the CEH. The United Nations provided advice and experts. Many Guatemalan human rights groups contributed.

66 Figures for killings of women and children come from *Guatemala Never Again: Recovery of the Historical Memory Project*, The Official Report of the Human Rights Office, Archdiocese of Guatemala, UK, CIIR/LAB, 1999.

67 *Guatemala Memory of Silence*, p. 19.

7 The End of the Cold War, 1989–2001

1   Murillo, L., *The Noriega Mess: The Drugs, The Canal and Why America Invaded*, California, Video Books, 1995, p. 28.

2   Drugs, Law Enforcement and Foreign Policy: A Report Prepared by the Subcommittee on Terrorism, Narcotics and International Operations of the Committee on Foreign Relations, United States Senate, December 1988 (hereafter Kerry Report).

3   Cited in Kerry Report.

4   Murillo, *The Noriega Mess*, p. 542.

5   Conniff, M., *Panama and the United States*, Athens, GA, University of Georgia Press, 2001, p. 161.

6   Raymont, H., *Troubled Neighbours: The Story of US–Latin American Relations from FDR to the Present*, Cambridge, MA, Westview Press, 2005, p. 294.

7   *Human Rights Watch World Report, 1995*, Human Rights Watch, New York.

8   'Implausible Deniability, State Responsibility for Rural Violence in Mexico', Human Rights Watch, April 1997.

9   Domínguez, J. and Fernández de Castro, R., *The United States and Mexico: Between Partnership and Conflict*, London, Routledge, 2001, p. 35.

10 General Accounting Office, 'Longstanding Problems Hinder US International Efforts', GAO/NSIAD-97-75, February 1997.

11 Domínguez and Fernández de Castro, *The United States and Mexico*, p. 49. Mexico bought seventy-three UH-1H helicopters from the United States in 1995, but returned them and replaced them with seventy-three Cessna 183 Skylab planes.

12 *Our Word is Our Weapon: Selected Writings of Subcomandante Insurgente Marcos*, Ponce de León, J. (ed.), London, Serpents Tail, 2001, p. 175.

13 DIA Weekly Intelligence Forecast, January 5, 1994, National Security Archive

Electronic Briefing Book No. 109, 'Rebellion in Chiapas and the Mexican Military', Document 8.

14 US Embassy in Mexico, confidential cable, May 11, 1995, 'The Mexican Army – Still Passive, Isolated and Above the Fray', National Security Archive Electronic Briefing Book No. 120, Document 8.

15 Henriksen, T., *Clinton's Foreign Policy in Somalia, Bosnia, Haiti and North Korea*, Stanford, Hoover Institute, p. 22.

16 Ibid., p. 24.

17 Congressional Record, Selective Leaks of Classified Information on Haiti, Senate Intelligence Committee, 5 November 1993. Press reports appended. See also Brune, L., *The United States and Post Cold War Interventions*, California, Regina Books, 1998.

18 Congressional Record, Selective Leaks of Classified Information on Haiti, Senate Intelligence Committee, 5 November 1993.

19 'Key Haiti Leaders Said to Have Been in CIA's Pay', *New York Times*, 1 November 1993.

20 Castro Mariño, S., 'US–Cuban Relations during the Clinton Administration', *Latin American Perspectives*, Vol 29, No 4, July 2002, p. 58.

21 1982–2006. Other human rights groups cite higher figures; Amnesty International cites 70,000 since the 1980s. Colombian Comisión de Juristas figures from: Violaciones de derechos humanos y violencia sociopolítica en Colombia, Derecho a la Vida. Ejecuciones extrajudiciales, homicidios sociopolíticos y desapariciones forzadas Julio de 1996 a Junio de 2006, CCJ, and Comisión Colombia de Juristas, *Colombia, derechos humanos y derecho humanitario*, Bogota, 1996. See CCJ data cited in Livingstone, G., *Inside Colombia: Drugs, Democracy and War*, London, Latin America Bureau, 2003, p. 30.

22 Charles E. Wilhelm, Testimony to the House Committee on Government Reform, Subcommittee on Criminal Justice, Drug Policy and Human Resources, February 15 2000.

23 For a comparison of the two Plan Colombias see Livingstone, *Inside Colombia*.

8 George W. Bush and the 'War on Terror'

1 General John Craddock, 'Governance and Security for the Americas in the 21st Century', speech to the First Annual Latin American Conference, University of Miami Center for Hemispheric Policy, 25 April 2006.

2 Duncan Hunter, Chairman, House Armed Services Committee (Republican), 16 March 2006, Hearing on the Fiscal Year 2007 Budget Request for the United States Southern Command.

3 The American Servicemembers' Protection Act (ASPA) 2002 suspends non-drug aid to states that do not grant to US forces immunity from the jurisdiction of the International Criminal Court on their soil. Countries are asked to sign bilateral pacts with the US granting their service personnel immunity. Isacson, A., Olson, J. and Haugaar L., *Below the Radar: US Military Programs with Latin America, 1997–2007*, Washington, LAWGEF, CIP, WOLA, 2007.

4 General John Craddock, 'Governance and Security for the Americas in the 21st Century', University of Miami Center for Hemispheric Policy, 25 April 2006.

5   General John Craddock, Speech at Florida University, 10 March 2005.

6   Donald Rumsfeld, State Department press release, 5 May 2005, 'Rumsfeld Hails Democratic Reforms in Latin America'.

7   Quoted in Haugaard, L., *Tarnished Image: Latin America Perceives the United States*, Latin America Working Group, March 2006.

8   General James T. Hill, Commander, United States Southern Command, testimony before the House Armed Services Committee, Washington, 24 March 2004.

9   'Secretary Rumsfeld's Remarks at the National Press Club', 2 February 2006 US Department of Defense, Office of Assistant Secretary of Defense, news transcript.

10 Frank C. Urbancic, Principal Deputy Coordinator for Counterterrorism, 'Venezuela: Terrorism Hub of South America?', statement before the House Committee on International Relations, Subcommittee on International Terrorism and Nonproliferation, 13 July 2006.

11 Clement, C., 'Confronting Hugo Chávez: United States "Democracy Promotion" in Latin America', *Latin American Perspectives*, Vol 32, No 3, May 2005, p. 65.

12 Ibid., p. 65.

13 Ibid, p. 66. The two IRI grants were worth US$194,521 and US$292,297.

14 Colin Powell, Secretary of State, Foreign Policy Overview and the President's Fiscal Year 2003 Foreign Affairs Budget Request, US Senate Foreign Relations Committee, 5 February 2002.

15 Ibid.

16 Golinger, E., *The Chávez Code: Cracking US Intervention in Venezuela*, London, Pluto Press, 2007, p. 60.

17 Wilpert, G., *Changing Venezuela by Taking Power: The History and Policies of the Chávez Government*, Verso, 2006. Pre-publication manuscript.

18 Cited in Golinger, *The Chávez Code*, p. 69.

19 The documents are available in Eva Golinger's book, *The Chávez Code*, and also on her website www.venezuelafoia.info.

20 Declassified document. Cable from US ambassador, Donna Hrinak to State Department, September 2001, 'Venezuela–US Business Council Requests Washington Meetings', published in Golinger, *The Chávez Code*, p. 152.

21 Golinger, *The Chávez Code*, citing declassified document: email from ACILS, Lourdes Kistler, to Department of State, Mary Sullivan, 11 February 2002.

22 Ibid., p. 161.

23 Clement, 'Confronting Hugo Chávez'.

24 Quoted in Golinger, *The Chávez Code*, p. 44.

25 In his testimony to the National Assembly the pro-Chávez General Garcia Carneiro reported seeing the two colonels in the fort on 11 April. See Wilpert, *Changing Venezuela*.

26 Gott, R., *Hugo Chávez and the Bolivarian Revolution*, London, Verso, 2005, p. 228.

27 Congressman Roger Rondon, quoted in Campbell, D. 'American navy "helped Venezuelan coup"', *Guardian*, 29 April 2002.

28 Ibid.

29 Declassified document. WHA Press Guidance, April 17 2003, 'Topic: Reich call to Pedro Carmona', published in Golinger, *The Chávez Code*, p. 185 (emphasis added).

30 Aharonian, A., 'Venezuela: A Coup with the Smell of Hamburger, Ham and Oil', in

Wilpert, G., *Coup Against Chávez in Venezuela*, Caracas, Fundación Venezolana para la Justicia Global/Fundación por un Mundo Multipolar, 2003, p. 123.

31 His report is available at http://www.uvm.edu/~wmiller/venezuelancoup.htm. See also Wilpert, *Changing Venezuela*.

32 Chávez anecdote in Wilpert, *Changing Venezuela*, and Golinger, *The Chávez Code*.

33 DeYoung, K., 'US Seen as Weak Patron of Latin Democracy', *Washington Post*, 16 April 2002.

34 NBC News Meet the Press, 14 April 2002, http://caracas.usembassy.gov/wwwh1789.html

35 Pers. comm., 2003.

36 Golinger, *The Chávez Code*, p. 93.

37 Kozloff, N., *Hugo Chávez: Oil, Politics and the Challenge to the United States*, Basingstoke, Palgrave Macmillan, 2006, p. 13.

38 Conclusions and recommendations of the Committee against Torture: Venezuela. 21/12/2002. United Nations. CAT/C/CR/29/2.

39 *Human Rights Watch, World Report, 2007*, Human Rights Watch, New York, 2007.

40 Frank C. Urbancic, Principal Deputy Coordinator for Counterterrorism, 'Venezuela: Terrorism Hub of South America?', Statement before the House Committee on International Relations, Subcommittee on International Terrorism and Non-proliferation, 13 July 2006.

41 John Negroponte, Director of National Intelligence, Annual Threat Assessment, Senate Select Committee on Intelligence, 2 February 2006.

42 Kozloff, *Hugo Chávez*, p. 36.

43 Ibid., p. 36.

44 United States Southern Command, General James T. Hill, Commander, testimony before the House Armed Services Committee, Washington, 24 March 2004.

45 Statement of Gen. Bantz J. Craddock, Commander, US Southern Command, Florida International University / Army War College / US Southern Command Conference, 10 March 2005.

46 'The return of an aggressive Cuban foreign policy', speech by Roger Pardo-Maurer at the Hudson Institute, Center for Latin American Studies, 26 July 2005.

47 *Hearing of the Senate Armed Services Committee on "Nominations", September 19, 2006*, Vice Admiral James G. Stavridis, USN, for appointment to be admiral and to be Commander, US Southern Command. Answers to written questions. In 2006, Bolivia still had fifty-nine soldiers enrolled in the School of the Americas.

48 Evo Morales on Latin America, US Foreign Policy and the Role of the Indigenous People of Bolivia, interview by Amy Goodman and Juan Gonzalez, 22 September 2006, www.democracynow.org.

49 Interview: Paul Trivelli, US ambassador to Managua, *Financial Times*, 14 September 2006.

50 'Advancing Democracy in Nicaragua', http://www.iri.org/lac/nicaragua.asp

51 'Opinion Editorial by Secretary Carlos M. Gutierrez on Progress in Nicaragua and Importance of Upcoming Elections', press release, Department of Commerce, Tuesday, 10 October 2006.

52 'USAID official says Ortega presidential win could cost Nicaragua aid', Associated Press, 29 October 2006.

53 'Mixed US Signals Helped Tilt Haiti Towards Chaos', *New York Times*, 29 January 2006.

54 Ibid.

55 Ibid.

56 'Human rights abuse and other criminal violations in Port-au-Prince, Haiti: a random survey of households,' *Lancet*, Vol 368, Issue 9538, 2 September 2006.

57 Préval won more votes than any other candidate. The announcement of the results was delayed because there was a high number of blank ballots. Following riots spurred by the fear that Préval would be fraudulently denied victory, the international observers and electoral authorities agreed to a solution in which the blank ballots were distributed evenly among all of the candidates, thus cancelling each other out and giving Préval over 50 per cent of the vote.

58 Castro Mariño, S., 'The Cuba–United States Conflict: Notes for Reflection in the Context of the War against Terrorism', in Zebich Knos, M. and Nicol, H. (eds), *Foreign Policy Toward Cuba: Isolation or Engagement?*, Lanham, Lexington Books, 2005, p. 205.

59 'US Expands Axis of Evil', 6 May 2002, http://news.bbc.co.uk/2/hi/americas/1971852.stm

60 Castro Mariño, 'The Cuba–United States Conflict', p. 198.

61 Haney, P. and Vanderbush, W., *The Cuban Embargo: The Domestic Politics of An American Foreign Policy*, University of Pittsburgh Press, 2005, p. 138.

62 Report of the Commission for Assistance to a Free Cuba, July 2006. Condoleezza Rice, Chair.

63 'The return of an aggressive Cuban foreign policy', 26 July 2005.

64 'US Southern Command General John Craddock visits Uruguay', 23 June 2005, US Embassy in Montevideo, http://montevideo.usembassy.gov/usaweb/paginas/431-00EN.shtml.

65 Joint press statement with CJCF General Peter Pace, Bogotá, Colombia, Military Club, 19 January 2007.

66 *The State of the World's Refugees 2006: Human Displacement in the New Millennium*, New York, UNHCR, 2006.

67 Colombian Commission of Jurists. 'Violaciones de derechos humanos y violencia sociopolítica en Colombia, Derecho a la Vida. Ejecuciones extrajudiciales, homicidios sociopolíticos y desapariciones forzadas Julio de 1996 a Junio de 2006'.

68 Codhes Informa, Boletín informativo de la Consultoría para los Derechos Humanos y el Desplazamiento, No. 50. Bogotá, 31 August 2004, 'The Patriot Plan'.

69 The information on US military aid and activity in these paragraphs comes from Vaicius, I. and Isacson, A., *The War on Drugs Meets the War on Terror. The US Military Involvement in Colombia Climbs to the Next Level*, Washington, Center for International Policy, February 2003, and from an interview with Adam Isacson, from the Center of International Policy, Washington, October 2006.

70 For example, Adam Isacson, Center for International Policy, Washington. Interviewed October 2006.

71 'Report of the High Commissioner for Human Rights on the Situation of Human Rights in Colombia', 16 May 2006. E/CN.4/2006/9. English version.

72 Ibid.

73 Colombian Commission of Jurists. 'Violaciones de derechos humanos y violencia sociopolítica en Colombia, Derecho a la Vida'.

9 Why US Drugs Policy Doesn't Work

1   Dirección Nacional de Estupefacientes figures in *Los Cultivos Ilícitos: Política Mundial y Realidad en Colombia,* Defensoría del Pueblo, Bogotá, August 2000, p. 35.

2   Centro de Investigación Formación e Información para el Servicio Amazónico (Cifisam), *Evaluación Económica de la Propuesta de Desarrollo: Granja Familiar Amazónica (Grafam)*, PLANTE/UNOPS/UNDCP, Caquetá, Colombia, 2000, p. 55.

3   Two studies cited in United Nations Drug Control Programme (UNDCP), *Annual Coca Cultivation Survey 2001,* March 2002, Country Office Colombia, p. 10. The studies were funded by the Colombian government development agency, PLANTE.

4   Klaus Nyholm, Colombia representative, UNDCP, press conference, 10 May 2001.

5   'Drug Control: Narcotics Threat from Colombia Continues to Grow', General Accounting Office, US Congress, June 1999

6   Statement by Donnie R. Marshall, Head of the Drug Enforcement Administration, Testimony to the Senate Caucus on International Narcotics Control, 2 March 2001.

7   Klaus Nyholm, press conference, 10 May 2001.

8   Pers. comm. with Klaus Nyholm, 22 November 2002.

9   'Effects on Health and the Environment of Herbicides Which Contain Glyphosate', speech by Elsa Nivia, November 2000, www.usfumigation.org.

10 US State Department Factsheet on Aerial Eradication of Illicit Crops, 6 November 2000, released by the Bureau of Western Hemisphere Affairs.

11 Branford, S. and O'Shaughnessy, H., *Chemical Warfare in Colombia: The Costs of Coca Fumigation,* London, Latin America Bureau, 2005, p. 79.

12 Colombian Ombudsman's Report: Resolución Defensorial Nacional, No 026. 'Derechos Humanos y Derecho Internacional Humanitario en el marco del Conflicto Armado y de las Fumigaciones de los Cultivos de Coca en el Departamento del Putumayo', 9 October 2002.

13 Departamento administrativo de Salud, Putumayo subdireccion de salud pública, 'Impacto de las fumigaciones aereas con glifosato en el Putumayo', Putumayo, Colombia, 2002.

14 Ibid.

15 Colombian Ombudsman's Report: Resolución Defensorial Nacional, No 026, 9 October 2002.

16 Ibid.

17 'Daños Genéticos en la Frontera de Ecuador por las Fumigaciones del Plan Colombia', study prepared by Dr Adolfo Maldonado for Dr Claudio Mueckay, Defensoría del Pueblo de Ecuador, investigation file 9067-DAP-2002, November 2003. Cited in Branford and O'Shaughnessy, *Chemical Warfare in Colombia,* p. 82.

18 Amicus Curiae, *Impactos en Ecuador de las fumigaciones a cultivo ilícitos en Colombia,* published by ten Eucadorean NGOs, including Acción Ecológica, Quito, December 2003.

19 Inter-American Drug Abuse Control Commission, a division of the OAS,

'Environmental and Human Health Assessment of the Aerial Spray Program for Coca and Poppy Control in Colombia', 31 March 2005.

20 'Peru's president recommends coca', BBC online, 20 December 2006.

21 Condoleezza Rice, Secretary of State, Hearing before the Committee on International Relations, House of Representatives, 16 February 2006.

22 International Narcotics Control Strategy Report 2006, INL, State Department, March 2006.

23 'EEUU reduce 25% la ayuda antidroga', El Diario, 21 December 2006.

24 Ibid.

25 'National Drug Assessment 2005 Summary Report', National Drug Intelligence Center, February 2005. The 60 per cent figure is a percentage of the world's total potential production destined for the United States (422 metric tonnes of a total of 655 metric tonnes in 2003).

26 Rydell, C.P. and Everingham, S., 'Controlling Cocaine: Supply versus Demand Programmes', Rand, 1994.

10 Money, Multinationals and Misery

1 United Nations Economic Commission for Latin America and the Caribbean (ECLAC), Social Panorama of Latin America 2005, ECLAC, 2006, p. 54.

2 O'Brien, T., The Century of US Capitalism in Latin America, Alberquerque, New Mexico Press, 1999, p. 1139.

3 Ibid, p. 159.

4 Peet, R., Unholy Trinity: The IMF, World Bank and WTO, London, Zed Books, 2003, p. 75.

5 The IMF first imposed wide-ranging conditions on the British Labour government in 1976. The extent of its interference in domestic policy convinced rich countries that borrowing from the IMF should be a last resort. See ibid., pp. 67–74.

6 Buira, A., Challenges to the World Bank and IMF: Developing Country Perspectives, London, Anthem Press, 2003, p. 25 and p. 28.

7 Economic Survey of Latin America 1996–1997, ECLAC, 1998.

8 Green. D., Silent Revolution: The Rise of Market Economics in Latin America, London, Cassell/ LAB, 1995, p. 63.

9 Social Panorama of Latin America 2005.

10 Ibid.

11 Ibid.

12 Economic Survey of Latin America and the Caribbean, 2004–2005, ECLAC, 2005.

13 See Foreign Direct Investment in Latin America: Perspectives of Major Investors, Madrid, IDB/Institute for European-Latin American Relations, 1998.

14 Foreign Investment in Latin America and the Caribbean 2004, ECLAC, 2005.

15 Bayliss, K., Privatisation and Poverty: The Distributional Impact of Utility Privatisation, Working Paper, London, DFID, January 2002, p. 11.

16 'Pipe Dreams: The failure of the private sector to invest in water services in developing countries', Ferney-Voltaire Wold Development Movement, briefing paper, London, March 2006.

17 Narlikar, A., *The World Trade Organisation*, Oxford, Oxford University Press, 2005, p. 46.

18 Ibid., p. 135.

19 Ibid.

20 Ibid.

21 *OECD Agricultural Policies at a Glance 2004*, Paris, OECD, 2004, Table 1.1, p. 18.

22 'A Round for Free', Oxfam International, briefing paper, June 2005.

23 Ibid.

24 Hurtado Guzmán, E., *El Camino de la Recolonización: hacia el ALCA*, Santa Cruz, Bolivia, 2003.

25 Hufbauer, G.C. and Schott, J., *NAFTA Revisited: Achievements and Challenges*, Washington, Institute for International Economics, 2005, p. 289.

26 *The Ten Year Track Record of Nafta: US, Mexican and Canadian Farmers and Agriculture*, Public Citizen Working Paper, Global Trade Watch, Washington DC, 2004, pp.1–4.

27 Ibid.

28 Hufbauer and Schott, *NAFTA Revisited*, p. 50.

29 Vera Cruz, A. and Dutrenit, G., 'Las Pymes ante las Redes de proveedores de la Maquila: Reto o Utopía?' in Carrillo, J. and Partida, R., *La Industria Maquiladora Mexicana: Aprendizajes Tecnológicos, Impactos Regionales y Entornos Institucionales*, Tijuana, El Colegio de la Frontera Norte, 2004, p. 222.

30 Hufbauer and Schott, *NAFTA Revisited*, p. 100.

31 *The Ten Year Track Record of Nafta: Jobs*, p. 1.

32 Conteras, O., 'Empleo y Trabajadores en La Industria Maquiladora', in Carrillo and Partida, *La Industria Maquiladora Mexicana*.

33 Hufbauer, G. C., *NAFTA and the Environment: Seven Years Later*, Working Paper, Institute of International Economics, Washington DC, October 2000, p. 41.

34 Grijalva Monteverde, G. and Covarrubias Valdenebro, A., *Las Mujeres en La Maquila*, Sonora, El Colegio de Sonora, pp. 21–90.

35 *Mexico: A Job or Your Rights: Continued Sex Discrimination in Mexico's Maquiladora Sector*, Human Rights Watch, December 1998, p. 34.

36 Armbruster-Sandoval, R., *Globalization and Cross-Border Labor Solidarity in the Americas*, London, Routledge, 2005, p. 117.

37 Ibid.

38 O'Brien, *The Century of US Capitalism*, p. vi.

39 *BP World Energy Review 2006*. All subsequent figures in this paragraph are from the same source.

40 Figures from Ibge, Brazil's official statistics institute, show that the country's inequality gap narrowed between 2001 and 2004. Figures cited in Osava, M., 'Brazil: Inequality Gap Narrowing at Last', IPS newswire, 15 June 2006.

11 Coca-Cola, Cartoons and Caricature

1 Cited in Schoultz, L., *Beneath the United States: A History of US Policy toward Latin America*, Cambridge, MA, Harvard University Press, 1998, p. xii.

2   Cited in Sharbach, S., *Stereotypes of Latin America, Press Images, and US Foreign Policy, 1920–1933*, New York, Garland, 1993, p. 12.
3   Cited in Schoultz, *Beneath the United States*, p. 35.
4   Sharbach, *Stereotypes of Latin America*, pp. 13–14.
5   Ibid., p. 11.
6   Ibid., p. 86.
7   Johnson, J., *Latin America in Caricature*, Austin, University of Texas Press, 1980.
8   Schoultz, *Beneath the United States*, p. 377.
9   Donald Rumsfeld, Defense Secretary, Remarks to 35th Annual Washington Conference of the Council of Americas, 3 May 2005, http://www.defenselink.mil/transcripts/transcript.aspx?transcriptid=3254
10 Schoultz, *Beneath the United States*, p. xv.
11 The examples from this section are taken from Reyes, L. and Rubie, P., *Hispanics in Hollywood: An Encyclopedia of Film and Television*, New York, Garland, 1994; Ramírez Berg, C., *Latino Images in Film: Stereotypes, Subversion and Resistance*, Austin, University of Texas, 2002; and Richard, A.C., *Contemporary Hollywood's Negative Hispanic Image*, Westport, Greenwood Press, 1994.
12 Reyes and Rubie, *Hispanics in Hollywood*, p. 31.
13 Ibid., p. 3.
14 Ramírez Berg, *Latino Images in Film*, p. 77.
15 Rangel, C., *The Latin Americans, Their Love-Hate Relationship with the United States*, New Brunswick, Transaction Books, 1987, p. 26.
16 Reid, J., *Spanish American Images of the United States 1790–1960*, Gainesville, University of Florida, 1977, p. 25.
17 Ibid., p. 42.
18 Martí, J., *Our America, Writings on Latin America and the Struggle for Cuban Independence*, New York, Monthly Review Press, 1977, p. 93.
19 Ibid, p. 85.
20 McPherson, A. (ed.), *Anti-Americanism in Latin America and the Caribbean*, New York, Berghahn Books, 2006; McPherson, A., *Yankee No: Anti-Americanism in US-Latin American Relations*, Cambridge, Harvard University Press, 2003; Sweig, J., *Friendly Fire: Losing Friends and Making Enemies in the anti-American Century*, New York, Public Affairs, 2006.
21 McPherson, *Anti-Americanism*, p. 271.
22 See Joseph, G., LeGrand, C. and Salvatore, R., *Close Encounters of Empire: Writing the Cultural History of US-Latin American Relations*, London, Duke University Press, 1998, and Shukla, S. and Tinsman, H., *Imagining Our Americas: Towards a Trans-national Frame*, London, Duke University Press, 2007.
23 Rodríguez, J. and Vincent, K., *Common Border, Uncommon Paths: Race, Culture and National Identity in US-Mexican Relations*, Wilmington, SR Books, 1997, p. 110.
24 Ibid, p. 106.
25 *Food Brands in Latin America 1997*, Seymour-Cook Ltd, Food Research International, UK, 1997 and *Food Markets in Latin America*, Euromonitor PLC, 1993, UK.
26 Fox, E. (ed.), *Media and Politics in Latin America*, London, Sage Publications, 1988, p. 13.
27 State Department memo, 1942, cited in Smith, P., *Talons of the Eagle: Dynamics of*

US–Latin American Relations, New York, Oxford University Press, 2000.

28 Fox, *Media and Politics in Latin America*, p. 19.
29 Sinclair, J., 'Geolinguistic Region as Global Space: The Case of Latin America', in Allen, R. and Hill, A. (eds), *The Television Studies Reader*, London, Routledge, 2004, p. 137.
30 Fox, E. and Waisbord, S., *Latin Politics, Global Media*, Austin, University of Texas Press, 2002, p. 11.
31 Becker, T., *Doing Business in the New Latin America*, Westport, Praeger, 2004, pp. 15–16.
32 Ibid. The statistics from this paragraph come from this source.
33 'Obama's Latino Vote Mandate', *The Nation*, 18 November 2008.

Index